# Sociology

# BY THE SAME AUTHOR

ALREADY PUBLISHED

*La Societat de Masses* (Barcelona: Dalmau, 1961)

*Historia de pensamiento social* (Barcelona: Ariel, 1967)

*Social Stratification in Spain* (Reading University, 1967)

*Contemporary Europe: Class, Status, and Power* editor, with M. S. Archer, and co-author (London: Weidenfeld & Nicolson, 1971)

*Sociedad Masa: ideología y conflicto social* (Madrid: Seminarios y Ediciones, 1971)


IN PREPARATION

*Mass Society* (London: Martin Robertson, 1976)

*Sociologie au XXième Siècle* editor and co-author (Toulouse: Editions Edouard Privat, 1972)

# Sociology

## *Salvador Giner*

Martin Robertson

The original Spanish edition was published in 1968 by Edicions
62 in Barcelona. A French edition was published in 1970 by
Editions Edouard Privat in Toulouse.

This edition, revised and translated by the author, was first
published in 1972 by Martin Robertson & Company Ltd, 17
Quick Street London N1 8HL.
Reprinted 1972 and 1975.

SBN 85520 0018 1 (case edition)
SBN 85520 0017 3 (paperback)

Printed by Western Printing Services Ltd
Avonmouth, Bristol

# Contents

PER A MONTSERRAT

# Preface

The aim of this book is to present in a brief and elementary way one of the social sciences, sociology. It is therefore directed to students who are approaching the subject for the first time as well as to laymen who feel an urge to discover its nature and its findings. Sociology is now a discipline fortunate enough to awaken widespread curiosity both among students and the wider public. This measure of popularity carries with it not a few disadvantages, of which sociologists are all too aware. One of them is the shallow interpretation of modern social life through commonplaces and clichés taken from introductory textbooks. No introductory work can avoid this risk, so the reader must keep in mind that things are always more complex than presented here and that sociological knowledge can only be faintly reflected in a brief presentation of its rich and ample field.

New introductions tend to begin with apologies from the author, who is at pains to explain why he is producing yet another introduction to the field. Happily this is not my case. I first wrote mine in my native tongue—Catalan—in 1967, and it appeared in Barcelona in the following year. In spite of the apparent parochialism of the event two translations ensued—one in French and one in Spanish. (A third Spanish edition has just appeared and an Italian translation is in preparation.)

Re-writing this book once more has given me the opportunity to improve it further. Inevitably, I have expanded it again, though not excessively, for it is not a treatise, but a mere introduction. My professional colleagues who may happen to glance at it will soon notice the systematic character of its contents but will equally detect some areas which are not covered by it. This is inevitable in a short text such as this, but I am fully responsible for my selection of omissions; such selection is part of the central criteria which underlie the plan of the book. It is unnecessary that such criteria should now be spelled out, for they will soon become apparent in the text. Let me only point out two things: first, while I considered that the text ought to be an invitation to regard sociology as an interesting mode of approaching human reality, I also decided to eliminate excessive speculation on this matter and to present instead a certain number of sociological findings, notions and contributions in the hope that they will speak for themselves convincingly enough. Secondly (and this is quite important) the reader will find in this book a number of theories, descriptions and definitions, often presented as if they were correct. But sociology is not a dogmatic science, and all its statements are tentative. It must be clear from the start that they appear here in this spirit, as statements about social reality which seem, in the light of our present knowledge, to be useful hypotheses and propositions.

References are to be found at the end of each section. Themes or issues referred to in one part of the book but which are developed further in another are followed by an indication in parenthesis. Thus (VII, 5) means that the reader is advised to turn to Chapter VII, Section 5 for a fuller treatment of the matter.

My debt to Mr Stephen Schenk and other friends, students and critics who have lent attention to this book is very great. I am very grateful to them. I would also like to express my thanks to Sr Josep M. Castellet (Edicions 62), M. Georges Hahn (Editions Edouard Privat) and, very especially, to Mr Ian Robertson (Martin Robertson) for their encouraging cooperation while each text was being written or prepared for publication.

S.G.

The University of Reading

Winter 1971

*Note about this edition.* A first reprint of this book in June 1972 gave me the opportunity to introduce a few amendments and corrections. This second reprint has allowed me further improvements, somewhat more extensive. I would like to thank Professor Phillip Levy, Head of the Psychology Department, University of Lancaster, and Professor Motohisa Kajitani, Visiting Fellow, Queen Elizabeth House, Oxford, for their very helpful suggestions and criticisms. I am very grateful to Mr David Martin (Martin Robertson & Co.) for his continued help. Finally I would like to point out that the Italian and Swedish editions of this introduction to sociology have been translated directly from the English version.

S.G.

University of Lancaster

Michaelmas, 1974

# I The Nature of Sociology

## 1 THE DEFINITION OF SOCIOLOGY

Sociology is one of the social sciences. Its purpose is the scientific study of human society through the investigation of the social behaviour of man. It therefore explores human processes of interaction, and their results. Phenomena such as social institutions, groups, collectivities and their relationships to each other are fully within the field of sociology; the same can be said of the study of individual behaviour in so far as it is explainable by the existence of these social patterns. The cultural basis of social behaviour—social values, meanings, norms—falls also within the field of interest of sociology. The subject of sociology is man as a social animal.

This definition is misleadingly simple, though, for all the social sciences have as a common starting point the fact that man is a social animal. Each social science, however, tends to confine itself to one zone of social reality. Thus, economics studies the processes of exchange, production and consumption of goods and services which one finds in every society or section of it. History describes past social events and establishes our knowledge of them. Political science explains government. By contrast, the aims of sociology appear to be much broader as it does not limit itself to one dimension of the social world. When an economist studies the development of market fluctuations in a given capitalist society he more often than not concentrates his attention only upon such processes as capital formation, rates of interest, wage levels, and the financing of the operations. The sociologist approaching the same area takes into account the people involved in the process, and he will inquire who gets which jobs, which social norms obtain in the capitalist order under scrutiny, which social classes and which social institutions are involved, which strategies of action they follow, and which cultural factors enter the picture of the economic behaviour present. (For methodological reasons he may be well advised not to study all these phenomena at once, but they are all legitimate subjects for investigation).

Set against the other social sciences, then, sociology appears to possess a greater degree of generality, as well as a certain difference in emphasis and point of view. But the distinctions are not substantial. In the first place, the methods and results of each social science are necessary to the others: there is a constant and natural osmosis between them. What is more, sharp distinctions between the diverse social sciences cannot be drawn and may lead to fruitless disputes. We admit distinctions as a matter of course because they prove convenient, but for no better reason. How can sociology be distinguished from social anthropology? From social psychology? When the economist is a practitioner of political economy, is he not 'invading' the realm of the sociological? And how can one distinguish history from sociology? Yet it is being asserted that sociology is different from these other disciplines in a degree of generality. There is no contradiction in this. We say simply that sociology is the meeting ground of the other social sciences, their common universe of discourse. This does not mean that sociology is in any way superior to them, in spite of the exalted position pretentiously assigned to it by some of its founders, such as Saint-Simon and Comte. The truth seems to be that it is only *logically* broader in scope. And, perhaps for the same reason, it depends more than any other on the methods, tools, achievements and experience of related disciplines. One could even say that it is 'parasitic' on the laws of others.[1] Sociology is not an autonomous discipline. The distinctions just drawn between the work of an economist and that of a sociologist still hold, but they must now be interpreted only as aspects of our conventional wisdom.

Those who approach sociology for the first time are often surprised by the great variety of its themes. There is a sociology of law, of education, of religion, of crime, of the economy. How can such an array of fields be covered by one discipline and still possess logical unity and internal coherence? Sociology achieves unity by never abandoning its central criterion: the study of social behaviour, the processes of human interaction. Whether he is exploring an army, a financial institution, or a church, the sociologist always looks for a central cluster of characteristics—social order, the distribution of authority, the channels of communication, the patterns of conflict and conflict resolution, and so on—as they are reflected in social behaviour and treats the other aspects of the area as secondary to this central purpose. In so doing, sociology is forced to *interrelate* phenomena which belong to several areas of social reality; sociology thus tries to establish the pertinent connections between the various realms of human life (religion, power, morality, labour, art welfare) as they influence each other in social interaction. Thus, when a sociologist studies a political ideology (VIII, 4) he is trying to establish which are the concrete class conflicts that engender it, what degree and kind of internal cohesion are produced amongst the groups which embrace it, and how its supporters act in front of those who do not subscribe to it. If he studies the spread of a new religion, he will look for its patterns of recruitment amongst the wider society, the numbers of its converts, its impact on economic life, the response of the established civil authorities, and so on. In every case there is a unity of purpose or perspective (social behaviour) combined with an interrelational approach.

The interrelational approach is so much in the nature of sociology that it has been identified with it. The *sociological imagination*,[2] the key to a sociological comprehension of human reality, is an attitude of mind which asserts the basic interdependence of all dimensions of social reality. The sociologist systematically refuses to analyse his problems in watertight compartments,[3] for he regards this interdependence as a principle. This, of course, poses some methodological problems, for the axiomatic interdependence of social phenomena cannot mean that each one of the factors present can be assigned the same weight in the establishment of causal laws, regularities and correlations (II, 1). However, the more the sociologist tries to unravel the intricacies of social causation the more it becomes clear to him that, no matter how prominent one or a few factors might be in explaining social reality, it is so rich and complex that any simplistic or monocausal formula pretending to explain it must be rejected forthwith. The sociological imagination, then, means the skill to relate mentally and methodologically what is related in reality. Religion, science, work, law, are different activities—different not only for the analytical mind but also for common people in everyday experience; and yet these activities of man are inextricably—if not confusedly—intertwined. They all meet in our consciousness, but they also meet in social behaviour.

Social behaviour has been mentioned as the central subject of sociology. Its concrete forms will be expounded in the pages that follow, but it is convenient to make clear what is understood by it: human behaviour that exists in relation to other human beings, their institutions and their groups or collectivities is social. It may entail actual physical social action, but it may also imply symbolic interaction. (Thus all forms of language are social behaviour.) It takes into account the presence of others, and can therefore be considered as a social bond[4] even when it is hostile, for that embodies our mutual interdependence as social animals. The 'presence' of others need not be physical. Men act not only in response to the actual social behaviour of others in their material presence, but also in response to their notions, hopes, fears, expectations and emotions about the realm of the social in which they live. Sociology studies this realm through its only concrete expression—social behaviour.

*NOTES on Chapter I, Section 1*

1. W. G. Runciman *Sociology in its Place* (Cambridge University Press, 1970) pp. 2 and 44. However, the assertion that sociology lacks autonomy *vis-à-vis* the other social sciences has been explicitly expressed in all the earlier editions of the present book. The opposite view is still maintained by a number of sociologists. See particularly R. Fletcher *The Making of Sociology* (London: Michael Joseph, 1971) Vol. 2 pp. 773–813.
2. C. W. Mills *The Sociological Imagination* (New York: Oxford University Press, 1959) pp. 10–11.
3. Cf. G. Le Bras 'Destin de la sociologie' in G. Le Bras *et alii, Aspects de la sociologie française* (Paris: Editions Ouvrières, 1966) pp. 10–11.
4. R. Nisbet *The Social Bond* (New York: Alfred Knopf, 1970), p. 18 identifies 'social bond' with all forms of social behaviour and its results: order, status, authority systems, etc.

# 2  THE SCIENTIFIC NATURE OF SOCIOLOGY

If the scientific method is the attempt to understand and explain logically and objectively a certain area of reality, if it involves the systematic posing and testing of hypotheses, then sociology is a science for it fulfils these requirements. So far, numerous social phenomena have not lent themselves readily to the same sort of treatment that natural science applies to its field of study; but it would be a fallacy to apply to social phenomena only the methods of algebra, botany or geology. The basic question is to establish whether sociology has or has not made serious progress towards our objective—the verifiable and rational knowledge of society. In the event of an affirmative answer, the scientific nature of sociology will have to be acknowledged. There have been serious arguments and debates about this matter, however, which cannot be ignored.

The controversy over the scientific character of sociology—or lack thereof—stems from the difficulty of verifying many of its propositions and theories. This becomes clear when one compares its achievements with those of natural science, especially if the same criteria of predictability, precision, measurement and quantification are applied to both, and if one denies sociology any methods other than those of the natural sciences. Certain sociologists who would like to see their discipline turned into just one more natural science have been extremely worried by this contrast. The standard explanation they give for the (in their terms) backward situation in which sociology finds itself is that of its newness. Sociology, in their opinion, is a very recent branch of knowledge, still feeling its way. They compare its present situation with that of, say, medicine just before the time Servetius and Harvey made their discoveries about the circulation of the blood. As they see it, the period prior to the growth of behaviourism in the psychological and social sciences before the First World War ought to be confined to the not very fruitful pre-history of sociology. This would mean that not only the work of such great sociologists as Montesquieu, Marx, Spencer, Ferguson, and many others would be practically ignored but also that of social thinkers of earlier times—Ibn Khaldūn, Hobbes, Aristotle, Machiavelli—whose lasting contributions to our knowledge of the social world do not seem to wither for those who care to read them. Nothing short of experiment, quantification and mathematical language can satisfy these critics. Being themselves sociologists by profession, they must feel very unhappy indeed, for it is evident that their discipline only partly meets their requirements. Besides, sociology has so far failed to produce anything like Newton's laws of universal gravitation, and there is very little evidence that such simple mechanical principles regulating society are likely to be discovered in the near future.

In contrast with this extreme positivist or behaviourist attitude to sociology stand those who consider that it pertains strictly to the humanities. The difficulties involved in the scientific study of man in society allegedly stem from his capacity for unpredictable action —the result, in turn, of his free will.[1] No matter how limited by nature or by his own society, man's liberty is an unpredictable variable which seriously curtails our capacity to make scientific statements about social life. Thus the world of knowledge is divided into two kinds of disciplines: those which study nature and those which study man, each with a different set of criteria. (The distinction was first clearly made in Germany—hence the frequent use of the expressions *Naturwissenschaften* and *Geisteswissenschaften* to refer to these concepts.[2]) While the 'sciences of nature' can be expressed in laws, those of the 'human mind' can only describe unique, unrepeatable events. At best the latter can speculate about human nature and the 'laws' of history and society, but they cannot spell them out in positivistic terms.

The truth of the matter seems to lie somewhere between these two extreme positions, or, rather, to contain a great deal of both. From the start the sociological apprentice will encounter quite solid, reliable statistical and quantitative information about social phenomena, coupled with a respectable wealth of first-rate descriptive material about peoples, tribes, social events and institutions of the utmost variety. (These descriptive features sociology, ethnology and anthropology fully share with other disciplines, from geology to zoology.) Systematic generalisations about human society—sociological theory—he will find much 'weaker' if he uses the same criteria, but in this field he is bound to encounter a few masterpieces of humanistic scholarship, worth studying not for their aesthetic merits only, but for their achievement in comprehending and explaining the human predicament. Some positivistically minded sociologist has said somewhere that his colleagues keep referring and going back to the early classics of sociology because their science is so imperfect. This is in contrast with natural scientists, who supposedly only work on the basis of very recent research. Thus in biochemistry the work of Pasteur is merely of historical interest —even if his discoveries are still profitably used by the food industry. So there must be something wrong if we are still consulting Tocqueville, Marx or Simmel with so much assiduity. In fact, there is nothing wrong; the classics of sociology, insofar as they are humanistic, retain the freshness of any classics in the humanities. This is a fact that no explanation can satisfactorily demonstrate— only direct contact with their works. If we accept this assumption, we must conclude that sociology is a bi-dimensional discipline, uniquely combining *naturwissenschaftliche* and *geisteswissenschaftliche* elements—if we are, for one moment, to accept this somewhat old-fashioned dichotomy. (And the burden of the proof that this is not so is not, incidentally, with the sociologists themselves.) Moreover some of us will not mind if our discipline is called a hybrid science; we may for that reason find it more enticing.

In order to avoid some of the logical pitfalls of the controversy about the scientific nature of sociology, Emile Durkheim, one of its modern classical proponents, used to insist upon the notion that social phenomena possess a reality *sui generis*, with specific properties and principles of causality, and that they are ruled by laws that do not find facile analogies in other zones of reality.[3] Now if we do not interpret the *sui generis* claim in an extreme way—i.e. that society has *nothing* in common with other realities—we shall be in a position to understand the apparent ambiguities of conceiving sociology as both a scientific *and* a humanistic discipline. Not only will they not appear as contradictory, but in fact they will complement each other most fruitfully. Sociology is part of the humanities because it is knowledge about man—and not about his physiology or his biology, but about his predicament; and it approaches the human condition with the tools of rational and objective explanation. This last characteristic is made possible by the traits of social behaviour and social institutions: they have a material or objective character of their own. When sociology attempts to grasp the meaning of social life in each instance studied, it is one of the humanities; when it attempts to disclose objective causal relations, correlations, and regularities, it is one of the natural sciences. Most of the time, though, it is both. In fact, it *must* be both if it wants to avoid being either an often shallow accumulation of data or a sheer speculation about a conjectural society.

In the last resort all science possesses a final, intimate unity of purpose[4] and a similar attitude of mind. Sociology is a science because it fulfils the basic requirements of what the Latin notion of *scientia* has come to mean: objective and rational knowledge of reality or, more strictly, consistent effort towards the possession of such knowledge. It is in this complex but definite sense that the discipline will be understood throughout this book.[5]

Keeping in mind what has been said, the following characteristics of sociology can be enunciated:

*I Empiricism* All aspects of sociological knowledge are either bound to observations made upon social behaviour or subject to the test of such observations. Conjectures, hypotheses and theories about reality are to be confronted with our experience of it. Given the special nature of social reality the methods of its sciences vary considerably (II, 1) but they all aim at the rigorous examination of empirical evidence.

*II Theory* A theory is a system of logically integrated propositions whose aim is to explain a certain area of reality. (The degree of logical integration is not always perfect, but the effort to make it so must be predominant.) Scientific theories try to explain the laws or regularities of such areas of reality. Sociological theory is the generalisation, in these terms, of the partial conclusions arrived at by empirical research or data collection. Its chief aim is to interpret and to interrelate sociological information in order to explain the nature of social phenomena, as well as to produce hypotheses whose final validity can only be checked by further empirical research.

*III Openness* Like all science, sociology is open, that is, non-dogmatic. Closed theories only admit exegesis and lead to scholasticism: they are typical of theology and of some forms of ideology. The authority principle has no place in sociology: all its propositions must be re-examined and are subject to systematic doubt and comparison with new experience and data. This has as a corollary the fact that sociology is a cumulative discipline. Less imperfect theories come to supersede the more imperfect; explanations which appear as more plausible than others are admitted in their stead. Obviously, this is not a simple, easy process since it is not always possible to decide in black and white terms about the merits and demerits of alternative explanations. In such cases theoretical integration becomes only a goal of sociological theory construction. In any case cumulativity in sociology, as a consequence of its adogmatism, is a fact; we simply know more about social phenomena in many fields today than we knew yesterday. Another corollary is that, while sociological schools do exist, none can claim to monopolise truth. Thus, if we accept expressions such as the 'sociology of Marx', the 'sociology of Weber', 'Marxist sociology', 'functionalist sociology', it is for mere convenience in order to highlight certain lines of approach, or the work of a given social scientist, or that of his followers. Yet, there is only one sociology and one of its chief criteria is the integration of all its valid knowledge.

*IV Criticism* Sociology is potentially a critique of society. A natural science cannot be called a 'critique' of nature. But a science of human affairs cannot escape this condition either. Thus even when sociologists study the most trivial and harmless themes their findings might not be liked by everyone concerned. And precisely because their work is based to a large extent on data, and often on sound reasoning, their activity finds constraints of all sorts, from the outright banning of the discipline in some countries to subtle economic and political pressures in others. It is interesting to note that even the most positivistically oriented sociologists—those who would reject the present statement about the nature of their discipline—do in fact put forward a very concrete idea of the social world and how it should be best organised for human happiness,[6] thus belying their own claims to aseptic social reasoning. Moreover, while it is true that not *all* sociological activity is a criticism of society, its results are in any case the material upon which any acceptable critique of the social world can be built.

*V Methodologically non-ethic* This means that, in the actual process of research, sociology does not make moral judgements; if it approved or condemned beforehand what it purports to investigate it would be unable to proceed in a scientific manner. However (and here lie some of its puzzling intricacies) one of the deepest sources of sociology is its moral concern for the human condition in the modern world, not just scientific curiosity about an area of reality, important though this last element might be. Because they study human relations—where responsibility and duty are paramount criteria of social action—sociologists must in one way or another come to terms with ethical problems; and very frequently their moral neutrality in research procedures is based on a conviction that there is, in our times, a morality of objectivity, or a rational morality based on a thorough knowledge of social situations.[7] Sociology is *not* the science of social reform, but it is not a mere coincidence that the history of the two has never been entirely independent.

Some of the points mentioned in this enumeration need elaboration, especially those related to ethics, to man's study of his own species—criticism—and to the nature of theory.

## NOTES on Chapter I, Section 2

1. On sociology and free will *cf.* S. Giner *L'estructura social de la llibertat* (Barcelona: Edicions 62, 1971).
2. The distinction is to be found—under different names—in the works of Wilhelm Wildenband, Heinrich Rickert and Wilhelm Dilthey. In sociology, Weber acknowledged the existence of the different methods implied in the distinction but rejected such division of the sciences.
3. E. Durkheim *Les règles de la méthode sociologique* (Paris: Alcan, 1894).
4. K. Popper *The Poverty of Historicism* (London: Routledge & Kegan Paul, 1957) pp. 130–43.
5. For a discussion of the scientific and the humanistic dimensions of sociology, E. Shils 'The Calling of Sociology' the final chapter in T. Parsons, E. Shils *et alii, Theories of Society* (New York, Free Press, 1961).
6. *Cf.* B. F. Skinner, *Walden 2* (New York: Macmillan, 1948).
7. M. Ginsberg 'On the Diversity of Morals' in his *Essays in Sociology and Social Philosophy* (Harmondsworth: Penguin, 1968) pp. 235–70.

## 3 THE ETHICAL AND VALUE PROBLEMS OF SOCIOLOGY

The goal of ethical neutrality in the process of social research is an essential condition of sociology. (Note that the distinction is explicitly drawn here between neutrality in method and procedure and the more problematic moral neutrality of the sociologist as a person choosing areas of study.) The introduction of moral judgements in sociological investigation is bound to diminish the scientific validity of the results. The fact that the researcher belongs, for instance, to a society where monogamy is the accepted form of matrimony is bound to prejudice his description and evaluation of family life in polygamous societies if he thinks that monogamy is the right form of marriage. Attitudes such as this would immediately disqualify him as a social scientist. In spite of the fact that sociologists who have overcome several forms of cultural parochialism are not hard to come by, it is not possible to affirm that *all* kinds of subtle prejudice have been eliminated by them. Besides, the notable degree of detachment of which man is sometimes capable in his consideration of human affairs does not invalidate the fact that at the same time as he contemplates the world he also evaluates it. Man possesses a moral as well as a descriptive map of his world, but these two maps are inextricably intertwined. This, of course, seems to run counter to the postulate of ethical neutrality in the process of research which is being put forward here. Therefore, it is not surprising that this has given rise to not a few debates and disputations. The very validity of sociology as a science has been made to depend on the solution to these apparent contradictions.

The sociologists themselves have been keenly aware of the dangers of evaluative distortion. When Durkheim recommended that social facts ought to be treated as if they were things (*comme des choses*) he wanted to root his discipline in a solid basis, but he also wanted to express the necessary degree of dispassionate detachment which must accompany the researcher if he wishes to attain credible results.[1] (Social phenomena are not 'things', for they have meanings, but Durkheim's pursuit of objective criteria of enquiry is what counts in the present context.[2]) It was Weber, though, who formulated with considerable clarity the goal of ethical neutrality, or value-freedom (*Werturteilfreiheit, Wertfreiheit*). For Weber freedom from value judgements is, on the one hand, an ideal towards which the social scientist must always strive, and not a condition easily attainable at every step of his investigation. On the other, though, the social scientist inevitably possesses some ultimate assumptions or commitments which must inescapably influence at least his selection of problems.[3] Weber's notion has often been interpreted as if he had meant that value-freedom is possible, while what he put forward is that the only way one can admit it is as a systematic effort towards objectivity. Complete value-freedom is unrealisable but a serious level of scientific objectivity results from a sustained effort towards it. In turn, as Weber made clear, such striving is something entirely different from moral indifference, and has nothing to do with it.[4] Thus the existence of the evaluative activity is an impediment whose nature is not absolute. In this connection it is interesting to note that our knowledge of the social has increased thanks to the exertions of men deeply committed to various ethical and political causes—and passionately at that. Let us only think of Tocqueville, Marx and Weber himself. Their basic commitments triggered in them—or at least reinforced—their passion for objectivity.

The paradigm of non-evaluation[5] does not mean that the sociologist can look with Olympian indifference at the troubles of the world. It is, rather, a norm for his work—hence the expression 'methodologically non-ethic' used above to refer to one of the traits of the discipline. The paradox is that the desire for methodological ethical neutrality stems from some ethical assumptions of the secular, rational modern mind. The weakening of religious commitment among scientists, intellectuals and the intelligentsia generally has often been accompanied by a desire to find new secular and solid criteria for morality: the effort towards objectivity in the study of the human world has provided a 'solution' for many scholars, as it has itself become a moral orientation. This can in part explain why some of the staunchest champions of value-freedom in sociology have also made important contributions in the field of social ethics. After all, some core problems of sociology—social cohesion, group loyalty, legitimacy—are also moral problems. To sum up, while the sociologist's basic assumptions about life and the social world are bound to be value-oriented (or ethical in nature), his actual methods of research must obey the rules of logical consistency and scientific enquiry.

Different, but not altogether unconnected with these questions, are the moral problems of social scientists in their professional capacity. The uses of sociology are many; a sociologist can put his talent at the disposal of unjust forces. The modern adviser to the prince may be a physicist, an economist, a sociologist. And in advising the prince he may consciously help him pursue reprehensible policies. Thus in the United States a vast research project sponsored by the Department of Defence, Project Camelot, was about to be started with the intention of investigating the causes of social upheaval and revolution in the Hispanic American countries. It soon became obvious that it was intended to help the government in anti-insurgency measures abroad. The United States is a pluralist polity where criticism and non-official campaigns are possible, and thanks to this Project Camelot never got under way, since a number of sociologists successfully exposed the whole affair.[6] In totalitarian countries sociology is under terrible strains—a palpable proof of the assertion that it always is or implies, a critique of society. The coming of what has been called Stalinism in the Soviet Union meant the expulsion of Russia's sociologists. Even Bukharin's marxist *System of Sociology*[7] was eventually banned while its author paid for his ideas with his life. Since then sociology disappeared from the Soviet Union, to be restored in the form of the Moscow Institute of Sociology in the 1960's. In the Soviet Union, however, sociologists have still to pay more than merely ritualistic lip service to the official doctrines of the Party; hence the present poverty of its results, even if it is true that the situation has improved by comparison with the past. In only one communist country, Poland, has sociology managed to thrive, although it still remains under the constant pressures of those who wield power.[8]

Less extreme and spectacular forms of professional bias are those which come from subtler ideological commitments to certain institutions. Funds may be provided for the most conformist and subservient social scientists. In Spain, rigged committees often decide the award of an university chair in 'delicate' disciplines such as sociology: favouritism and faction politics pervade the struggle for it. Notable exceptions in that and other countries only confirm the sad truth. Moreover much that goes under the name of 'social research' is actually market research carried out for private enterprise with only lucrative ends in mind. The findings of social psychology and sociology have often proved to be of great interest to the world of business. Many such examples could be cited, but those quoted are sufficient to make the point. However it would be wrong to conclude from them that sociology is unable to face these problems. In the first place they are common to all branches of knowledge, and scientists of all fields are becoming more and more aware of their moral responsibilities and their need to be independent from partisan interests. Sociological bodies—often at an international level—have often made open statements about professional ethics or particular issues, and a constant (and on the whole healthy) stream of criticism has been produced by sociologists about all these kinds of alienated sociology.[9] No matter what standpoint these sociological critics of sociology might take—and they certainly are often at loggerheads with each other in these controversial matters—they all agree on one thing: that a deep moral concern for the predicament of modern man and for the sanctity of human life must preside over the endeavours of the social scientist, while his actual research must always be carried on in accordance with the dispassionate rules of the scientific method.

*NOTES on Chapter I, Section 3*

1. E. Durkheim *op. cit.*
2. Cf. J. Rex's discussion on this matter in his *Key Problems of Sociological Theory* (London: Routledge, 1961) pp. 1–15.
3. E. Shils & H. Finch eds. and trans. *Max Weber on the Methodology of the Social Sciences* (Glencoe: Free Press, 1949) pp. 1–47.
4. A. W. Gouldner 'Anti-Minotaur: the Myth of Value-Free Sociology', in I. L. Horowitz *The New Sociology* (New York: Oxford University Press, 1964) p. 198.
5. Thus called by S. L. Andreski *Elements of Comparative Sociology* (London: Weidenfeld, 1964) pp. 77–78.
6. I. L. Horowitz *The Rise and Fall of Project Camelot* (Harvard: M.I.T. Press, 1967).
7. N. Bukharin *Historical Materialism, a System of Sociology* (New York: Russell, 1965, reprint of 1925 English translation).
8. S. Ossowski *Class Structure in the Social Consciousness* (London: Routledge, 1963, English translation from Polish) pp. 192–93.
9. E. Shils 'The Calling of Sociology', *op. cit.*; C. W. Mills *The Sociological Imagination*, *op. cit.*; A. Gouldner *The Coming Crisis of Western Sociology* (London: Heinemann, 1971); H. S. Becker 'Which Side are We On?' *Social Problems*, Vol. 14, no. 3, 1967; Statement of Professor Jan Szczepanski, President of the International Sociological Association on its forthcoming congress in Varna, Bulgaria, reproduced in many journals, e.g. *Acta sociologica* Vol. 12, no. 4, pp. 232–33; *cf.* also the debate between O. Fals Borda and A. Solari in *Aportes*, nos. 8 (April, 1968), 13 (July, 1969), 15 (January, 1970) and 19 (January, 1971); N. Glazer 'The Ideological Uses of Sociology' in P. Lazarsfeld *et alii The Uses of Sociology* (London: Weidenfeld, 1967) pp. 63–77; P. Halmos ed. 'The Sociology of Sociology' *Sociological Review Monograph* no. 16, September 1970.

## 4   EPISTEMOLOGICAL PROBLEMS

Ethical and value questions are also epistemological questions (that is, problems about the acquisition of true knowledge), since emotions, prejudice and moral judgements often act as barriers to, or distort our perception of, external reality. Yet they do not exhaust the number of hindrances which have to be overcome. Outstanding amongst them is our tendency to erratic, non-rigorous thinking in social matters. One way to begin correcting this is, of course, to abide by the principle of publicity; our findings and method must always be open to scrutiny and criticism. Another, and equally important, way of overcoming epistemological difficulties is logic. Now logic, in the social sciences, must be understood in all its possible senses. Thus it is desirable that the procedure of social enquiry should withstand the tests of verification established by formal logic as far as possible; and it is even more desirable that common sense—intuitive logic—should also be applied throughout sociological discourse and research. One factor which powerfully enhances the chances of logical thinking is that it should be couched in clear and simple language, although one must hasten to say that clarity is not always synonymous with readability, or with an easy access for the uninitiated to sociological literature. The vice to be avoided here is the hiding of trivialities behind a screen of pomposity or apparent profundities. Yet when the complexities of the issue at hand demand it a certain degree of difficulty in expression will inevitably be involved; in such cases the sociologist does not have to make any concessions to his public. Aside from this, however, it should be noted that in sociology not a few interesting theories or revealing insights have suffered from nebulous or unnecessarily esoteric presentation. It is understandable that scholars and students alike should be put off—or even infuriated—by such theories. Besides, obscure language being the hallmark of poor thought, the danger exists that the reader or the audience of such relevant though cryptic contributions may take them for what they are not.

Apart from maximum possible clarity and conceptual precision (II, 1), sociology requires the use of a conventional language to serve as a platform upon which all social scientists can understand each other and understand reality. All branches of knowledge have developed their jargons as a matter of course, and with no evil intentions. (Ancient Egyptian priests had their hieroglyphic writing as a monopoly and a privilege whose inaccessibility to others helped them maintain their exalted position; the many jargons of science today still serve some people's desire for social prominence in the academic and technological world, but this is an entirely peripheral phenomenon.) Every science needs a vocabulary which is peculiar to it; when it cannot take its terms from ordinary language, it must invent them, or take them from languages other than the mother tongue of the researcher himself. Perhaps, then, there exists a jargon which one may call 'sociologese' and which is justified. Yet one must distinguish it carefully from the 'sociologese' which is the unnecessary and mistaken use of words and notions possessing a sociological flavour. The popularity of sociology has aggravated this problem: journalistic treatment of social issues tends now to be bursting with such language, much to the detriment of the quality of rich languages, which already have ancient concepts and words to refer to most questions at hand. It is worth noting that the classics of sociology have very often avoided such pedantry. Besides, sociologese can easily be misleading: why use 'status seeking' for 'envy' or 'ambition' if one of these words more precisely describes a given situation? Why speak of 'mores' if we are loosely talking about social habits? Why employ the dubious term 'mass society' every time reference is made to 'the modern world'? Sociology must coin words or use old ones in a new sense— after having defined them with precision—only if it is absolutely necessary. Thus, for instance, 'status seeking' is one aspect of social action which, though related to ambition, does not denote the same thing—it must therefore be used only when necessary.

The problem of language in sociology is important because the very words with which we denote certain social phenomena carry with them several connotations which are references to emotional perceptions of that which is explicity referred to. Thus the effort towards conceptual clarity is an effort towards the elimination of harmful connotations. On another level, the existence of this semantic problem (the dichotomy denotation/connotation) points to the fact that through the social sciences man contemplates his very nature: hence the duality (or even duplicity) of his language. Admittedly one cannot have emotional connotations in the study of geodesics, but the same cannot be said of the study of the role of slaves in the sugar plantations of the Spanish Main. Now the point here is not just to go back to the question of value freedom, but to realise which other epistemological snags are to be encountered by virtue of the fact that sociology is man's study of man. Herbert Spencer claimed that sociology is the only discipline which entails the self-observation and study of groups and collectivities of which the spectator is a living part.[1] Although this might be unjust to the other social sciences and to philosophy, the contention is sound. An answer can perhaps be found for the problems involved if we remember that, for all practical purposes, it has been admitted that there are two distinct dimensions in social life: the objective and the subjective.

The objective dimension is clear. Although it might not always be easy to decide what constitutes a social fact[2] it is obvious that social data can be gathered with varying degrees of reliability. A great many social phenomena possess the same traits of natural phenomena, that is to say they can be statistically treated and factual generalisations can be made about them, for they appear in collectives.[3] We can thus classify them, analyse them statistically, plot them in graphs, make inventories with them. The subjective dimension, though, poses a problem. If we admit not only that the various aspects of social life have a meaning for its participants and that such meanings ought to be grasped if one is to make any sense of human social behaviour, we shall have to come to terms with this problem; if we do not, embracing instead some form of extreme positivism or behaviourism, our sociology will be the poorer. Following Weber the process which leads to an understanding (*verstehen*) of the social situation can be explained as the comprehension of the meaning of the social behaviour of the participants in a social situation by imagining oneself to be actually in that situation, and thus obtaining a basic insight into it. (Technically, this is often called 'role taking'.) Many factors intervene in the success of a sociological understanding: they cover sufficient scholarship or erudition but also demand a certain capacity for empathy for which no formulae can be provided in textbooks. In any case, and without in the least belittling our constant necessity for the more accessible objective data, it would prove wise to admit with Weber that 'subjective understanding is the specific characteristic of sociology'.[4] As he points out:

> Statistical uniformities constitute understandable types of action ... and thus constitute 'sociological generalizations' only when they can be regarded as manifestations of the understandable subjective meaning of a course of social action . . . It is unfortunately by no means the case that the actual likelihood of the occurrence of a given course of action is always directly propor-

tional to the clarity of subjective interpretation. There are statistics of process devoid of meaning such as death rates, phenomena of fatigue, the production rate of machines, the amount of rainfall, in exactly the same sense as there are statistics of meaningful phenomena. But only when the phenomena are meaningful is it convenient to speak of sociological statistics. Examples are such cases as crime rates, occupational distributions, price statistics, and statistics of crop acreage. Naturally, there are many cases where both components are involved, as in crop statistics.[5]

Far from being a barrier to our scientific knowledge of social reality, our capacity to understand the subjective meaning of the social world for other human beings, in situations entirely different from ours, is a guarantee for the validity of sociology. As Alfred Schütz remarks:

> . . . the subjective point of view must be retained in its fullest strength, in default of which . . . a [sociological theory of human action] loses its basic foundations, namely its reference to the social world of everyday life and experience. The safeguarding of the subjective point of view is the only but sufficient guarantee that the world of social reality will not be replaced by a fictional non-existing world constructed by the scientific observer.[6]

Needless to say, this is a condition sociology fully shares with other social sciences such as social psychology and history, and which further explains the initial contention (I, 1) that it is often hardly distinguishable from them. A final point must be made: if the understanding of subjectivity in social behaviour is as necessary as it is claimed here, it is also necessary to combine it, without confusing it, with the establishment of objective data. Both elements must constantly be present in our task, each correcting and checking the accuracy of the other.

All this does not exhaust the general epistemological problems of sociology. Several others will still have to be treated or referred to in the pages that follow (see Chap. II), which are devoted to the nature of sociological theory and to the various aspects of the methods employed by the discipline.

## NOTES on Chapter I, Section 4

1. H. Spencer *The Study of Society* (Ann Arbor; Michigan U.P., 1961 ed.); R. König 'Die Beobachtung' in R. König *et alii Handbuch der empirischen Sozialforschung* Vol. I (Stuttgart: Enke, 1967) p. 120.
2. Cf. Durkheim *Règles* . . . *op. cit.*; and J. Rex, *op. cit.* pp. 1–26.
3. M. Duverger *Méthodes des sciences sociales* (Paris: P.U.F., 1961) p. 36.
4. M. Weber *The Theory of Social and Economic Organisation* (New York:

Free Press, 1947; English translation, Vol. I, *Wirtschaft und Gesellschaft*) p. 104.
5. *Ibid.* p. 100.
6. A. Schütz, 'The Social World and the Theory of Social Action' in D. Braybrooke, ed. *Philosophical Problems of the Social Sciences* (New York: Macmillan, 1965) p. 58.

# 5  SOCIOLOGICAL THEORY

Sociology, it is affirmed, is a theoretical discipline. This means first of all that it avoids intuitive and impressionistic speculation about human society as much as the presentation of loose masses of data, in spite of the fact that both elements—insight and raw collections of factual information—do play a part in the early stages of any cognitive process. Thus the aim of sociology is to elaborate theories about social reality. Theories are sets of interrelated statements about reality which are logically integrated, and are empirically verifiable. Logical consistency, integration and empirical confirmation do not have to be absolute, but if any or all of these three elements are poorly represented in a given 'theory' it is better to consider it as a mere set of unproved hypotheses.[1] These principles are valid for any science. It is clear from them that, since no rigid criterion can be established to delimit the line at which an 'interesting hypothesis' begins to be a 'theory', or vice versa, the question must be left as idle. It must be borne in mind that in the social sciences mere sets of hypotheses are, unfortunately, often presented as theories, when in fact they are far from qualifying for such status.

Zetterberg has distinguished theory proper from sociological taxonomy. The latter—very important for the elaboration of theory —entails classification and precise definitions. But theory implies 'systematically organised, lawlike propositions about society that can be supported by evidence'.[2] Taxonomies are important because they allow us to diagnose the place of a phenomenon in the system of classification that we have devised; and when such diagnosis is not possible we receive a serious hint that the system might be wrong or in need of refinement. Propositions, on the other hand, spell out dynamic relationships between phenomena, which we shall call variates.[3] (Variates are specific values of factors entering into play in a situation; these factors are called variables (II, 1).)

Basically propositions try to establish relations of cause and effect, or at least of correlation. 'The greater the amount of money a man of humble origins has, the higher will be his chances of being admitted in the circles of the upper class' is such a proposition, though a very simple one. In fact, as Zetterberg indicates, it is multivariate propositions—much more complex—which make up theory. Their value is highly informative, but they are also more vulnerable to criticism and more difficult to obtain.[4] If the reader goes beyond the Second Chapter of this book, he shall see that precise and acceptable definitions as well as fruitful taxonomies are not rare in sociology, whereas theoretical propositions—let alone well grounded, elaborate theories—are harder to come by. The abundance of ordinary propositions—presented as theoretical ones—is what has inclined some superficial observers to think that sociology consisted of common sense statements about social phenomena, uttered under a scientific veneer. This is false, as one hopes a minimum familiarity with the contents of the discipline will prove.

The more general the range of a theory the harder is its empirical test. Very general and comprehensive theories abound and often enjoy widespread acceptance for all sorts of reasons, often of an ideological nature. Comte's 'Law of the Three States' (X, 2), Marx' conception of the history of mankind (VI, 3), Sorokin's explanation of cultural change (IV, 2), are theories of this kind. The development of such theories is far from objectionable, especially if their creator possesses sufficient genius and a notable command of great quantities of material. As a matter of fact, and as will be seen throughout our presentation of sociology, some of these theories not only possess a certain degree of plausibility at the greatest level of generality—especially if they are not taken dogmatically—but they entail numerous partial insights, hypotheses and smaller theories which are most valuable to the researcher. From another point of view these theories provide a necessary link between sociology and social philosophy generally. In modern, culturally creative societies, these two related fields of endeavour constantly cross-fertilise each other.

As a contrast, theories with an extremely low degree of generalisation hardly deserve that name, since they fragment our conception of reality and say very little about it. A theory must have a minimum degree of generality; only thus can phenomena begin to make some sense. How, then, can we find a solution to the dilemmas involved in simultaneously avoiding excessive amplitude and narrowness? As an answer, Robert Merton has put forward the idea

that, in the present historical moment of the development of sociology, our aim ought to be the elaboration of 'theories of the middle
range'. These are theories which cover limited aspects of social
reality, sets of variables and phenomena which can be covered
by the scientific observer without ever losing sight of the results
of empirical research. Such theories

> lie between the minor but necessary working hypotheses that
> evolve in abundance during day-to-day research and the all-
> inclusive systematic efforts to develop a unified theory that will
> explain all the observed uniformities of social behaviour, social
> organization and social change.[5]

Theories of the middle range, Merton says, are meant to explain
limited areas of reality such as the dynamics of social class, group
conflicts, fluctuations of power, interpersonal influence, rather than
to search for a simple formula from which to derive all these and
still other phenomena. Of course the widest theories are as necessary
as the special ones—and this is a trivial truth. A debate about the
respective merits of both kinds of theories would be barren if each
side tried to show the meaninglessness of the other. In the first place,
limited or 'middle range' theories are necessary; in the second,
general theories about society, mankind or history are here to stay;
man needs a general picture of his world, an explanation of his
cosmos. It is a fact that this is found in every society, though in
many different forms. As for the possible contradictions between
both types of theory, Merton's observations are, once again, apposite.
Many theories of the middle range are not

> inconsistent with such broad theoretical orientations as Marxist
> theory, functional analysis, social behaviourism, Sorokin's integral
> sociology or Parsons' theory of action. This may be a horrendous
> observation for those of us who have been trained to believe that
> systems of sociological thought are logically close-knit and
> mutually exclusive sets of doctrine. But in fact, . . . comprehensive
> sociological theories are sufficiently loosely-knit, internally diversi-
> fied, and mutually overlapping that a given theory of the middle
> range which has a measure of empirical confirmation, can often
> be subsumed under comprehensive theories which are themselves
> discrepant in certain respects.[6]

Merton's plea for concentration on theories of the 'middle range'
can be understood as a demand that a theory must stay close to
empirical findings and also that empirical research must unfold
within a theoretically relevant framework. This should not be taken
to mean that the most general level of theory and sociological specu-

lation ought to be abandoned altogether, for the explicit formulation of the desirability of theories of the middle range pushes further a trend started much earlier by the first generation of sociologists who, without abandoning their very general preoccupations about society, began to isolate problems or problem areas for their study. The justly famous study of suicide by Emile Durkheim is an excellent example of this, precisely because it is also grounded in the author's general preoccupation with the 'moral state' of modern society, its widespread unhappiness and its specific malaises *and* the sources of its cohesion and order. Because of this double nature, Durkheim's *Suicide* (a study in general theory *and* an investigation attempting 'middle range' theorising) can be summarised to illustrate further both types of approach in the field of theory.[7]

Durkheim took a limited phenomenon, the apparently completely private act of suicide, and interpreted it sociologically. To be entirely sociological such an interpretation (explanation of causes, theory) had to exclude all elements appertaining to individual psychology, as well as less likely influences such as climate, race or geographical location. Even other possible causes such as 'suggestibility', 'imitation' and so on had to be discarded, for they seemed vague, or unscientifically mysterious. (By the way, Durkheim discarded such possible 'causes' after having scrutinised them fairly thoroughly. For example, although statistics showed that suicides were far less frequent in the warmer climates of Europe, Durkheim proved that this variable—climate—could not be a proper cause.) He was then left with only social factors to explain suicide. 'The causes of the suicidal aptitude of each society' had to be sought in the 'nature of the societies themselves'. This was, however, only a preliminary step for, he still did not know whether suicide was the consequence of a single, unitary social trend, or the effect of a combination of social trends. In order to clarify this point, it proved necessary to classify suicides not by the manner of death, but by the motives and motivations that originated them. By doing so, the diversity of suicidal acts fell into a limited number of cases.

By relating suicide rates to the characteristics of the social milieux—religious belief and practice, family structure, political environment, occupational groups and so on—Durkheim was able to establish three main types of suicide which he called egoistic, altruistic and anomic.

*Egoistic suicide* is that form of suicide which is 'inversely proportional to the degree of integration to be found in the groups of which the individual is a part'. In separate sections Durkheim shows how the intensity of religious, domestic and political ties act as factors against suicide. An important fact was that suicides are more common among Protestants than among Catholics. In the former communities the degree of social integration tends to be lower than amongst the latter, as the individualistic, competitive ethos had made greater inroads in the Protestant—also more industrialised—lands than in the Catholic ones. At the time Durkheim was writing, Jews, with their strong ethnic and family allegiances, showed a much lower rate of suicide than Protestants and, very often, a slightly lower rate than Catholics. Yet, as the processes of modernisation penetrated the tight web of Jewish society, it also lost integration. From about 1870 on, Durkheim notices, Jews 'have lost their old privilege' of committing the smallest number of suicides in every European society, and their rates begin to converge with those of the most urbanised, modern, social milieux in gentile society. Parallel reflections can be made comparing rural and urban society, educated and uneducated strata, married and unmarried people.

*Altruistic suicide* represents the opposite case; it varies in direct proportion to the degree of integration of the group. Suicide here is not proscribed but prescribed in certain cases. We only find it in tribal societies—where social cohesion is extremely high—or, in modern times, in very militant groups. It is the case of the soldier who gives his life in an heroic act. Altruistic suicide is more common among the peoples who show low degrees of egoistic suicide.

*Anomic suicide* is the third type. It is the consequence of the weakening of social ties in a situation of social anomy (IX, 4) or lack of a clear definition of norms. Typically, its frequency varies with economic fluctuations. Both economic crises and states of economic euphoria undermine certain forms of social cohesion. When this occurs, it is the least integrated members who suffer most. The suicide of the bankrupt businessman is characteristically anomic.

Once this taxonomy had been established it could be seen that in the three cases suicide was related in some regular way to one single underlying element: the internal cohesion and affective integration of the group whose member had chosen to end his life. Durkheim then hypothesised that the 'moral constitution of society' (the degree of internal moral solidarity and integration of each group or collectivity) would in turn determine its suicide rate, that is, the percentage of members committing the act in each given historical moment. And the logic and coherence of the methodology

—if not entirely watertight—was sufficient to explain actual rates of suicide. Thus, to return to the relationship between religion and suicide rates, Durkheim's argument follows certain explicit, logical steps. When studying Germany, he noticed that suicide was much lower in Rhineland and Bavaria than in Saxony and Prussia. He reasoned thus:

1. In any collectivity, egoistic suicide varies directly with the degree of individualism. (Theoretical postulate).

2. The degree of individualism varies with the incidence of Protestantism. (Hypothesis).

3. Therefore the suicide rate will vary with the incidence of Protestantism. (Theoretical consequence).

4. The incidence of Protestantism in Bavaria is low. (Known fact)

5. Therefore the suicide rate in Bavaria is low. (Confirmation of postulate.[8]

We can thus see how cause-and-effect hypotheses, combined with an interrelational approach and backed by an accurate taxonomy and a fair and skilful use of documents and statistics can result in a plausible theory. Obviously Durkheim's theory of suicide is imperfect, but it *is* a theory. It has, in addition, been a point of departure for the elaboration of a more reliable understanding of the problem. Since Maurice Halbwachs began a systematic revision of his teacher's theories about the causes of suicide, a whole tradition has developed around this problem,[9] whose review is unnecessary in the present context. What is significant now is to stress how (*via* Durkheim's work) sociological theory is possible and fruitful. It is also worth noting that the theory so sketchily presented here contains a predictive element: given the social structure of a group and the degree of its cohesive moral strength, we shall be able to predict its suicide index in each circumstance. The predictive element is as important in social theory as in theory of any other kind.

Theory orients empirical research; research, in turn, elevates mere working hypotheses to the category of theoretical propositions. Each needs each other. It is upon their mutual interrelationship that the creativity of sociology depends. The activity that links them is called methodology.

## NOTES on Chapter I, Section 5

1. D. Willer *Scientific Sociology* (Englewood Cliffs: Prentice Hall, 1967) p. 9.
2. H. L. Zetterberg *On Theory and Verification in Sociology* (Totowa: Bedminster, 1965 3rd edn.) p. 22.
3. *Ibid.* pp. 25 and 64–65.
4. *Ibid.* p. 80.
5. R. K. Merton *On Theoretical Sociology* (New York: Free Press, 1967) p. 39.
6. *Ibid.* p. 43.
7. What follows is taken from E. Durkheim *Le suicide* (Paris: Alcan, 1897); (the 1970, P.U.F. edition has also been used). Other authors have also placed Durkheim's study at the beginning of their introductory works to sociology; eg P. Sorokin *Society, Culture and Personality* (New York: Cooper Square, 1962) pp. 8–13; D. Willer *op cit.* pp. 10–12; W. L. Wallace *Sociological Theory* (London: Heinemann, 1969) pp. viii–x; also G. C. Homans 'Contemporary Theory in Sociology' in R. E. L. Faris *Handbook of Modern Sociology* (Chicago: Rand McNally, 1964) pp. 951–953. Durkheim's *Suicide*, in fact, shows the essential connection between general level' and 'middle range' theory. As Sorokin remarks (*op cit.* in this footnote, p. 8) 'even such a minor phenomenon as suicide cannot be adequately understood, especially in its causes, without a study of its occurrence in man's socio-cultural universe as a whole'. For the explicit connection of suicide with the very general problem of the ultimate nature of modern society cf. Durkheim's *Suicide* (Book III, Chapter III, Section IV).
8. As set out by G. C. Homans *op. cit.* p. 951; he uses Spain as an example, not Bavaria of the areas examined by Durkheim. Bavaria seems even more significant as it is part of a religiously pluralist country.
9. Cf. J. D. Douglas *The Social Meaning of Suicide* (Princeton University Press, 1967).

# II The Methods of Sociology

## 1 METHODOLOGY AND METHODS

Methodology is the systematic study of the methods used by a science. Such study involves, on the one hand, the logical analysis of research procedure and, on the other, critical assessment of its basic assumptions. Methodology, then, is not oriented towards the development of new knowledge but rather towards the improvement of the scientific conditions that lead to it. Obviously, methodology and theory are very closely related: many of the issues we have just encountered above are also methodological problems. (The question of *how* a theory should be built to be effective is one instance of this.) It should be clear by now why methodology is important in the social sciences, and also why sociologists are so much concerned with it. Here all former observations about the complexities of their subject matter and the implications of the subjective-objective dimensions of social reality need to be recalled. The greater the danger of going astray in a discipline, the greater the necessity for awareness in these matters. Thus it is a good sign—and not a symptom of stagnation—that discussions about anti-scientific views in social enquiry, about what values are and what their significance is in research, about the use of and abuse of statements of mere chance, and so forth,[1] still continue to occupy the minds of a number of social scientists and are inscribed in most programmes of study.

In a less strict, although unfortunately quite common, sense, 'methodology' denotes the whole of the various series of methods employed by sociology. Yet this popular meaning of the term points to the fact that there is no unitary or unique method which is peculiar to sociology. *The* sociological method—if it exists—must be spoken of in the abstract; this is why some prefer to speak, at most, of a sociological imagination or stance—that is, of the spirit of the discipline, which has been already defined as being based on an interrelational approach to social reality. All this is reflected in the methods of sociology. They are many and very different. Some are highly qualitative, others are quantitative; some are based on experimentation, others on the observation of data as one encounters them. And the only criterion common to all of them is utility. As far as methods are concerned sociology is thoroughly utilitarian: if a method proves useful, it is used. But what is a method?

A method is the process of research which the mind must follow in order to increase its knowledge about something. Several sciences possess their own methods, but hardly any method is confined entirely to one science only. Methods tend to be transferable. Some of them, like statistics (first developed, by the way, in the social sciences), are common to all disciplines. Sociology uses practically all the methods employed by the other social sciences. Perhaps the only difference in some cases is the general orientation of the research project, the kinds of questions which different investigators try to answer in each case.

By and large sociological research procedures follow the same pattern as that of any other science. First they start with a *hypothesis* (or a set of connected hypotheses). A hypothesis is a supposition of causality or interconnection between phenomena. It is a tentative statement: truth or falsity are not affirmed, for it is the following phases of research that are meant to confirm or invalidate it. There is an obvious intuitive element in hypotheses: they are hunches, strong feelings that a hitherto non-apparent situation is in fact the case. But it is also obvious that fruitful or creative hypotheses do not generally occur to the layman. There is evidence that they come with greatest frequency to minds trained in the study of a given area, fertilised by disciplined reflection, observation, experimentation and the gathering of information. A hypothesis is formulated with the help of *nominal definitions*. These are not statements about the essence of some phenomenon ('real' definitions) but definitions which give sets of attributes to the phenomena at hand, so that there can be no mistake about what one means. In the social sciences these definitions are vital, particularly in view of the vagueness with which many of their themes are treated in everyday life. Let us suppose we want to start a study on the voting behaviour of a given population in order to find out which social class votes most heavily, and that we postulate, for reasons A, B, and C, that it is the middle class, and that the highest degree of voting is to be found amongst the lower middle class precisely. Now this would be entirely meaningless if we did not start our investigation with clear definitions of what we mean by 'social class', 'democracy', 'electoral behaviour' and so on. We have only to consider the number of meanings ascribed to the word 'democracy' by all sorts of people. (In the present case we ought first to be meeting the needs of liberals, anarchists, conservatives and communists, among others.) The only way out of an endless previous discussion about the 'real' essence of democracy (and that of the other terms) is a nominal definition—a definition without metaphysical pretensions. Of course, in developing his nominal definitions, the researcher will be well advised to draw from the strength of an already extant consensus in sociology and use his concepts in already accepted meanings, if these prove correct. After all, sociology is a discipline showing cumulative growth and the coining of terms must be backed only by a genuine need for them. Closely related to nominal definitions are *operational definitions*, which allow us to point out clearly the criteria used in our research procedure. For instance a given educational background, combined with a minimum income level, may be used as a device to define membership of a certain social class. Only by the combined use of clear nominal and operational definitions shall we succeed in ensuring that our particular piece of research be understood in its own terms and not by criteria freely introduced by observers alien to it.

Definitions point to the question of *conceptualisation*. Solid definitions are based on concepts slowly elaborated by the cumulation of sociological theory, and tested time and again by research. Concepts are 'the irreducible elements of theory'[2] and it is upon their accuracy that in many ways the fate of the theory depends. Scientific conceptualisation in a cumulative discipline must imply *codification*, which in Robert Merton's words is 'the orderly and compact arrangement of fruitful procedures of inquiry and of the substantive findings that result from their use'. Such effort implies the 'identification and organization of what has been implicit in the work of the past rather than the invention of new strategies of research'.[3] Codification—a term coined by Lazarsfeld —thus implies the systematic ordering of past scientific experience. And it should not be confined to procedure alone but to concept formation, theory formulation and sociological ideas generally. A deep knowledge of the past experience of a discipline such as sociology is necessary in order to avoid many pseudo-discoveries, and considerable wastage. In this connection the role of the history of sociological theory in the framework of the discipline can hardly be exaggerated. Research must start by a review of past experience and a statement of the 'state of the matter', except in the very few cases when this is manifestly unnecessary.

Before beginning research it is often necessary to elaborate *ideal types*. As Max Weber pointed out, ideal types are mental constructs which express the fundamental traits of the phenomena to which they refer, and they do this in the abstract—that is, they do not exist in objective reality, but prove necessary for its comprehension. In economics, the notion of 'perfect competition' is equally abstract and necessary for the explanation of certain kinds of market. Yet, a market with 'perfect competition' does not exist anywhere. In psychology, for example, individuals have been classified in series of bodily types, in order to help us understand and explain their personalities as they are correlated to physical characteristics. Thus the 'cyclothymic' and 'schizothymic' biotypes, or the 'pycnic', 'leptosomatic', and 'athletic' constitutional types of Kretschmer on the one hand, and Sheldon's somatotypes— 'endomorphs', 'mesomorphs' and 'ectomorphs'—do not correspond to any concrete and real individual but—at a given moment in the history of psychology—have helped us to understand the relationships between personality structure and organism in real individuals.[4] Sociology also needs ideal types of this sort. It must build elaborate notions of 'bureaucracy', 'feudalism', 'sect', 'clan', 'lineage', and so on. These ideal types—often called 'models', though strictly speaking different from them, as we shall presently see—are sets of definitions conveniently put together in an interdependent whole. They stand between discrete definitions and theories, and they are heuristic devices of great importance. In order to avoid repetition no elaborate examples are needed at this stage for ideal types will appear throughout this presentation of sociology.

Models differ from ideal types in that the former are explanations of complex systems of social relationships; models try to explain the patterns of relationship to be found in the social world. Thus models are also heuristic devices, but they attempt to explain sets of rather more complex and ample phenomena than mere ideal types, although both are ways of ordering or structuring our perceptions of the world in some meaningful whole. Sociology has used a wide range of models; one of its schools—the Social Darwinist school—used the 'evolutionary model' to explain social change. Likewise today the 'general systems' perspective (III, 7) uses a number of models, and several mathematical models have been

worked out for specific areas. And one can often use given theories
—or parts of theories—as models. There is, for instance, the case of
the 'Marxian model' of class conflict, when used to explain certain
types of revolutionary situation. It is not always easy to distinguish
between models and theories. Indeed initial notions, definitions,
ideal types, models and theories (including hypotheses) are more a
continuum than a chain of separate mental stages. They are all
phases which precede actual research, and which in turn are set
in movement again by the results of research. Research receives from
such activities a meaning it would otherwise lack; it is through
them that concrete research is sociologically interpreted.

Attention can now be turned towards some of the fundamental
methods of social enquiry, which can only be mentioned at this
stage rather than explained in detail. The methods and the tools of
sociology—most of them also used by its neighbouring disciplines
—have been subdivided here under four rather arbitrary headings:
'descriptive', 'psycho-sociological', 'historical and comparative' and
'experimental and mathematical'. This classification is arbitrary
because practically all sociological methods taken in isolation incorporate techniques and approaches used by the other sociological
methods. Moreover the methods chosen in each case depend on the
whole design of the research programme.[5]

*NOTES on Chapter II, Section 1*

1. A clear general treatment of these problems is to be found in Q. Gibson
   *The Logic of Social Enquiry* (London: Routledge, 1960).
2. G. J. Di Renzo 'Conceptual Definition in the Behavioral Sciences' in
   G. J. Di Renzo *et alii Concepts, Theory and Explanation in the Behavioral
   Sciences* (New York: Random House, 1966) p. 6.
3. R. K. Merton *op. cit.* p. 69.
4. O. Klineberg *Social Psychology* (New York: Holt, 2nd edn. 1954) pp. 327–
   351.
5. For a clear statement about the complexities of social research, sociological explanation and measurement, of H. M. Blalock *An Introduction
   to Social Research* (Englewood Cliffs: Prentice Hall, 1970).

# 2 DESCRIPTIVE METHODS

Descriptive methods are those whose chief aim is to present a clear
image of a given area of social reality. This description is neither
an easy nor a pre-scientific task. In most cases we are confronted

with a conglomerate of phenomena whose mere 'photographical' reproduction already entails problems for our understanding of the situation. Even if we succeeded in obtaining a fairly good picture of that situation, it cannot be satisfactory if the elements left in the shade are invisible. Thus, the adjective 'descriptive' applied to method implies also the bringing to the fore of non-apparent phenomena. This is, for instance, quite clear in statistics. To say that a particular piece of work, then, is 'merely descriptive' does not imply criticism, for correct description is often very difficult. Descriptive methods cover the whole gamut of research work, from those which are portrayals of perceived social facts or are sociographic, to the more evaluative, such as content analysis and statistical induction. All these methods often appear together in sociological description.

## Sociography

The most descriptive of sociological methods is sociography. Though introduced by Roberto Michels, the term received recognition through Sebald Steinmetz who used it to refer to the borderline area of sociology and geography.[1] Yet, this zone lends itself to studies rather more complicated than those of sociography, as ecology and human geography demonstrate. Under Ferdinand Tönnies' efforts sociography became an accepted part of much sociological work. For him sociography was a non-evaluative representation of a limited field of phenomena; such representation requires a certain analytical level and may not be limited to space, as it can include an account of events. Tönnies himself demonstrated his conception of sociography with several descriptions of criminality in Northern Germany and with an elaborate description of the power struggles that took place during the great strike of the Hamburg docks in 1896 and 1897.

Basically, though, sociography means the ordered presentation of collected data, as they appear and without omitting any that may be relevant to the case: territory, climate, population, life conditions, income levels, customs, types and indices of delinquency, distribution of public offices and political power, and so on. The tools employed in such descriptions are extremely varied: they may include aerial photography, inventories of goods owned by families, measurement of living space, compilation of lists of dates and data on duration of rituals, and collection of statements made by other observers. Very often, then, sociographical tasks turn out to be factfinding expeditions.

Frequently sociographical work appears under other names, especially, in the English-speaking countries, that of 'social survey'. Of course social surveys and other sociographic tasks were around quite a long time before the notion crystallised in an explicit method. Often social surveys were carried out in order to expose very bad social conditions and injustices, either with the intention of promoting reform[2] or of adding more wood to the revolutionary fire. Frederic Le Play's *Les ouvriers européens* (1855) and Charles Booth's *Life and Labour of the People of London* (1892–1897) are examples of the first kind of social survey, and Friedrich Engels' study of working class conditions in Manchester and England (*Die Lage der arbeitenden Klasse in England 1844*) which appeared in 1845, is typical of the second. From the very beginning it became obvious that good sociography could hardly be kept at the strictly descriptive level. This became fully evident with the sociographical work of the ecological research carried out by the University of Chicago during the 1920s, as well as in the more anthropological studies by Robert and Helen Lynd in an Indiana town in 1929 and 1937. Today none of the sociologists who try to follow the example of these pioneers would admit that their task is only sociographic. This is so because sociography and the social survey have become more of a stage than an end in themselves in the ongoing procedure of research.

## Statistics

Statistics is a series of methods whereby numerical data are classified, collected and related to each other. When they can be used, these procedures allow a clearer presentation and measurement of phenomena.

There are basically three kinds of statistics. (1) *Descriptive statistics* gather numerical information about certain phenomena as they appear in a given social area. They tell us how many doctors there are in a town, or have been over the past decade, per year. They also give information about the simplest averages; for instance, percentages of population receiving higher education, numbers of cars per thousand inhabitants, rates of divorce, infant mortality, and so on. These are elementary data, but very important for research, especially if they are reliable. (Some of the weaknesses in Durkheim's study of suicide stem precisely from the unreliability of official statistics in his day.) This is the kind of statistics which is most characteristic of sociography and social survey methods. (2) *Inductive statistics* are based on samples. A *sample* is a portion of the total number of phenomena showing a certain trait or set of traits. (The total number is called *universe* or *population*.) When the entire population cannot be studied a sample is taken of it, and this is used to study the population. (3) *Statistics of relationship* are methods used to establish relationships between two or more variables. The key idea here is that of correlation, which means that this is the field in which statistics are relevant for the establishing of causal relationships. (Yet, mere correlations only hint at cause-and-effect phenomena.) These three types are called parametric statistics, as they are all based on parameters—the summary measure of a given population, e.g. a mean, or a coefficient of correlation.[3]

Since descriptive statistics are not always possible, given the great numbers of data often involved in an investigation, sampling has become a central technique. The chief task in this respect consists of obtaining reliable samples which are as truly representative of their population as is feasible. In fact, the attempt to reduce errors of all sorts in sampling techniques takes a great deal of effort in all statistical enquiries. Most samples are *random*—a simple device that helps avoiding subjective bias, for in such cases each datum is nearer the ideal situation of having an equal chance of being picked for the sample. Randomness in an entire population may be refined by what is called the *stratification* of the sample. This means that the population is subdivided in categories or 'strata', each with its own particular characteristics. For instance in studying an electorate we may prefer to draw random samples from each one of several age groups; we shall be thus getting a clearer pattern of voting behaviour in the area concerned. This can be made more complex. We can introduce a further 'stratification' of our electoral sample by organising it according to social class, ethnic origin, regions, professions, sex. At this point, though, statistics cease to be only descriptive and classificatory and become also mathematical.[4]

An important notion in statistical work—and indeed in all sociological research—is that of the *variable*. In every situation under scrutiny we speak of 'intervening factors' that determine it. In a revolution, for instance, we may observe famine, a previous war, people unemployed, a hesitant and weak government, a strong and militant social movement struggling against that government, and so on, and we suspect that these are 'factors' precipitating the revolution. But we may want to establish our hunches on a more scientific basis as historians or sociologists. What we do—if enough solid data are available—is to quantify information and transform our impressionistic perception of factors into variables. Famine will be expressed in numbers of deaths by starvation, the social movement in question will be expressed in numbers of militants and rates of recruitment at different stages of the crisis, unemployment figures will be collected. And all these will be plotted on tables —graphical and numerical—so that correlations can be more easily visualised. A variable, then, is a trait that is common to a number of phenomena—or individuals, groups—and that shows growing or diminishing degrees of magnitude over time and space.

There are several kinds of variables, but the important distinction is between the dependent and independent ones. The latter, the *independent* variables, are those which can be considered as causes of the situation at hand. Thus the presence or change in magnitude of the independent variable results in corresponding changes in the dependent ones, and it is through these that we try to establish its social significance. Suppose that we want to know the effects of a new teaching method. In such a case we would introduce it in one classroom—keeping another of practically identical conditions as a control group—and watch the results. The introduced new method would in this case be the independent variable (that is, if our experiment has been correctly carried out) the cause of the perceived changes in the learning processes of the pupils. The effects, once measured, we would call *dependent variables*. A dependent variable appears and changes according to the presence and changes of other (independent) variables or sets of variables. Cause-and-effect relationships between variables are often inferred, but in general it is preferable to speak of correlations. *A correlation* is the established relationship between variables, i.e. the increase in magnitude of variable X (independent) means the decrease or increase of variable Y (dependent). Correlations, of course, are not always simple, or linear, though these are very widely used in sociology. Curvilinear and other, more complex, types of correlations soon appear in the process of social research.

Thus, what begins by an inventory of the various ways in which a population can be classified ends by becoming an interpretation of quantitative relationships, or multivariate analysis, which can be defined as the study of complex interrelations among a multiplicity of characteristics.[5]

*Content analysis*

The systematic description of the elements which make up the products of culture—whether implicit or explicit—is an important task for certain social sciences. This method is widely used by all branches of the sociology of culture and by cultural anthropology. With few exceptions traditional, artistic, literary and ideological forms of criticism meant that the manifestations of certain sets of values were being judged through the prism of other sets of values. Now, with the technique of content analysis the possibility of studying values, attitudes and general orientations with a greater degree of objectivity has arisen. Some psychologists—such as Freud and Jung—opened a path in this direction as they began to analyse the contents of consciousness, as well as those of dreams, myths and symbols. For their part, sociologists and anthropologists have for a long time tried to study the contents of works in which contents of cultures appear, so to speak, materialised or 'reified': ideals, values, collective goals, beliefs, and even social structures themselves.[6] In order to extract such contents, two principal methods are employed. They are not mutually exclusive.

*Quantitive content analysis* refers to the frequencies with which certain cultural units appear reproduced in the object studied. If one wants to study the fluctuations or rhythm of increase of anti-semitic propaganda in Nazi Germany one can examine the space devoted to this in newspapers published in that country before 1945, the percentage of anti-semitic allusions or statements in the public speeches of the fascist leaders, and so on. A second, more meaningful step would be to relate the curves and averages thus obtained to historical events, to see if there are any correlations among them. Not only political propaganda, but aesthetic values, fashion, sexual morality, religious attitudes and dogmas, can be studied with the help of this method, which very much centres around the scientific treatment of *documents*—printed, televised, or broadcast. Calculating machines—as in other fields of sociological research—have come to save much tedious work in the long reckonings implicit in such kind of analysis.

*Qualitive content analysis* refers to the internal structure of the cultural phenomenon under scrutiny and to its connections with the society in which it appears. There is a long tradition behind this kind of analysis. Marx put it into practice while studying the ideology of the German intelligentsia of his time (VIII, 4). Weber did the same thing in his investigation of the causal relationships between the Calvinist ethic and the growth of Western capitalism (VIII, 3). But qualitative content analysis was incorporated formally into sociological research later on, after the Second World War, when the study of the mass media of communication and the culture thus transmitted—'mass culture'—became more wide-spread. A good example of this new tendency is Bernard Berelson's *Content Analysis in Communication Research,*[7] which appeared in 1952. Whether or not they mention it in their publications the majority of ethnologists, anthropologists and sociologists of culture make use of qualitative content analysis to understand and explain their documents. They 'read' and interpret the cultural phenomena at hand. Thus, Claude Lévi-Strauss' deciphering of the mythologies of tribal societies has not only helped us to understand their social structure and behaviour, but also the meaning of life and the world for those human beings who are so far removed from the universe of modern man. Julio Caro Baroja has increased our capacity to comprehend the 'magic mentality' through his analyses of documents relating to trials carried out by the Catholic Inquisition; indirectly, his work has shed further light on the difficult question of 'orthodoxy' in belief and allegiance.[8] There are other studies which present a lower degree of interpretation and which leave much of the analysis to the reader. The work of Oscar Lewis among some of the lowest strata of the Mexican or Puerto Rican societies is an example, of this trend.[9] In this case the researcher limits himself to the verbatim reproduction of oral culture, thus producing valuable documents. He may accompany this with his own hypotheses or theories, but in principle these do not enter the presentation itself, except in the external design of the research project.

*NOTES on Chapter 2, Section 2*

1. S. R. Steinmetz *Geloof en Misdaad* (Amsterdam, 1913), and R. Michels *Il proletariato e la borghesia nel movimiento socialista italino: saggio di scienza sociografico–politica* (Turin, 1908).
2. C. Madge *The Tools of Social Science* (London: Longmans, 1953) p. 17.
3. For this classification cf. W. M. Kolb in W. M. Kolb and J. Gould *A Dictionary of the Social Sciences* (London: Tavistock & UNESCO, 1964) p. 692.
4. Cf. R. Boudon *L'analyse mathématique des faits sociaux* (Paris: Plon, 1967).
5. Cf. P. Lazarsfeld *et alii The Language of Social Research* (New York: Free Press, 1964) pp. 111–99.
6. A. Silbermann 'Systematische Inhaltsanalyse' in R. König *et alii op. cit.* p. 572.
7. (Glencoe: Free Press, 1952).

8. C. Lévi-Strauss, *Mythologiques* (Paris: Plon, 1964, 1966, 2 vols.). J. Caro Baroja, *Vidas mágicas e Inquisición* (Madrid: Taurus, 1967, 2 vols.).
9. O. Lewis *The Children of Sánchez* (New York: Random House, 1961), and *La Vida* (London: Secker, 1967). For the shortcomings of this method, however, cf. Víctor Urquidi 'Luis Oscar Sánchez' in *Los hijos de Jones* (University of Texas at Austin, 1969).

# 3 PSYCHO-SOCIOLOGICAL METHODS

The methods which, for the sake of convenience, have been called descriptive observe easily identifiable traits of human behaviour (such as language, aggressive actions, migrations) as well as the material consequences of such behaviour (the work of art, the political pamphlet, the totem). Next to them stand those methods whose aim is the exploration of the psychological dimension of social life. Inevitably such exploration must also have as a starting point data which possess a minimum degree of objectivity. The contents of social consciousness in man can only be inferred from those data.

The methods of sociology are, in this context, also those of social psychology; this is a discipline in its own right, but it is also a bridge between sociology and psychology.

*The interview*

Interviews and questionnaires admirably reflect the spirit of curiosity about the human predicament and the respect for each person's opinions which inspires the discipline of sociology, for these techniques express a basic attitude of humility before the motivations and reasons which impel men to act as they do. Interviews and questionnaires show that the social scientist abstains from passing judgement over that which seems most obvious without first having asked the people involved for their views about the situation. Members of the bourgeoisie, prostitutes, soldiers, wizards, labourers, engineers, missionary nuns, aristocrats—they all possess a point of view, a vision of the world and its events, a life experience, which the questionnaire and the interview may help to bring to the fore and to record.

*Questionnaires* are ways of sounding out a given population—frequently through a sample. A set of questions is answered by willing respondents, who fill them in, or answer them verbally. Of all techniques employed by sociologists, questionnaires are the most widely known by the public, as many private firms and public corporations use questionnaires for their own market or opinion studies. The motivations behind these studies often impairs their scientific value. The use of questionnaires can very easily lead to erroneous results, so that very strict rules must be used throughout in order to obtain the minimum representativeness of the sample, the good quality of the questions themselves, the sincerity of the respondents, and the most suitable place and time for the operation. Besides, the questionnaire must correspond to the central elements of the hypothesis which inspires it. In order to meet these conditions, social scientists begin with one or several pilot interviews to help them revise and refine the final questionnaire and sample. And once the returns are all in, classification, quantification, codification, and interpretation of results (by establishing the pertinent correlations) takes place. These final results are then looked at in the framework of relevant sociological theory.

The *interview* proper offers greater scope than questionnaires, which are rigid and brief, thus often oversimplifying complex problems. Interviews entail a longer meeting between the researcher and the interviewee, and possibly a whole series of meetings. It is for these reasons also that interviews vary greatly, depending on the type of information needed and the whole design of the research project. Apart from the interviews which are strictly characteristic of psychology (clinical, therapeutic, and diagnostic interviews) one finds those which are closer to sociology and social psychology. One of the most characteristic is the *focused interview* which concentrates on a given theme; the subject expresses his reactions to a specific phenomenon. One can analyse for instance the reaction of an audience to a film they have just seen, or the effects of commercial advertising or political propaganda on the opinions held by different groups of people. Using the interview, 'the validity of the hypotheses derived from content analysis and social psychological theory' can be tested, and 'unanticipated responses to the situation, . . . giving rise to fresh hypotheses' can be ascertained.[1] Another widely used type is the *informal interview* which gives the subject the opportunity to express himself freely for hours, days, and even months. (For obvious reasons this has also received the name of *non-directive interview*.) The work of Oscar Lewis just mentioned is based on this kind of protracted and free interviewing. Normally this intensive technique cannot be used on a large scale as it would involve great numbers of interviewers and a very painstaking and slow process of codification of answers, resulting in a very costly programme of research. Yet it is valuable as an aid to the *participant observation* by field workers who live for long periods in a given social environment in order to study and comprehend it from the inside. Using this method those elements which must inevitably be overlooked by statistical data are brought to the fore. The reconstruction of *life histories* by reproducing the accounts given by one or several subjects to the researcher is a technique based on such intensive interviewing. If then the sociologist relates the case or cases studied to wider theory and known generalisations—e.g., migration trends, economic fluctuations, historical events—the study may become very enlightening, as it fills the gaps of 'impersonal' sociological considerations.[2] Finally, a third type of interview can be mentioned, the *free-answer interview*: this technique involves the careful elaboration of a questionnaire which nevertheless gives entire freedom to the interviewee in his answers. The questions being the same for each subject interviewed, final codification is made easier.

Together with questionnaires, interviews are the most frequently used of sociological techniques, though they are not (as some sociologists tend to believe) the most important. It would indeed be very hard to prove that any one is paramount in importance. The difficulties in interviewing are as great as in other fields of inquiry —if not greater. Many difficulties, to give the obvious example, are cultural. Let us only think of the awkward situation of an interviewer trying to ask questions about politics in Sicily, sheet of questions in hand, as if he were canvassing in an English town. Or that of an interviewer asking 'middle class questions' to lower working class people. In order to possess a minimum of validity questionnaires and interviews must meet a series of personal, cultural and psychological requirements, which vary from place to place and over time.

*Attitude scales.* Human beings possess attitudes which can be defined as predispositions towards real or imaginary phenomena, that appear with a certain amount of persistence in given individuals, groups or collectivities. They are concrete and discrete, even if they appear in clusters, and can be assumed to respond to more general beliefs and values. These, though, can only be inferred from attitudes, as only attitudes are fully detectable. They can often be measured through *attitude scales*. These were first developed by Thurstone and his collaborators, and later improved and simplified by Likert.[3] Each type of answer is related to a numeric score and the sum of these scores gives us the degree of intensity of the attitude in question. In other words, attitudes are established through a series of attitude statements. We can thus establish the intensity of racial prejudice, the degree of acceptance of a set of moral conventions, the intensity of xenophobic feelings in a community, and so on. Theodor Adorno and his associates employed a scale of authoritarian attitudes with which they successfully measured the degree of anti-Semitism as well as that of authoritarianism in individuals. Their investigation led them to the formulation of the notion of the 'authoritarian personality' which combines clusters of certain attitudes, such as conventionalism, submission, superstition, aggressiveness, cynicism or moral indifference, and prudery.[4] Thanks to Adorno's scale (the F scale)[4] and its general research design, new aspects of totalitarian political phenomena have become clearer.

In this field of research it soon became apparent that there are very high positive correlations between various types of attitudes. The presence of attitudes A, B, C, . . . in an individual or category of individuals often implies the existence of another series, N, P, Q, . . . It was thus that Louis Guttman developed his *scalogram analysis*, an attitude scale designed to establish whether attitudes can be arranged along a certain continuum. Thus acceptance of any statement or item on the scale ought to imply acceptance of any statement or item below it. This means that all attitudes in the Guttman scale must relate to one dimension of social experience. If items are so different that they cannot be ranked, attitudes cannot be scaled either.

Lazarsfeld, for his part, realised that most measurements were based on overt statements. He set out to analyse the *latent structures* which underlie manifest attitudes. Correlations between diverse attitudes are explained by their supposed connection to the latent structure. Ethnocentrism, for instance, can only manifest itself in concrete attitudes towards one's own country, towards the individuals of other countries, or a vision of contemporary history as understood by the subject. 'Ethnocentrism' would be the 'latent structure' behind all these expressed attitudes. This brings us back to values and beliefs; perhaps what Lazarsfeld calls latent structures are what have all along been called values. But even if this is so, the rigour of the approach is essential. Moreover, all scaling and attitude measuring methods have steadily advanced in formalisation, refinement and mathematical elaboration.

*Sociometry.* The term and basic notion of sociometry were in the making for quite a long time[5] before Jacob Moreno finally perfected this method of social research. Sociometry, said Moreno, 'deals with the mathematical study of psychological properties of populations, the experimental technique of and the results obtained by application of quantitative methods'.[6] (In this context 'population' means group or network of groups.) Basically, sociometry is a method of measuring certain individual interrelationships, though the results will tell us as much about the individuals as about their groups. Animal societies can also be investigated with this technique.

Sociometry starts by enquiring into the sympathies, antipathies and feelings of indifference detectable in a group. This allows us to represent graphically a system of affective relationships, which is in its turn related to the authority, leadership and communication patterns of the group. Such graphic representation is called a *sociogram* and is interpreted with the help of a series of notions such as 'social distance', 'leadership' and 'isolation'. If values are assigned to each one of these concepts and they are then related to the numbers of individuals or relationships at hand, final measurements can be made. In spite of the excessive claims for sociometry made by Moreno—who thought it could be applied to the larger society —it has mainly proved fruitful as a technique for the study of small groups, some of whose structural aspects are eloquently reflected by the sociogram. Sociometry also illuminates some aspects of the internal dynamics of groups and their behaviour towards other groups, and allows for some measurement of the status of individuals (III, 4). Some of the techniques associated with it have also proved useful for therapeutic purposes and for the development of sociological insights into the problems of everyday life. Such is the case of the *psychodrama* and the *sociodrama*, whereby the subject or subjects act out in a play their real situations. In spite of all its advantages, it seems clear that sociometry fails to explain the causes behind the situations it so often so clearly exposes, while it tends to give a far too static vision of group structure.[7] As with many other sociological methods, when used alone it provides only a biased and incomplete view of the subject. Most research projects require the imaginative use of several methods before the central questions of sociological enquiry can be answered.

*NOTES on Chapter II, Section 3*

1. R. K. Merton and P. Kendall 'The Focused Interview' (*Am. Jnl. Soc.* 1946), reprinted in P. Lazarsfeld *et alii The Language . . . op. cit.* p. 477.
2. J. F. Marsal *Hacer la América* (Buenos Aires: Instituto Di Tella, 1969), especially his chapter 'Historias de vida y ciencias sociales' pp. 409–34.
3. W. S. Togerson *Theory and Methods of Scaling* (New York: Wiley, 1958).
4. T. Adorno *et alii The Authoritarian Personality* (New York: Harper, 1950); the F stands for 'fascist'.
5. A. Coste *Les principes d'une sociologie objective* (Paris: Alcan, 1899).
6. J. L. Moreno *Who Shall Survive?* (New York, Beacon House, 1953 edn.) p. 53. In Moreno's mind sociometry (or rather 'socionomy') is also a philosophy, and a therapy for ailing mankind; only the technical aspects are mentioned in our book.
7. M. Cornaton *Groupes et société* (Toulouse: Privat, 1969), p. 54.

# 4 HISTORICAL AND COMPARATIVE METHODS

*History and sociology*

It is not unusual to find the sciences—and especially the social sciences—classified in two categories, the nomothetic and the ideographic. According to this classification the ideographic sciences would be those which study unique and unrepeatable events, while the nomothetic sciences would be those that attempt to make generalisations. Also according to this classification sociology is a nomothetic science, whereas history is ideographic. And, on the face of it, this describes what the practitioners of these two sciences often do. Thus a historian might investigate such phenomena as 'the reign of Catherine II of Russia', 'the maritime trade of Barcelona during the Middle Ages', 'the origins of the Inca empire'. Yet, if it is the sociologist who becomes interested in the same themes, it is very likely that he will try to subsume them under wider issues, and study them as further evidence and illustration for his own concerns; he will probably study them under headings such as 'despotism and social change', 'the rise of a mercantile bourgeoisie', and 'civilisation as a social system'. The historian will try to increase our accurate knowledge of unique phenomena of the past, whereas the sociologist will try to correct and increase what we know of certain uniformities of social behaviour under specific conditions. This is, in principle, the difference between the two methods. But a closer scrutiny substantiates our earlier contention that sociology shows a very considerable degree of dependence on other social sciences (I, 1). History is a case in point. But if sociology lacks autonomy in relation to history, the latter, in so far as it now tries to generalise, is also losing such autonomy and becoming more sociological. If it is true that many historians would still refuse even to sketch a few shy generalisations about the nature of human affairs over certain periods of time and in certain kinds of situations, many now realise the necessity for using sociological notions and ideal types if fragmentation as well as conceptual confusion are to be avoided. Clear concepts of the meaning of 'social stratification', 'charismatic authority', 'estate society', 'social mobility' and so on cannot hinder the historian's task.

Some of the early sociologists included in their theories grand designs about the history of mankind, its general 'laws' and even its future (X,2). Perhaps as a reaction to such imperialist claims, later sociologists often became excessively ahistorically oriented, and only studied current phenomena, without inquiring about the sequence of events that had made them possible. This second phase can now be said to be over. The data of history are now intensively used by sociologists and—and this is indicative of the quality achieved by sociological work—historians are relying increasingly on historical work done by sociologists.[1]

### The comparative method

The analyses of social change in history are carried out with the help of several methods, of which the most favoured by sociologists is the comparative method. The comparative method entails the study, side by side, of different groups, collectivities, communities or institutions which present some important similar patterns. Total diversity precludes comparison, but relative diversity allows us to establish the factors that cause differences in structure and in the trend of events. The comparative method—also widely used in studies of contemporary societies—does not have to be restricted to coetaneous societies, hence the significance of historical data. Karl Wittfogel has drawn a picture of several civilisations—all far apart in time and space, but all based on bureaucratic despotism and on the control, by the central power, of the natural resources of the territory. This has allowed him to produce a number of important generalisations about the characteristics which are common to all these vast sociopolitical units. And Barrington Moore, in another comparative and historical study, has investigated the lines of change which have taken place in several countries leading towards modernisation either through the path of dictatorship or through that of political pluralism.[2] These sociologists are actually following in the steps of men like Weber, who often tried to answer important questions with the help of the comparative approach. Why did a bourgeois capitalist class appear and succeed in post-Medieval Europe and why did it never develop well, let alone succeed, in other highly developed societies, such as China and Imperial Rome? Still earlier, Alexis de Tocqueville, tried to explain the growth of a democratic, individualistic and comparative society by studying the then young United States, as well as, in another work, the remote origins of the French Revolution. Both studies, which are now classics of nineteenth-century sociology are inspired by the comparative approach. For example, cultural comparisons between the Spanish and the English conquests of America led Tocqueville to reflections that are still valid for an understanding of the very different societies which have flourished south and north of the Rio Grande. But basically he studied the advance of a new system of economic, political and cultural relationships—something one could call 'modernity' (X, 3)—under different social conditions, on both sides of the Atlantic. These examples are typically macro-sociological, and it goes without saying that the historical comparative method has often been applied to much more limited subjects.

The comparative method is amply used in anthropological and ethological research. (Thus *cross-cultural* research is nothing else but the name used by social anthropology for its own brand of comparative studies.) George P. Murdock, realising the necessity for storing the information which was continually building up and the importance of having it at the disposal of social scientists everywhere, opened a 'Cross Cultural Survey' at Yale University. Today, the Human Relations Area File has been developed on the basis of Murdock's idea and material, and is one of the principal 'data banks' which social scientists possess. (Incidentally, in the Victorian age, Herbert Spencer had already begun an important systematic inventory of information about social institutions in a great number of countries.) Today, all sorts of data banks are developing in various places, making important factual information readily and widely available.

The importance of the comparative method in sociology need hardly be emphasised—as Durkheim used to say, it is *the* method. It is an essential corrective to one of sociology's worst biases—

parochialism. It would be extremely risky, for instance, to make generalisations about the social mobility of skilled workers in all industrialised societies if one had only studied, say, the upper working class of Sweden. Thus even if a given research project is not specifically comparative, it is advisable that it should be put into perspective and its results contrasted with those of similar studies in other areas with similar characteristics.

*NOTES on Chapter II, Section 4*

1. R. Nisbet *The Social Bond* (New York: Knopf, 1970) p. 344.
2. K. Wittfogel *Oriental Despotism* (Yale University Press, 1956); B. Moore, Jr. *The Social Origins of Dictatorship and Democracy* (London: Allen Lane, 1967).

# 5 EXPERIMENTAL METHODS AND QUANTIFICATION

The *experiment* is an operation in a controlled situation which tries to discover the unknown effects produced by the introduction of one factor amongst other known factors. In terms of variables, the experiment can also be defined as the observation of the variation of one or several dependent variables in the presence of one independent variable (II, 2). In experiments we are able to control the situation, that is, to decide which are going to be the dependent variables and to choose which is going to be the independent one, and how and when it will be introduced. This entails the active participation of the researcher and his capacity to manipulate factors. Now, in the social sciences the barriers to the unbounded use of these methods are considerable, for their 'material' is composed of human beings who cannot be manipulated as objects or animals.

Yet there are some areas of research in which social science experimentation is quite feasible and has already yielded interesting results. Notable examples are available from the sociology of education and small group research. The effects of new educational techniques, new kinds of school organisation, new avenues of social integration in school or college, and so on, can be (or, rather, must be) first tried out experimentally. In small group research, students often lend themselves to harmless experimentation as 'guinea pigs', and mentally disturbed patients or prisoners also often very willingly cooperate in it. As mentioned earlier, experimentation requires the presence of at least one control group, that is, a social unit of characteristics as similar to those of the experimental group as possible, and which is not submitted to the introduction of the new factor.

There are techniques, which can be called *quasi-experimental*, that have some, if not all, of the advantages of full experimentation. Such are *projective techniques*, or tests used to check the reactions of the subject to objects presented to him by the investigator. This type of test has the advantage of circumventing the element of insincerity which often beclouds the answers given to a questionnaire. The notion of psychological projection has a Freudian origin, and it can be defined as the process whereby feelings and emotions come to the fore—manifest themselves—in a transformed version, since the conscious level of our mind—the ego—rejects and represses them in their original form. Some of these techniques—such as the 'thematic apperception test', or T.A.T.—are very well-known. The T.A.T. invites the subject to 'invent' a story on the basis of a minimum set of data—usually a collection of pictures depicting ambiguous social situations. This test studies personality, but may be relevant for sociology as some of the information obtained is directly about patterns of social interaction, such as racial discrimination. Sociometry, mentioned above, is also a quasi-experimental technique, as combinations of individuals chosen by the observer play a paramount part in it. *Ex post facto* experiments can also be mentioned within this category. They can be used in sociology where a social situation is well-known and then an event occurs which alters it. Questionnaires, interviews and all sorts of reliable records are put into use to study the effects of the event in question (independent variable). The intensity of technological change in the modern world provides us with the opportunity to study the social effects of some new factors entering the life of certain communities or collectivities in an essentially '*ex post facto*' manner. If the researcher knows that, for example, television is going to be introduced in an area, he can study the relevant elements before and after it appears, and tell us much about the social consequences of this important medium of communication.[1]

All these methods, like many mentioned earlier, try to give a mathematical or geometrical expression to their findings. In many cases such expression is only ancillary to the main train of thought, in others quantitative language is vital.[2] If we accept the notion of sociology as it has been put forward here, it will have to be recognised that the degree of quantification and 'mathematisation' needed will vary in accordance with the premises and requirements of the study and the research design. There is no shorthand formula to express the degree of quantification and mathematical language needed in each case. Let it be clearly stated—especially in the present introductory context, where only the most elementary examples of statistical tables or data will be presented—that the highest *relevant* amount of quantification and mathematisation is always called for, and that the student of the discipline will be well advised to familiarise himself with such language and methods. It must be added, however, that a purely mathematical sociology offers a very poor interpretation of man in society. But if *all* social reality cannot be reduced to algebraic operations, equations and matrices, neither can these be ignored; still less can one ignore the data of national accounts, censuses, demographic studies and econometrics. They *must* be used but, as Aaron Cicourel has correctly pointed out they should not be taken as 'given', for they are largely the product of census bureaus, correctional agencies, welfare offices and business concerns with only relative claims to objectivity.[3] They must therefore be used in conjunction with other criteria of sociological analysis, as it would appear that once all these quantitative data have been duly taken into account, ultimate sociological generalisations about the world of man always entail a humanistic element which still calls for a language of its own.

*NOTES on Chapter II, Section 5*

1. H. T. Himmelweit *et al. Television and the Child* (Oxford University Press and The Nuffield Foundation 1958).
2. R. Stone *Mathematics in the Social Sciences* (London: Chapman, 1966) pp. 1–18; P. Lazarsfeld *Mathematical Thinking in the Social Sciences* (Glencoe: Free Press, 1954); V. Capecchi, 'La misurazione in sociologia' in F. Alberoni ed. *Questioni di sociologia* (Brescia: Scuola Editrice, 1966, vol. II) pp. 697–740.
3. A. V. Cicourel *Method and Measurement in Sociology* (New York: Free Press, 1964) p. 36.

# III  The Elementary Forms of Social Life

## 1  THE FRAME OF REFERENCE

Each zone or aspect of human society possesses a set of qualities which are peculiar to it and can be found in other areas only in a diffuse or secondary way. These phenomena naturally call for special branches of social science, such as social biology, demography, human ecology, the sociology of occupations, the study of labour relations, economic history, and so forth. Next to this long array of clusters of phenomena (which, by the way, only the mind of the scholar isolates) one finds another set of social phenomena which always appear with the same degree of prominence and which are the common denominator of any social situation. We could call them primordial dimensions of human society or perhaps, in plainer words, elementary forms of social life. (And when the word 'elementary' is used here it is not meant that they are simple, but that they are the basic forms upon which the web of social life is built.) These elementary forms cover the whole spectrum of social science in general, and of sociology in particular.

Sociology has developed a system of primary concepts and theories for the purpose of understanding these phenomena and making them amenable to use in research situations. Such primary concepts and theories denote universal social phenomena found at virtually all levels of society. Primary concepts of the elementary forms of social life can also be defined as those which are equally necessary to all areas of sociology, cutting across its conventional sub-divisions and sub-disciplines. Fortunately, owing to their very general nature, these concepts are few. They are always under fire from critics, and subject to continual elaboration, for they belong to the most theoretical level of the discipline. They are its core, and they constitute the most problematic area of sociology.[1] Logic demands that this area be treated first in spite of the danger of deterring the reader with dry abstraction—something that does not arise when dealing with the much more specific problems of the specialised branches of sociology.

The present treatment of the elementary forms of social life will attempt to be systematic, but will not be bound by the limits of the present chapter. There are notions—such as 'social change', 'culture', 'division of social labour'—which are also primary in the sense here employed, but that lend themselves more readily to separate treatment elsewhere, even though they also possess the characteristics of universality (in that they are found everywhere in society) and generality (in that they affect the whole social situation). The concepts (and theories related to them) which will now be presented are: social group, social action, social position (including norms, roles, status and social control), social function, social conflict, social order, structure and system.

*NOTES on Chapter III, Section 1*

1. What I call 'elementary forms of social life' must be distinguished from the 'constitutive central ideas of the sociological tradition' as presented, for instance, by Nisbet. However, there is a very high degree of overlap between the two. Cf. R. Nisbet *The Sociological Tradition* (London: Heinemann, 1967).

## 2  SOCIAL GROUPS

Groups are a datum so central to sociology that a number of its practitioners define the discipline simply as the science of human groups. Even if others prefer to emphasise the social behaviour aspect of sociology as central to its definition, it is still possible to agree with Enrique Tierno that the group 'is the initial observable structure of sociology'.[1] A *social group* may be defined as a number of individuals who find themselves in a state of mutual and relatively lasting integration. 'Integration' means here that they share norms, common goals of action, and a feeling of belonging to the group—regardless of the degree of intensity with which these phenomena occur, or the reason why they occur. The numerical element also varies. A group may consist of two individuals (for instance, two lovers) but it may also consist of a vast national community (say, the Italians). These collectivities are groups in so far as their members belong to them with a clear degree of awareness of such belongingness and hence act in a way that reveals the existence of that group, or if the behaviour of their members cannot be satisfactorily explained without regarding them as part of a group.

A group is not a category of individuals, even though in some cases the word 'group' is used in this misleading sense. What population studies call an 'age group' is not a group, but a manner of 'grouping' statistical data from a demographic standpoint (hence the use of the concept of 'cohort' in demography to describe a collection of people having a common trait or set of traits). This fact does not prevent group formation based on common traits, though. In a given society we may find that all males above a certain age (a category) form a real group, such as a council of elders. What is important here is not only the criterion for membership— age—but the fact that there is a durable integration, recognised also by those who are outside the group. A less simple example is that of a social class; it can be a merely taxonomic criterion based on objective observable data, but it can also be a group if it shows sufficient awareness of its position in society to affect the social behaviour of its members. To make things more complicated the degree of 'class consciousness' (VI, 3) varies considerably not only in intensity but also in quality. At the lowest point in consciousness a class is a collectivity which is nearly an aggregate (aggregates are not groups), whereas at the highest it is a very structured group. Both extremes are rare, and the degree of 'groupness' of such collectivities as social classes fluctuates according to certain other factors, studied by the field of social stratification. In general, groups are such an elementary fact that to affirm their existence is literally only to recognise the oldest axiom of social science—that man exists only through social groups. Outside them human life is simply not possible. (Those who believe that hermits and Robinson Crusoe do live outside groups should read on, until they come across the notion of the 'reference group'.)

A first important distinction in looking at groups is that of *groups* and *subgroups*. Only the *dyad* (a group of two individuals) is a group that cannot be subdivided. All other groups, starting with the *triad* (a group of three individuals) possess subgroups, that is, sets of relationships that bind together sections of the wider group. The distinction between groups and subgroups is also a question of perspective, since practically all groups are subgroups of others. Besides, the existence of a system of subgroups does not have to be only a *de facto* situation, as with the cliques of friends we find in classrooms and schools generally, but it can also be a *de jure* one: an army is prescriptively divided into battalions, brigades, divisions. Between these two poles, a wide range of institutionalisation is possible. Informal cliques of workers in a factory may become, in a situation of labour unrest, sources of 'unofficial power' with whom both management and official unions must come to terms. There are subgroups, whose life within the group may be peaceful and even called for by the group structure itself, cooperating with it in the attainment of its goals and strengthening its integration; but under certain circumstances they may well conduct hostilities against it, undermine it, or secede from it. Most of the efforts of sociology are directed, one way or the other, towards explaining how it is that all these phenomena occur.

The only group that is not a subgroup is *society* itself. A 'society' is the widest possible group, and just for that reason, it can be rather diffuse and imprecise. Society is a much clearer concept if it coincides with a collectivity whose boundaries are easy to delimit, as happens with certain tribes. Modern inter-state and inter-nation interaction has made this concept less precise. We shift its area of coverage at our convenience when we say 'Western society', 'Scottish society', 'Soviet society'. Nevertheless it is a handy concept, and few sociologists want to split hairs over it.[2] The 'group' definition of society seems acceptable enough. The adjective *societal* is often used to refer to social characteristics that are to be found throughout a whole society—in contrast with the familiar 'social' which refers to any level of generality.

The distinction between groups and subgroups conforms to a system of supra-ordination and subordination which can often be easily distinguished by the external observer, as well as by the actual members of these collectivities. The latter, though, being emotionally involved in their situation make other distinctions that are vital for the description of the social behaviour produced. There is the distinction between *in-group* and *out-group*, to use William Graham Sumner's expression. The greater the loyalty and identification felt towards the in-group, the greater its strength and internal cohesion, often accompanied by an intensification of feelings of differentiation toward other groups, or out-groups, perceived as external and alien. This elementary distinction is based on the 'we' feeling and the 'they' feeling which one finds wherever groups form and thrive.

The 'we' element becomes an integral part of one's own consciousness of the ego. Very rarely, if ever, does man think of himself as detached from his entire social world; he takes it for granted that belonging to a certain country, being a scion of a given family, a member of a party or social movement, employed in a certain firm, are aspects of his ego. Even if he feels alienated from one or various of those aspects (VI, 2) he will still identify with others, thus maintaining some important group attachments. In-group and out-group feelings produce several phenomena. One of the most important is ethnocentrism—another word coined by Sumner—which refers to the belief that one's in-group is superior to comparable out-groups. Ethnocentrism at a national level may degenerate into chauvinism and jingoism, and is often identified with these exacerbated feelings, but racial and aristocratic prejudice are also, strictly speaking, extreme forms of ethnocentrism.[3] However, a certain mild degree of ethnocentrism—in the sociological sense of the term—may be necessary for the self-respect and inner loyalty which are necessary to any minimally cohesive group.

The problems posed by the existence of in-groups and out-groups lead directly to the question of *reference groups*, a notion whose origin is to be found in social psychology. Individuals behave and judge their social world not only in relation to the members of their own group but also in relation to other groups and their members; social behaviour must be understood in such terms[4] if it is to make any sense. Reference groups, as out-groups which are used to orient social behaviour, are of two different signs. They are positive if they are seen as embodying norms, values, and life-styles which are desirable, coveted or envied. The *nouveau riche* who strives to be fully accepted by 'high society' and snobbishly apes its members thinks of it as a positive reference group. A *negative* reference group shows the opposite characteristics; it embodies norms, values and life-styles that must be avoided. Our hypothetic snob may consider his own group of origin (for instance a poor family in a rural community) as a negative reference group, membership of which is to be hidden or severed because it is socially degrading. In this situation, what is important is not how groups really are but how they are imagined by other groups. Converted Jews in sixteenth-century Castile did not possess many of the characteristics gentiles attributed to them; even less did those of Eastern Europe who suffered from pogroms in the nineteenth century. Afrikaaners in South Africa attribute certain characteristics to peoples of Indian or negro origin whether they possess them or not; they have even institutionalised those feelings in the form of discriminatory laws.

From this example it is clear that the term 'group' is occasionally imprecise. In some situations it is not strictly a group that is the referent; it may be anything from a single person to an abstract idea, as Runciman points out. What is important is that a person (or collectivity) will orient his behaviour towards (or away from) that referent. Within this framework the notion of *relative deprivation* is crucial. Positive reference groups appear to possess something which we lack, so we experience a feeling of 'injustice'. Runciman defines it in the following manner:

> Relative deprivation may be broadly defined by saying that a person is relatively deprived when (1) he does not have X, (2) he sees some other person or persons, which may include himself at some previous or imagined time, as having X (whether or not they do have X), and (3) he wants X (whether or not it is feasible that he should have X) . . .
> On the basis of this definition we may say that the further the positive referent (or its equivalent) from a given person, the greater his relative deprivation.[5]

Relative deprivation and reference groups are related phenomena which are important for the explanation of the dynamics of social inequality (VI, 2, 3). They illustrate the cleavages caused by the process of social differentiation and the feelings and behaviour which they arouse. The fact, however, that people make efforts to enter other groups, or try to bar people from gaining access to their own, does not mean that different groups (not just groups and subgroups) cannot interpenetrate each other on a peaceful and often mutually advantageous basis.

Georg Simmel approached this question when he investigated the problem of what he called 'intersection of social circles',[6] that is, the overlapping and intertwining of groups as seen from the standpoint of the individual in whom all these 'circles' meet. Socially, groups and subgroups may remain distinct but, as far as individual members are concerned, at least in modern society,

> the person belongs first of all to his parental family, then to his family of procreation and thereby also to the family of his wife. Beyond this he belongs to his occupational group, which often involves him in several interest-groups. For example, in an occupation that embraces both supervisory and subordinate personnel, each person participates in the affairs of his particular business, department office, etc., each of which comprises higher and lower

employees. Moreover, a person also participates in a group made up of similarly situated employees from several, different firms. Then, a person is likely to be aware of his citizenship, of the fact that he belongs to a particular social class. He is, moreover, a reserve officer, he belongs to a few clubs and engages in a social life which puts him in touch with different social groups. This is a great variety of groups. Some of these groups are integrated. Others are, however, so arranged that one group appears as the original focus of an individual's affiliation, from which he then turns toward affiliation with other, quite different groups on the basis of his special qualities, which distinguish him from other members of his primary group. His bond with the primary group may well continue to exist, like one aspect of a complex image, which retains its original time-space coordinates though the image itself has long since become established psychologically as an objective configuration in its own right.[7]

This fact of multiple intersection is basically dynamic but, for the individual in complex societies it is also a process of increasing definition of his social space. Simmel adds:

> The groups with which the individual is affiliated constitute a system of coordinates, as it were, such that each new group with which he becomes affiliated circumscribes him more exactly and unambiguously. To belong to any of these groups leaves the individual considerable leeway. But the larger the number of groups to which an individual belongs, the more improbable is it that other persons will exhibit the same combination of group-affiliations, that these particular groups will 'intersect' [in a second individual] . . . To speak platonically, each thing has a part in as many ideas as it has manifold attributes, and it achieves thereby its individual determination. There is an analogous relationship between the individual and the groups with which he is affiliated.[8]

Groups, then, are frames of reference for man's social life.[9] They define his social space, orient his behaviour by providing him with a map of his world and his goals, and life chances. In other words, they are the concrete frameworks of social action.

## NOTES on Chapter III, Section 2

1. E. Tierno Galván *Conocimiento y ciencias sociales* (Madrid: Tecnos, 1966) p. 137.
2. For a discussion of the meaning of the notion 'society', cf. T. Geiger 'Gesellschaft' in A. Vierkandt's *Handwörtabuch der Sozialwissenschaften* (Stuttgart: Enke, 1931) pp. 202–11.
3. W. G. Sumner *Folkways* (Boston, 1907).
4. R. K. Merton *Social Theory and Social Structure* (New York: Free Press, 1967 ed.) p. 282.

5. W. G. Runciman 'Problems of Research on Relative Deprivation' in H. H. Hyman & E. Singer *Readings in Reference Group Theory and Research* (New York: Free Press, 1968) p. 70. Runciman's statement that 'the further the positive referent . . . from a given person, the greater his relative deprivation' is only so if the person sees the position of the referent as accessible. For further qualification on this point cf. IX, 3 especially pp. 244–5 and X, 3.

6. G. Simmel 'Die Kreuzung sozialer Kreisen' in his *Soziologie* (Munich: Duncker & Humboldt, 1922) pp. 305–44. For difficulties in translating this expression—which is also the title of the chapter mentioned—cf. R. Bendix's remarks in G. Simmel *Conflict and the Web of Group-Affiliations* (New York: Free Press, 1964) p. 123.

7. G. Simmel *Web of Group-Affiliations, op. cit.* p. 138.

8. *Ibid.* p. 140.

9. For an attempt to draw up a critical inventory of the numerous ways in which groups have been classified cf. Lucio Mendieta *Teoría de los agrupamientos sociales* (Universidad Autónoma de México, 1963, 2nd ed.); also A. Vierkandt *Kleine Gesellschaftslehre* (Stuttgart: Enke, 3rd ed. 1961, 1st ed. 1936).

# 3   SOCIAL ACTION

Social behaviour occurs whenever one or several individuals act in a way that cannot be explained without reference to other individuals; non-social behaviour belongs to the area of biology of psychology where the presence of the other members of the species seems to be irrelevant. This area—entirely unaffected by society—is very restricted, especially if one allows that certain activities which appear as non-social (the prayer of the hermit, the task of the lonely scientist in his laboratory) are deeply social, even if this is not their only nature. Thus if a Catholic is receiving holy communion, an observer who belongs to his faith will define the event as an act whereby he is receiving the sacrament of Eucharist; another observer, either less pious or a member of another faith, may say that it is merely an act of social conformity; still another, more cautious perhaps, may add that both things are true. A sociologist would not take sides in a question such as this, but he would affirm that any behaviour including people and relating them to each other—in our example, the faithful, the consecrating priest, the communicant —has an undoubted social dimension or bond, and that this is the focus of his concern.

This bond always becomes apparent in behaviour. Sociologists have made distinctive efforts to isolate its most elementary characteristics. In the first place some principles can be established about people's activities, which seem to be universally valid. Here are five basic propositions about them, as formulated by George Homans:

I. The more often a person's activity is rewarded, the more likely he is to perform the activity.

II. If in the past the occurrence of a particular stimulus, or set of stimuli, has been the occasion on which a person's activity has been rewarded, the more similar the present stimuli are to the past ones the more likely the person is to perform the activity, or some similar activity, now.

III. The more valuable the reward of an activity is to a person, the more likely he is to perform the activity.

IV. The more often in the recent past a person has received a particular reward the less valuable any further unit of that reward becomes to him.

V. When a person's activity does not receive the reward he expected, or receives punishment he did not expect, he will be angry and, in anger, the results of aggressive behaviour are rewarding.[1]

These propositions are obviously very elementary notions about human interaction sometimes verging on the tautological, which cannot be taken in isolation if a proper theory of society is to be developed but neither can they be ignored. By themselves, they can only lead to a stimulus-response oversimplified scheme of human conduct. Would they satisfactorily explain the example of the Catholic sacrament with which we started? Perhaps an answer can be found if some distinctions are introduced into the notion of social behaviour. So far, only 'social behaviour' has been mentioned when referring to human interaction.

Social behaviour is a conveniently loose expression, for it includes both the animal level of the human species and that level which seems to distinguish it from other animal societies—culture (IV, 1). At the level of culture, it is perhaps more adequate to speak of *social action*. Max Weber's has become the standard definition: Social action (*Handeln*) 'is any attitude or behaviour (*Verhalten*) . . . in so far as the agent or agents attach a subjective meaning (*Sinn*) to it'.[2] 'Social action', Weber adds, 'implies, in accordance with the subjective sense of the agent or agents, the activities and acts of others, and is oriented towards them'. The outstanding aspect of this definition is that it hinges upon the assumption that one cannot separate the meaning attached to behaviour from behaviour itself. If man is a cultural animal, his conduct cannot always be explained by his biology (IV, 1); it must also be traced to the significance he attaches to certain ways of behaving—to his fears, ambitions, aesthetic values, rational inclinations, loyalties, and principles—in short, to a subjective dimension of his life about which some remarks have been made earlier on. We also saw how this hypothesis is vital for a fully fledged sociology.

The intricacies of social action immediately become apparent. Meaningful social behaviour—that is behaviour which is not merely reactive—may include an 'abstention from taking any action' on the part of the agent or actor: conscious abstention and passive acquiescence are also forms of social action. Then, some actions and action sequences seem to follow a certain foreseeable pattern —the student who spends several years at a university, taking prescribed courses and examinations according to a set of academic regulations—whereas others are much less predictable, and yet very meaningful indeed to the persons involved, as in the case of men engaged in a tavern brawl. Furthermore, action is not just directed to present situations, but also to either the past or the expected future social behaviour of others. With all these complexities in mind can one classify social action in some fairly simple manner? Weber himself tried the following subdivision of social action according to its 'mode of orientation':

1. *Rational social action* (*Zweckrationalität*) is oriented towards the attainment of goals through the rational appraisal of the expected behaviour of others. This behaviour is taken as a means or condition of planned behaviour.

2. *Value-rational social action* (*Wertrationalität*). Rational social behaviour involving belief in some absolute value (religious, moral, aesthetic), for its own sake, and independently from possible material success.

3. *Affectual social action.* Guided by an emotional element (*affektuell*) of love, loyalty, hatred, and so on.

4. *Traditional social action.* Custom oriented.[3]

This fourfold classification implies, in fact, that there are two main sources of meaningful social behaviour—'rational' and 'non-rational' action. Other authors, such as Vilfredo Pareto, preferred to start from that dichotomy, at the risk of oversimplification. For him there are two main categories of social action—'logical' and 'non-logical' to use his misleading vocabulary. ('Logical' corresponds to rational social action and 'non-logical' to non-rational and irrational social action, but the definite acceptance of these labels would lead to confusion, since non-rational and irrational behaviour have an undeniable logic of their own.) 'All operations which are logically united towards an end, not only from the point of view of the subject who carries them out but also from that of those who possess a wider knowledge of it, are logical actions'; or, put in a more concise way, 'logical actions are those in which the subjective and objective coincide'.[4] 'Non-logical', non-rational social action is simply that which does not possess such traits. By taking into account the fact that social action may also be subjectively logical and objectively non-logical (if the subject does not know certain vital facts about his world) or *vice versa*, Pareto combines and subdivides the types of action possible, clearly implying, however, that no pure type is to be found in real social life—a view shared by Weber, who was also describing ideal types of social action. Although it is more difficult to prove that 'non-logical' actions are, as Pareto says, far more abundant in human society than 'logical' ones, it is clear that they have a very great weight in social life, especially when one considers those actions which are actually irrational but that are presented under a rational veneer, a point exhaustively and eloquently developed by Pareto.[5] Yet, it is in its Freudian version that this question has come to be widely known in the human sciences. Freud's relevant concept here is that of *rationalisation*, which is an attempt to justify behaviour or intended behaviour by alleging motives different from the real ones; the subject is not necessarily lying, for in genuine cases of rationalisation his motives and motivations are unknown to himself, remaining repressed and unconscious. Whether one subscribes or not to this psychoanalytical hypothesis, it is clear that men often sincerely 'give reasons' for social action which do not correspond to their real causes. Men and their institutions, show a need to legitimise their social behaviour, through constant reference to higher norms or principles (III, 4).

Talcott Parsons and Edward Shils have made an effort to unify social action theory. To this end they have distinguished between the actor, the situation in which he finds himself, and the orientation he takes towards it. Orientation, they observe, is composed of two elements: motivation and value. *Motivational orientation* is based on needs which prompt the subject to act. They are of three different kinds. (1) Cognitive motivations; these are based on the actor's perception of his situation, and on the way he thinks it can satisfy his needs. (2) Cathectic motivations; cathexis, a term first used by Freud, is an emotional response, negative or positive, to something (an institution, a person, a valued object). Cathexis orients our behaviour towards gratification and the avoidance of harm, punishment, or any other obnoxious effects of our conduct.

But it is also more than a mere automatic reaction to concrete situations, as it must include an emotional attraction (or repulsion) to an object which may elicit complicated sequences of behaviour. (3) Evaluative motivations imply a choice, by the actor, as to which of his interests he is going to pursue. *Value orientations* of social action are those which originate in the compliance of behaviour with the norms regulating the situation in which they arise. 'Correct' social behaviour is the source of the motivation here, whether it refers to trivial situations or to the basic moral principles upheld by the group concerned.[6]

A basic property of social action is that it does not consist only of mere *ad hoc* responses to particular stimuli present in a given situation; rather, the actor is surrounded by a whole system of expectations of action related to the social configuration of which he is a part.[7] His actions must be understood in terms of this system of values, norms, and the general social structure in which he finds himself not forgetting the continuous 'negotiation' that goes on in everyday life between human beings, whereby they arrive at plausible arrangements for living together.[8] The cultural orientations of social action are paramount to its right understanding (IV, 3) and preclude any simplistic interpretation of it such as the one represented by radical behaviourism, which attempts to reduce all social action to the level of conditioning processes of the stimulus-response scheme, explicitly discarding cognition and meaning. However there are signs that in some quarters of sociological theory students are becoming impatient with even the most elaborate behaviourist interpretations. Social thinkers of the past tried to explain our social world and human nature in terms of 'passions', and the modern classics of sociology were not impervious to such interpretation. Vilfredo Pareto and William Thomas developed, each in his own way, special notions to describe basic human sentiments of 'wishes'.[9] Within this tradition, a remarkable attempt has been recently made by Helmut Schoeck to develop an interpretation of social life based on one apparently timeless passion, envy.[10] Schoeck's 'envy theory of society' is inevitably one-sided, but the very perspective taken by the author provides us with new insights into those aspects of relative deprivation, emulation, and status seeking which more orthodox sociology fails to illuminate. The plea here is not that one ought to go back without reservations to classical approaches to human nature but that they should not be neglected. An effort to integrate their most lasting achievements with contemporary sociological theory is bound to prove fruitful.

Social action is teleological—even when non-rational—which means that it is oriented towards the attainment by the actor or actors, or their institutions, of certain close or distant goals. Here mere cathexis is insufficient to explain the complexity of the phenomenon: people often seek those goals down extremely painful paths, and are ready to make enormous sacrifices for them. We have only to think of religious or revolutionary movements to realise this. To accept teleology in social life does not require us, however, to affirm, or to deny, the existence of a general teleology in mankind or in human history—that is, to subscribe to some form of historicism. This is a matter for certain brands of social philosophy, and not for sociology. Yet sociology does not refuse to study long-range social trends and historical processes (X, 1, 2). It attempts to do so, however, without embracing any prophetic or mystical assumptions about the ultimate fate of our race.

*NOTES on Chapter III, Section 3*

1. G. C. Homans 'Fundamental Social Processes' in N. J. Smelser *Sociology* (New York: Wiley, 1967) pp. 32–41.
2. M. Weber *Wirtschaft und Gesellschaft* (Tübingen: Mohr, 1925) Vol. I p. 1.
3. For an English translation cf. M. Weber *The Theory ... op. cit.* pp. 115–118. The four types have been abridged from the German edition, *op. cit.*, note 1 pp. 16–22.
4. V. Pareto *Trattato di Sociologia Generale* (Milan: Communità, 1964; 1st ed. 1916) Vol. I, paras. 150 and 151.
5. *Ibid. paras.* 154 and ff.
6. T. Parsons and E. Shils *Toward a General Theory of Social Action* (Harvard University Press, 1951), pp. 3–110.
7. T. Parsons *The Social System* (London: Routledge, 1951) p. 5.
8. H. Garfinkel *Studies in Ethnomethodology* (New York: Prentice Hall, 1967).
9. V. Pareto *Trattato, op. cit.*; W. I. Thomas *The Unadjusted Girl* (Boston: Little, Brown & Co., 1923).
10. H. Schoeck *Der Neid, eine Theorie der Gesellschaft* (Freiburg: Karl Alber, 1966).

# 4 SOCIAL POSITIONS AND NORMS

*Positions: role and status*

Society is never a homogeneous mass of identical individuals. There are several causes which account for the internal differentiation of societies into institutions, occupational categories, ranks, and the like. Let us look at the most elementary form of internal social differentiation that can be found: the diversity of social positions occupied by individuals within every conceivable social structure (III, 7). No two individuals have the same prestige, power, knowledge and influence, nor do they perform exactly the same activities within their groups. They are located somewhere in social space, and this location differentiates them from each other and their groups and institutions internally. We say they occupy social positions. The definition of a *social position* is simple, yet the notion entails a certain amount of complexity. A social position is the place an individual or a series of individuals occupy within a social structure.

Social positions entail the presence of two dimensions which are —it must always be kept in mind—the two faces of one single phenomenon; these are role and status. *Role* is an interdependent set of activities which are carried out by the occupant of the social position in question, and which are normatively established. The role of a physician, for instance, would be to carry out a series of activities—healing—which are not independent of each other, as they form a whole, namely the art and science of curing the sick and caring for them. This is what we call 'the exercise of the medical profession'. The exercise, we say, is normative, that is, there are laws, bylaws, written rules, unwritten ones, professional oaths, which bind the physician and make explicit which are his professional duties. Quacks and witchdoctors are thus excluded from the position occupied by doctors; they occupy other social positions, and have other roles, even if they may sometimes overlap with the roles of doctors. When they do overlap, and in so far as they do, conflict is bound to arise. In some societies physicians are struck off the list of authorised practitioners if they violate the rules of their role. Other roles—for instance the role of a father or, even more, the role of uncle or cousin—are often much less clearly defined in terms of duties, but are equally important, and a close examination will show that in such cases role expectations (the kind of behaviour that is asked for and expected from a role occupant by other people) are not capricious or vague.

Roles are sometimes incompatible. A doctor cannot be a quack, and the suspicion that he may be one creates all sorts of tensions in his profession which may lead to an official inquiry about his 'unprofessional' activities. Very often, though, roles coexist in one individual; a woman may be a teacher, a mother, an aunt, a member of a socialist party, and the treasurer of a local voluntary association of neighbours. Not only may they coexist, but in many societies or sections of societies there may be a very high degree of *congruence* between roles. This congruence can be *prescribed* role congruence—a phenomenon quite common amongst tribal societies. A young man is expected to become a father and husband, a hunter, a dancer in the festivals, and not to assume roles that are prescribed for his elders, adolescents, or women. The intensity of prescription in role congruence may be weaker in modern societies, but is still common. Thus, in theory, being an assembly worker in a car factory does not require a man to be a member of a given labour union; yet forced membership of unions is far from a rare occurrence in Western industrial societies. In the Soviet Union it is not always prescribed that membership of the Communist Party is necessary for the occupation of certain highly placed jobs, it is simply a fact—enforced by a custom called 'cadre' ceiling—to which exceptions are very rare indeed.

The phenomena of role congruence, compatibility and incompatibility are often clear-cut cases. Catholics, for example, do not admit that the sacerdotal and the marital roles are compatible, except for Roman Catholic priests in the Levant who belong to the Oriental Rite; elsewhere the marriage of a priest means the cessation of his sacerdotal condition. Just as often, though, role incompatibility is a matter of degree, which results in a certain amount of ambiguity in social action. In consequence much activity in individuals is directed towards the solution of role strains and conflict.[1] In extreme cases this conflict may lead to the disintegration of personality or to other serious psychological troubles. More often, common neuroses result from role conflicts. Thus sociology helps to explain certain psychologically harmful processes whose cure must be sought outside the individual, in the social world in which he lives. This is why crime and suicide among other 'social problems' fall directly within the field of sociological research.

Ralph Linton, who introduced the concept of role, also distinguished and introduced its complementary concept, status.[2] *Status* is the set of rights and obligations possessed by an individual in the framework of a society. It implies certain behaviour expectations both on the part of its occupant and on that of the persons coming into contact with him. On the one hand status is tied to notions of rank, prestige, degree of social prominence, degree of authority, and therefore to the amount of obedience or the nature of deference[3] due to the incumbent of the status position. On the other hand status is characteristic of any individual in society, regardless of his formal rank in an institution. Thus an army general has a status as a member of the armed forces—or, rather, several: one depending on his official rank, another depending on the degree of prestige accorded professional soldiers in his country, and so on. An English gipsy, who certainly is not a member of a hierarchical and formal organisation, also has a status; so do social categories such as housewives, foreigners, children, in every society. What has just been said about role congruence and compatibilities can also be extended to statuses, and more will be said on this point later (X, 3). For the moment it is sufficient to emphasise that the conventional degrees of prestige earned by 'formal' status can be greatly affected by the incumbent's performance in office (or his social position); that is, by how he exercises his role. A university professor may be held in little respect by his scientific colleagues, or be disliked by a group of students, while retaining the status that his office confers upon him. The correlation between intellectual excellence and official status is rarely perfectly positive—and this is true of every other field of institutionalised social inequality. Part of the reason for this is that status distribution in a society is tied to the distribution of power and authority. Finally, one of the main functions of status is that it enables us to anticipate people's behaviour. Status tells us who is our superior, who is our inferior, who is our equal (our colleague, tribesman, co-religionist, comrade), and how to treat him, as well as what to expect from him, that is, which kinds of roles he will perform. Often one single status explains at one stroke a whole plurality of roles to the people who meet its occupant. Merton has called this plurality a *role-set* or complex. A role-set differs from the phenomenon of the multiplicity of roles referred to above, and largely overlaps with the notion of role congruence, but it is not the same thing, for a role-set is an interdependent system of roles. Merton gives the example of the status of the medical student, who not only has the obvious role of student, but also a series of other roles 'relating him diversely to other students, physicians, nurses, social workers, medical technicians, and the like'.[4]

It may be said that statuses represent the static side of social positions, while roles are their dynamic aspect. Status is the place a person occupies in a social arrangement and role the system of action expected from the occupant. But this is a serious oversimplification for status is itself a source of activity. People who have what they regard as a low status may try to attain a higher one.

Sociologists recognise two kinds of status—*ascribed* and *achieved* status—and the tensions between the two are a constant source of social mobility (VI, 3) and social conflict. Ascribed status is not based on the ability of the individual to perform certain roles, but it is assigned to him, often by inheritance. Thus by being born into an Irish Catholic family a person has a special status for the Protestants in Ulster; a great number of them will act in a certain way towards this person regardless of his individual characteristics. The areas covered by achieved and ascribed statuses vary from society to society and over time. It is not easy to determine which are these areas. For instance some sociologists—and journalistic social science—speak of modern society as an 'achievement oriented' society. If it is true that many occupational rewards are based on achievement in some contemporary societies, a glance at historical records shows that status achievement was not unusual in the past too. Entire new social classes emerged during the Roman Empire through trade, or military activity. India, with that most 'static' of social structures has witnessed in its long history a subtle set of patterns of status achievement circumventing the rigidity of the caste system (VI, 3). Every revolutionary period in the past has abundantly served status achievement through political means (IX, 3). Perhaps the characteristic of modern society is the unprecedented institutionalisation and legitimation of certain new forms of achievement and upward social mobility (X, 3).

The theatrical viewpoint provides an additional insight into the role-status complex. Shakespeare wrote, 'All the world's a stage and all the men and women merely players', while another classical playwright, Calderón, produced two plays largely devoted to exploring this theme—*The Great Theatre of the World* and *Life is a Dream*. Luigi Pirandello's *Six Characters in Search of an Author* points to the permanence of the modern dramatist's concern for the purely theatrical dimension of social life. Like the dramatic, the sociological imagination fosters the growth of such view in the minds of the social scientist. Although the sociologist does not accept the extreme view that society is a stage, the development of the kindred notions of social position, role, and status, coupled with the idea of the social actor, has formed the theatrical perspective in sociology. The sociodrama, defined earlier, is an example of this approach. And Erving Goffman has investigated social interaction from the stage angle, looking into the 'presentation' of our 'selves' in everyday life or under more testing circumstances.[5] Rational and value-rational social action requires manipulation of people and the strategic use of social situations; these, in turn, require role playing, 'hypocrisy', 'white' lies, and so on. Custom—traditional social actions—demands rituals, routines, and other crystallised forms of interaction. Our egos move within that world, never entirely identified with those situations, rarely entirely 'taken in' by them. Social life is play, and it is a play, as Huizinga's sociological classic *Homo ludens* has proved, in every sense of the word: game, comedy, amusement, drama, and tragedy.[6]

One can hardly exaggerate the importance of the notions of social position, status and role in sociology. They occupy a central place in the sociological imagination. All social sciences make an abstraction of some aspects of man in order to focus on their area of interest. Economists have developed the notion of *homo oeconomicus* and political scientists that of *homo politicus*. If there is a *homo sociologicus* he is the man who occupies and lives his social positions or, rather, the total social position which results from the combination of all his roles and statuses. *Homo sociologicus* is our particular kind of abstraction,[7] and also our particular bias. We must ward against it, and handle it with care, for our discipline cannot claim to exhaust human reality.

## Norms: social control, institutions, consensus

Implicitly or explicitly, norms have frequently been referred to in this book. Social behaviour (including social action) is not chaotic: it shows patterns, continuities, uniformities. Roles and statuses carry with them expectations of conduct from all concerned, and sanctions are imposed upon those who violate the rules of such behaviour or deviate from them. All social life is permeated with a normative order; it obeys laws. These laws, though, must be understood in the modern sense of observable uniformities and not in either the juridical sense or the sense of immutable and absolute principles. Social scientists, for this reason, much prefer to use the term *norm*, which implies a guideline for action. It is in this sense that it is asserted that social behaviour is always normative, even when it appears 'lawless'. Bandits are outlaws who seem to live outside the law-abiding society, yet they must conform to rigid rules within their own delinquent gangs, not to speak of the 'rules of the game' which apply in their relations with the world off which they live as plunderers or parasites. And revolutionary movements, which attempt to overthrow regimes and social systems, though branded as 'lawless' and 'unprincipled' by the established powers, aim at creating a new social order, that is, a new system of norms for social life. In a word, every social group—from the dyad to the widest society—presents systems and networks of norms which order and canalise behaviour. These standards of conduct, however, must be distinguished from *statistical norms*: the latter only point to the observed or hypothetical frequencies of events. Social norms occur with regularity, and can often find statistical expression, but the two concepts are distinct, even if they are compatible.

As with the other elementary forms of social life, the range and variety of norms is immense. Some are very explicit (positive laws) while others are embedded in the unspoken life of groups, being only 'understandings' of social behaviour. Many are customs, but these are very different in nature too; when strongly binding, sociologists call them *mores*, especially if they relate to moral principles; and if they concern 'proper' behaviour (including manners) they are called *folkways*.[8] These, together with civic regulations, state constitutions, trade-union statutes, canon law, international law, and every other conceivable kind of standard of behaviour indicate the range and complexity of the normative universe.

Norms do not appear in isolation. They are not an array of regulations, they appear in systematic wholes, mutually interdependent clusters of standards of behaviour. These are called social institutions. *Institutions* revolve round tasks or sets of tasks or roles. We thus find economic, religious, educational, political institutions; but we also find families, confraternities, clubs, voluntary associations, which equally are institutions. Their members come and go but, unless the turnover is excessive for the institutional system, institutions remain, even though they are all subject to change over time. In a factory workers are hired, or laid off; management and engineers are promoted, demoted, or find other jobs; a number of employees die, or retire. Yet the system of norms (rules for production, delimitation of hierarchies, work shifts, salaries and wages, etcetera) remains relatively unaltered over periods of time sufficiently long for us to consider the institution as a 'permanent' entity. Some institutions, like the Greek Orthodox Church, have lasted for centuries, and one marvels at their resilience and their capacity for maintaining certain basic traits. The study of the forces that work towards the maintenance and stability of social institutions in the face of change is one of the important tasks of sociology.

Man lives, then, in a world of norms, most of them related to concrete institutions, which from the very beginning of his life tell him what to do and which way to act—unless he is confronted with a situation of normative conflict (III, 6). These norms are objective, external to him in at least one sense; if he deviates from them he is bound to perceive them as external. He does not feel them as external, though, so long as they have been internalised by him (IV, 3), that is, made part and parcel of his own social consciousness and system of values. Whether it is psychological internalisation or sheer external coercion that is at stake, the individual or the group is made to conform to norms and institutions through a process called *social control*. This refers to the means used to make people adhere to norms. Once again, being an elementary phenomenon, the means of social control range from the most brutal forms of coercion to the mildest expressions of disapproval; from the highest rewards to the smallest signs of approval. Social control, aimed at the maintenance of the existing institutions or at the development of new ones, is exercised by all interested groups and individuals through vast, and not always perfectly integrated, systems of gratification and deprivation.

The control over social life which norms and institutions exercise is made possible not only by coercion but by the great amount of consensual behaviour which occurs within every group and between groups. Consensus is an accord over the aims of social action and the norms which it must follow. As Shils says, relating it to beliefs (VIII, 2):

> Consensus is a condition of agreement in the interindividual and in the intergroup structure of beliefs in a society . . . Consensus exists when a large proportion of the adult members of a society, more especially a large proportion of those concerned with procedure and substance of the allocations of authority, status, rights, wealth and income, and other important and scarce values about which conflict might occur are (1) in agreement in their beliefs about what decisions should be made about these issues and about the range about which they may disagree, and (2) when they also have some feeling of affinity with each other and the larger society as a whole. Consensus exists when there is acceptance of the institutions through which disagreed decisions are made or executed. Consensus exists when 'objectively' deprivational allocations are accepted on grounds other than the expectation of coercion for the enforcement of acceptance.[9]

*NOTES on Chapter III, Section 4*

1. W. J. Goode 'A Theory of Role Strain' *Am. Soc. Rev.* 25 (1960) pp. 483–496.
2. R. Linton *The Study of Man* (New York: Appleton, 1936) pp. 113–14.

3. For the important and little explored question of deference cf. E. Shils 'Deference' in J. A. Jackson ed. *Social Stratification* (Cambridge University Press, 1968) pp. 104–132.
4. R. K. Merton 'The role-set: problems in sociological theory' in *Brit. Jnl. Soc.* June 1957, 8, pp. 106–20.
5. E. Goffman *The Presentation of Self in Everyday Life* (Garden City: Doubleday, 1959); *Where the Action is* (London: Allen Lane, 1969).
6. J. Huizinga *Homo Ludens* (London: Routledge, 1949, English translation). It is alarming that this work, though very well known internationally, is systematically ignored by sociologists in studies which directly bear on matters explored at length by the great Dutch humanist.
7. R. Dahrendorf *Homo sociologicus* (Cologne: West-deutscher Verlag, 1958).
8. W. G. Sumner *op. cit.*
9. E. Shils *Consensus* mimeographed, 7th World Congress, *Int. Pol. Science Assn.*, Sept. 1967, p. 2.

# 5 SOCIAL FUNCTIONS

We have seen that social action is far from random, not only because it is teleological, or goal-oriented, but also because it occurs within systems of social positions in and between groups. Social action fulfils certain ends, which are called functions. In a general sense, a function is the characteristic or normal activity or manifestation of any entity. ('Activity proper to anything, mode of action by which it fulfils its purpose' says the Oxford Dictionary.) In sociology the meaning is analogous. The word was originally employed by Spencer, who drew certain parallels between social and organic life and their respective modes of organisation.[1] Durkheim wrote in this vein when he said that the function of a social institution was the correspondence between it and the 'needs of the social organism'.[2] (The idea of a social organism was rejected long ago and Durkheim's words are more easily understood if we substitute for 'social organism' such concrete notions as 'group', 'tribe', 'government', 'community', and the like, depending on the situation in which functions are observed to exist. A function may also exist for a society as a whole.) Some social anthropologists adopted the Spencer-Durkheim definition of function, believing that it could be improved. Thus, Radcliffe-Brown admitted it, with the proviso that Durkheim's 'needs' should be translated as the 'necessary conditions for existence' of a given group. This meant that the functioning of each social unit—individuals, institutions and groups—was understood to preserve the social structure of which they were a part. In turn, 'social structure' meant a set of interdependent social functions; every aspect of society was seen as interlocked with every other aspect—a characteristic of organisms. Another anthropologist, Bronislaw Malinowski, made the point explicitly: just as organisms have biological needs, so societies have needs, and they are both of a biological nature. This proposition was more tenable in his field—the study of primitive societies— than in the study of larger and more complex social systems, and it proved to be relatively useful to conceive of isolated tribes as closed, unchanging systems of interdependent functions.[3] Parsons has followed in this 'biological' tradition; although he has gone beyond the simple organic analogy, he still insists that 'the concept of function is central to the understanding of all living systems ... from the unicellular organism to the highest human civilisation'.[4] Now, this tradition in sociological theory has some serious problems, for it tends to see social action as always strengthening the structure in which it takes place or, rather, which has produced it. Thus 'functionalist' sociologists speak of functions as creations of social structures; Marion Levy defines social function as 'a condition or state of affairs, resultant from the operation ... of a structure through time'.[5] However, it is worth noting this view, for it sheds some light on important features of any social structure: its inter-locked system of functions does form a pattern with tendencies to maintain itself. But this is only one aspect of a very complicated problem (III, 7). Perhaps it can begin to be tackled if we first look into other aspects of the nature of social functions.

Functions, as manifestations of the presence of one social unit within a social system may have two types of consequences. On the one hand they can integrate the system further and serve some of its purposes, in the sense intended by the school of thought just mentioned. Every time that, say, the postman delivers a letter, his behaviour reinforces the structure of his institution (the General Post Office), and its functions (the carriage of mails); thereby he is helping citizens to communicate with each other and documents to circulate, and is assisting the smooth 'functioning' of a given social order. Yet there is another whole category of social action which corrodes the structure of sections of society. Suppose the postmen go on strike: countless people and institutions are bound to suffer from this. For them, the orders given to its members by the leadership of the (hypothetical) Trade Union of Postmen are not functional. The observable consequence of this type of action are what Merton has called *dysfunctions*: they erode or undermine a given social structure.[6] What is interesting about dysfunctions is that they may still be functional for certain institutions or groups. Our hypothetical postal strike may strengthen the Union of Postmen, it may even win them a salary increase, and recruitment into the organisation may grow as a consequence, no matter how dysfunctional it has been for the citizenry as a whole and for the state. As a matter of fact, the degree of inconvenience caused may itself be most functional in the end for all concerned, if adequate social change is brought about by those in authority. War is an excellent example of the function-dysfunction dichotomy. At first sight nothing appears more dysfunctional than war; yet it brings a number of blessings to those who manufacture weapons, capture booty, or gain military honours, not to mention entire organisations which thrive on it, or its possible occurrence—intelligence services, armies, ministries. This shows the two-dimensional nature of functions, and is in itself a first warning against the hasty interpretation of social equilibrium.

Another distinction (also made by Merton) must be drawn between two chief kinds of functions (and dysfunctions): manifest and latent. *Manifest functions* are 'those objective consequences for a specified unit (person, subgroup, social or cultural system) which contribute to its adjustment or adaptation and were so intended'. When the function is manifest it is recognised as a function from the start. *Latent functions* are those which are neither recognised as functions nor so intended. To use an example given by Merton himself, the Hopi Indians of North America have certain dances to bring about rain. The manifest function of these dances is precisely this, 'to make rain'. But the rain dance has unrecognised functional effects upon the tribe: it strengthens group solidarity, it gives the tribe moral cohesion before the draught, and provides an occasion for people to meet.[7] Processions in Andalusia or Southern Italy imploring a patron saint or the Virgin Mary to send rain are similar examples; whether rain is forthcoming or not, the frustrations and low morale engendered by danger to the harvest are partially allayed by the villagers' collective ritual sublimation. The notions of manifest and latent functions are not entirely new; for instance, Karl Marx' conception of ideology (VIII, 4) assumes that the doctrines or world-views held by the ruling classes are oriented towards the preservation of the established system of social inequality. In so far as the ruling classes are conscious that they indoctrinate the ruled and that their ideologies are misrepresentations of reality, the integrative function of such ideologies is not latent, on the contrary they are recognised as serving that purpose, but it *is* latent for all those who are unconsciously integrated into the prevailing social order by wholeheartedly believing in them. Machiavelli thought that the prince ought to use and manipulate religious sentiments in this way, once the ruler had recognised the enormous potential of the implicit social functions of beliefs. Consequently in any complex society, the relationship between explicit functions and implicit ones is very subtle: the degrees of awareness about the several real effects of one type of behaviour, belief, ritual or institution will vary from individual to individual, and from group to group.

No general classification of the principal kinds of functions which social action must perform has been developed which satisfies everybody. For some a way to confront this problem has been to look first at societies rather than at their subgroups, as these may be specialised and therefore omit functions in their activity. For Marion Levy, who has followed this approach, 'the functional requisites of any society' are:

1. provision for an adequate physiological relationship to the environment and for sexual recruitment (the biological needs);

2. role differentiation and role assignment (social positions, and systems of social inequality);

3. communication (learned, shared and symbolic modes of transmission of meaning);

4. shared cognitive orientations (knowledge of phenomena);

5. shared articulated set of goals (values);

6. regulation of affective expression (social control of emotions);

7. adequate socialisation (inculcation of the social structure on an individual) (IV, 3);

8. effective control of disruptive forms of behaviour (social control of deviant behaviour, crime and delinquency, as defined by the group) (IX, 5);

9. adequate institutionalisation (the existence of institutions is itself a functional requisite for the existence of a society).[8]

More simplified taxonomies are still possible but, for the same reason, are necessarily more abstract. As an example, Parsons' classification may be recorded, with the double caveat that no elaborate argumentation can accompany it in the present context and that, as has often been remarked, empirical proof or disproof are both highly problematic. For Parsons, there are four 'functional problems' which every society must solve. They are the following:

1. goal attainment—the 'control and coordination of social action within a whole collectivity'. This is the political function.

2. adaptation—the production, consumption and distribution of scarce commodities. This is the economic function.

3. pattern maintenance—the conservation and development of the value system. This is the cultural function.

4. integration—the conservation and development of the system of standards of behaviour governing social interaction amongst the members of a society, including the containment and control of deviance and of any threats to conformity with the institutionalised role expectations. This is the normative function.[9]

In considering classifications such as these it must be remembered that no social institution ever performs only one social function. A factory is an economic institution, and is therefore assisting in the adaptation of society to the physical environment by the transformation of raw material into goods for consumption. But the factory must have a policy—must define the goals to be attained—as well as maintain a social order within its boundaries and among its employees. So the factory has several functions, but one function —in this case the economic one—is preeminent. Similarly most social institutions can be considered as bundles of social action seeking the fulfilment of one chief function, but incorporating a range of other functions. All organised collectivities must adequately perform these secondary social functions before they can fulfil their main function, and before they can survive, let alone thrive. A religious community of monks, a primary school, an army regiment, a publishing house—no matter how much they may differ, they all must cope with certain basic common problems: order, authority, the allocation of resources, the distribution of rewards, the definition of collective goals, internal discipline.

## NOTES on Chapter III, Section 5

1. H. Spencer's chapter on 'Social Structure and Social Functions' in *The Principles of Sociology* (New York: Appleton Century, 1897) pp. 471–489.
2. E. Durkheim *Les régles de la méthode sociologique* (Paris: Allen, 1895).
3. B. Malinowski 'Culture' in *Encyclopaedia of the Social Sciences* (New York: Macmillan, 1930) Vol. IV, p. 624.
4. T. Parsons 'Some Problems of General Theory in Sociology' in J. C. McKinney and E. A. Tiryakian eds. *Theoretical Sociology* (New York: Appleton Century, 1970) pp. 29 and 35.
5. M. Levy *The Structure of Society* (Princeton University Press, 1952) p. 56.
6. R. Merton *Social Theory . . . op. cit.* p. 51.
7. *Ibid. pp.* 191–98. See V. Pareto *Trattato . . . op. cit.* para 1864 and 2115–2134, who much earlier made the same distinction, but called manifest 'intended' functions and latent 'incidental' functions. (J. Lopreato *Vilfredo Pareto* (New York: Crowell, 1965) pp. 2–22.)

8. M. Levy *op. cit.* pp. 149–98; cf. also D. Aberle 'The functional pre-requisites of any society' *Ethics* Vol. LX no. 2, Jan. 1950, pp. 100–11.
9. T. Parsons and N. Smelser *Economy and Society* (Glencoe: Free Press, 1956) pp. 16–19; T. Parsons *The Social System* (New York: Free Press, 1951) esp. Ch. 2. Mine is a very simplified rendering of Parsons' scheme.

# 6   SOCIAL CONFLICT

Several references have been made to disturbances in the social order, as well as to the presence of coercion, dysfunctions, norm transgression, and deviance in society. These phenomena point to the existence of yet another elementary form of social life: conflict. It may surprise some that conflicting behaviour is accepted as a 'form of social life'[1] when it seems to negate coexistence. Yet, as Simmel once showed, conflict is used 'to resolve divergent dualisms ... is a way of achieving some kind of unity, even if it be through the annihilation of one of the conflicting parties'.[2] Thus the enslavement of one people by another is a social process which produces a new social order, slave society. Internal family tensions leading to divorce result in new structures. The very notion of legal divorce indicates that channels of conflict resolution—sources of new order —exist.

Conflict is an all pervading phenomenon whose manifestations include occurrences as varied as litigation, competitive games, economic and political struggles, warfare, intrigue, antagonistic gossip and slander. This variety in kind and form of conflicting behaviour makes definition difficult. Coser has characterised social conflict as 'a struggle over values and claims to scarce status, power and resources in which the aims of the opponents are to neutralise, injure or eliminate their rivals'.[3] This is satisfactory if the expression 'neutralise' is also meant to cover certain forms of active subjugation and continued oppression, such as enslavement, as the struggle to subjugate people is usually more than an attempt to neutralise them, it is also an effort to exploit them as the tame serfs of the groups aspiring to domination. For another definition, found in a dictionary of sociology, conflict is the 'direct and conscious struggle between individuals and groups for the same goal'.[4] Our example of slavery would certainly not fit this definition as the slave hunter and the men escaping prospective bondage are not at all struggling for the same goals, although a superficial observer may say that they both want the same thing: the hunted man's freedom, the one in order to destroy it, and the other in order to keep it. This is only partially so, since the reason why the hunter wants the human prey is perhaps to sell it in the market, as a commodity, the destruction of freedom being only ancillary to slave hunting, breeding and trade. Freedom itself is a value to the slave, with a different meaning for the slave-owner. These distinctions are important to the study of conflict, since the contending parties often give very divergent versions of the issues at stake, and this cannot always be attributed to their obvious emotional involvement. Conflict may be about the same things as well as about different things which are, nevertheless, interdependent, or appear to be so to the contending parties. Rulers have often persecuted the followers of certain religious doctrines for fear that their spread could be harmful to their power, regardless of the fact that, seen objectively, this could not happen. Much conflict arises out of fear of imagined threats: the stuff of social conflict is often made up of misunderstandings.

Conflict is a hostile contest for or against domination, control, and self-preservation. Domination may be sought over goods, values, thought or behaviour. It may involve the annihiliation of one collectivity or the harmless striving for first place in a competition where the losers lose nothing or very little. More often, it is aimed at a re-arrangement of the relationships and hierarchies of power and authority in a given social structure. Control is a notion close to domination: a strike for higher wages results from conflict between workers and management over the apportionment (control) of company profits. Even though the workers may have no intention of questioning the existing patterns of power and authority, they may be seen as doing so by management, which thinks its prerogative is being threatened. In varying degrees, this threatening and defence of man's autonomy (including his status, authority and power) together with any perceived danger to his physical and moral authority is the common dimension of all social conflict. Its sources must also be related to certain aggressive tendencies in man towards whose explanation sociology contributes, as will be seen later. Because conflict is such a central category of social life, it needs separate and special attention (IX, 1).

*NOTES on Chapter III, Section 6*

1. 'Form of social life' a translation of Simmel's *Vergesellschaftungsform*; K. Wolff translates it as 'sociation'; cf. G. Simmel 'Conflict' in *Conflict etc. op. cit.* p. 13. All references to this English translation.

2. *Ibid.* p. 13.
3. L. Coser *The Functions of Social Conflict* (Glencoe: Free Press, 1956) p. 8.
4. G. A. Theodorson and A. G. Theodorson *A Modern Dictionary of Sociology* (New York: Crowell, 1969) p. 71.

# 7   SOCIAL STRUCTURE AND SOCIAL SYSTEM

*Order*

It is a truism that society is not possible without order. All the elementary forms of social life imply the existence of some kind of order: status, when it develops, creates a hierarchy; meaningful social action entails a given pattern of values and notions about society; conflict is the struggle to replace one system of power and authority by another; and so forth. Thus, social order is a prerequisite of society, a precondition of social life. Obvious as this might look at first glance, the problem of order is not a simple one. It has, basically, two aspects: the first must answer the question, how is society possible? The second must answer the question, which is the right order for man? Both questions have been paramount in the minds of social thinkers and critics of society of all ages, and cannot be answered by sociology alone; this is especially true of the second question, which is fundamentally a moral one. The first problem is one of the central concerns of theoretical sociology, and it has perhaps been best formulated by Thomas Hobbes who, realising that 'societies are not mere meetings, but bonds' set out to answer precisely the question, 'what are the conditions of society'?[1] (His conclusion favouring authority and coercion may not satisfy everyone today, but this is another matter.) The recent transformation of world society has added further complexity to this fundamental question. There is not the space to explore it here, for some familiarity with the achievements of modern social science is necesssary if such an endeavour is to meet with success.

The expression 'social order' is frequently found in sociological literature. Too often it is used as a synonym for 'social organisation', 'social structure', 'social system', and even 'society' itself. While this may be justified for the term 'social organisation', it cannot be so in the other cases, as will presently be seen. For us, social order will remain defined as the condition whereby a society requires patterning, hierarchies of norms, values and institutions. Social order includes the systems and networks of internal supra-ordination and sub-ordination, and differentiation of individuals, groups, collectivities and institutions,[2] their ecological and territorial distribution, and their cultural orientations and communication networks, as well as the biological arrangements of the species, which cannot be contradicted (IV, 1) by the other levels of social reality.

## Structure

A relatively stable pattern of relationships between interdependent elements is a structure. A *social structure* is a relatively stable set of relationships between social institutions, groups and individuals. These relationships include social action, roles, statuses, and a normative system. What is characteristic of structures is that they are wholes which are not the mere sum of their parts, that is, they are not mere aggregates or congeries; by being interdependent their parts cannot be explained outside the structure. Structures themselves must be studied as wholes by social science.[3] Another element is their relative permanence through time. If we observe, say, the status of the nobility in a feudal society we shall be able to determine their privileges, rights and obligations in spite of a certain amount of change, which is always present. This assumes that there is something ('the social structure of feudalism') which has been enduring enough to allow us certain generalisations.

To admit the relative permanence of social structures is not to subscribe to any static conception of the social world, just as to admit the necessity of a structural approach to social phenomena is not to belong to a 'structuralist' school of thought.[4] In a sense the question whether one should or should not be a structuralist is meaningless, for all sociologists must have a structural view of the problems they study; social phenomena, taken in isolation, are sociologically meaningless. Our own definition of sociology as a science that interrelates social phenomena means that the discrete components of social wholes cannot be completely understood in isolation. Equally the nature of the larger unit needs to be illumined by the study of its individual components. Thus the size, economy and authority patterns of families will tell us much about the general social structure of the society in which they live; conversely, a macrosocial picture of that society is bound to explain many aspects of the families which live in it. In structures one element always mirrors the rest, as well as the whole. There are some difficulties in proving this assertion for very large and complex societies, because they often contain several general social structures, or 'regions' of the wider society. In Assam and Kerala, two Indian states, one finds matrilineal societies (where descent is traced through women), but this cannot be said to 'mirror' Indian social structure generally. It is quite important, therefore, to delimit the range and 'space' of a general social structure, and even of its substructures, in order to make valid statements.

Social wholes or structures are perceived and then interpreted by their student. We arrange a series of data about phenomena so that these become meaningful and coherent to us, and then try to see if they will withstand further scrutiny. Claude Levi-Strauss has gone so far as to say that the 'fundamental principle' in this context is to recognise that 'the notion of structure does not refer to empirical reality, but to the models built upon it'. By this Lévi-Strauss does not mean that there is a complete divorce between social reality and our intellectual constructs of it. He means, rather, that we ourselves order the information delivered to us by the data about social reality. We infer social structures in a world whose complexity cannot be completely assimilated by theoretical interpretation; 'it can be said that data reveal a structure in so far as they present a defineable articulation, an ordered distribution of their parts'.[5]

*System*

Next to social order (which is a vague and general term, and encompasses the entire population of a society) and social structure (which refers to its concrete patterns, elements and relationships) is the somewhat more complex notion of social system. The often imprecise use made of the three notions, which sometimes appear as synonymous, make a separate definition the more necessary.

A system is a complex of elements which interact according to a set of principles.[6] Anatol Rapoport states that a system can be defined as:

(1) something consisting of a set (finite or infinite) of entities (2) among which a set of relations is specified, so that (3) deductions are possible from some relations to others or from relations among the entities to the behaviour or the history of the system.

According to this definition, he adds, both the solar system or a language are systems:

In the former, the entities are the sun and the planets; the relations among them are specifiable as position and velocity vectors and forces of gravitational attraction. Other relations (e.g. Kepler's laws of planetary motion) and the history of the system, past and future, are derivable from the given relations. In a language, there are also identifiable entities—phonemes, morphemes, sentences, and the like—and relations among these are given in terms of syntactic rules. In a larger sense, a language system may also include the referential world and even the speakers. In this sense, semantic and pragmatic relations are added to the syntactic ones.[7]

Rapoport's examples show that systems are not confined to one level of reality. An entire trend of theoretical inquiry, 'General Systems Theory' has arisen from this assumption, combined with the realisation that some systems (especially in the organic world) are open, that is, they transform themselves while maintaining their structure. As Ludwig von Bertalanffy points out, the living world seems to go against the second law of thermodynamics (which says that the world is always consuming and losing energy, and not creating any). The living world however 'shows, in embryonic development and in evolution, a transition towards higher order, heterogeneity, and organisation'.[8] Living systems when confronted with changes in the environment must at once re-establish their internal equilibrium, maintain their boundaries, and develop a new relationship with the external world. By so doing, they change. In the long run their early structure is itself relatively changed. Thus living systems over a given period of time possess three elements: a structure ('being'), a behaviour ('acting') and a history ('becoming').[9] All this appears to be relevant to the understanding of human societies.

A social system is a paradigm of human interaction. A social system is conceptually distinct from a social structure in that the system is abstract, whereas the structure is concrete. If structures are real social units in a given pattern of interaction, the system in which they operate includes the general principles at work. Thus, the social structure of a given family must be composed of a definite number of living individuals, with concrete identifiable roles and statuses: for instance, it may include three sisters, one brother and a father. The family as a social system, though, is the model upon which the several real family structures are built in a given society, each particular family adapting its own human resources to the more abstract pattern or paradigm, with different degrees of fidelity. The social structure of a factory will include a number of concrete people and groups in different jobs (manager X, workers M, N, P,

Q..., clerks A, B, C, and the like) but its social system will rather refer to a given occupational order, geared to the achievement of a series of economic goals, operating in a changing economic and political environment. What it is essential to understand in this context is that both notions are complementary and mutually necessary; that 'system' is a broader concept; and that if it is more abstract it does not mean that it is less real.

As early as 1773 the Baron d'Holbach, writing his *Système social*, began to grapple with the problem of society as a set of interrelated 'principles' rather than concrete elements.[10] But it was the development of notions such as homeostasis in biology and cybernetics in communication theory which, applied to society, have made the 'social systems aproach' possible and necessary.[11] This approach means that social systems are understood to possess not only self-regulatory, feedback and structural properties, but particularly to generate change in themselves. As Walter Buckley says:

> ...we are concerned with the fact that an isolated physical system typically proceeds to its most probable state of minimal organization (equilibrium), and that organic systems ... characteristically work to maintain a specific, genetically given structure within fairly definite limits (homeostasis) whereas systems on the phylogenetic, higher psychological, and sociocultural levels, are characterized primarily by their morphogenic properties. That is, these latter are distinguished precisely by the fact that, rather than minimize organization, or preserve a given fixed structure, they typically create, elaborate, or change structure as a prerequisite to remaining viable, as ongoing systems.[12]

It is true that some social thinkers have, in the past, viewed social structures and systems also as 'morphogenetic'; that is, as calling forth change by the very nature of their arrangements. Marx' macrosociological interpretation of the stages of class conflict is one example. And Comte's scheme for the explanation of history also presents stages in the evolution of mankind as containing the seeds of their own future, which will not just be a repetition of earlier phases. Yet the modern social systems conception does not start from a previous philosophy of history while still trying to explain change and conflict. (Systems theory conceives of certain forms of conflict as generated by the system itself—another idea that can be traced to Marx' conception.) A systems approach to social reality necessarily implies two notions. First, that social action is teleological, and second that man 'is always trying to live beyond his means'.[13] Thus it is not cosmic forces but man, too, compelling change in society. It is for this reason that the human species is the only one that presents such a bewildering variety of social orders, cultures, and conceptions of the world. There is no single 'social system' in human society: in contrast with other living systems, we must define it anew every time that we face a specific social situation.[14] These varieties of social life, however, are no insurmountable barrier to valid, if difficult, generalisations.

## NOTES on Chapter III, Section 7

1. T. Hobbes *De cive* (New York: Appleton Century, 1949) p. 21 and p. 21n.
2. G. Simmel *Uber sociale Differenzierung* (Leipzig: 1890. New edition—Amsterdam: Liberac, 1966).
3. J. Piaget *La psychologie de l'intelligence* (Paris: Colin, 1947) p. 186.
4. W. G. Runciman *Sociology in its Place, op. cit.* pp. 45–48.
5. C. Lévi-Strauss 'La notion de structure en ethnologie' in *Anthropologie structurale* (Paris: Plon, 1958) pp. 302–52.
6. L. von Bertalanffy defines system as 'a complex of interacting elements'; *General System Theory* (New York: Braziller, 1968) p. 55. This definition coincides with our definition of structure and it is, therefore, confusing.
7. A. Rapoport 'General Systems Theory' in *Int. Encyclopedia of the Social Sciences* (1968) Vol. 15, p. 453.
8. L. van Bertalanffy *op. cit.* pp. 40–41.
9. A. Rapoport *op. cit.* p. 454.
10. 'General systems theorists' and writers on 'the social system' systematically ignore Holbach's contribution. The very title of his important treatise ought to have made them interested in it. Cf. P. H. Th. d'Holbach *Système social* (Hildesheim: Olms, 1969, facsimile ed.).
11. W. B. Cannon *The Wisdom of the Body* (New York: Norton, 1939); N. Wiener *The Human Use of Human Beings: Cybernetics and Society* (Garden City: Doubleday, 1954).
12. W. Buckley *Sociology and Modern Systems Theory* (Englewood Cliffs: Prentice Hall, 1967) pp. 4–5.
13. H. A. Thelen, quoted by W. Buckley, *ibid.* p. 51. Cf. also D. Lockwood 'Social Integration and System Integration' in G. Zollschan, W. Hirsch eds., *Exploration in Social Change* (London: Routledge, 1964) pp. 244–257.

# IV Culture and the Process of Socialisation

## 1 HUMAN SOCIETY AND CULTURE

*Animal society and human society*

Men live in society not because they are men but because they are animals. The social way of life is a stage in the evolution of life prior to the appearance of the human race. What is distinctive of man is that he has developed the social way of life far more than any other animal species, so that there is a giant step in complexity between the most elaborate non-human society and the most elementary society of men. Human society shares characteristics with animal societies: it is formed by a given population of individuals, all belonging to the same species; it shows an internal specialisation of tasks, and a hierarchical order; individuals interact as members of the same species, and possess a common language which sets them apart from other species; and the population is perpetuated by means of biological reproduction and by constant struggle with the physical and biological environment. These similarities[1] become very conspicuous when human society is compared with that of other primates.

The contributions of ethology (the science that studies emotion and its expression in animals and man) have forcefully shown the common ground on which all animal behaviour, including that of man, moves. The traditional criterion for the distinction of human society from all other societies was that the latter were exclusively based on 'instinct' while ours was also based on the symbolic transmission of cultural meanings. There is still some truth in this assertion, but it cannot be accepted in its entirety any longer, as it is now known that some groups of animals may evolve a new code of signals to elicit a certain type of behaviour and transmit it to their offspring; this code will henceforth be found only in that group and not in the other groups of the same species. This phenomenon is, of course, most typical of man, whose tribes, clans, nations and families show a marked tendency to create their own particular codes of signals,[2] but the fact that its characteristics can be found in other animal societies is vital for a correct perspective of this point.

Man is unique because he has developed the cultural potentialities of animal nature to unprecedented levels, and not because he alone possesses the gift of culture. What ethological and anthropological research has established is that the difference between the most rudimentary forms of culture and the most elaborate of man's cultural achievements is a matter of degree, even though the gap between the two is enormous. From the sub-human to the highest human level, culture varies in complexity according to the complexity of its biological background. At one stage it looks as if the world of culture, to use Herbert Spencer's expression, were 'super-organic', a discrete world of norms, symbols, languages, tools and objects. Yet this world is thoroughly grounded in the biological realm.[3] Culture and nature are different things, but the first cannot contravene the laws of the second.

The recognition of this basic fact has led some students with a bias towards biology to extrapolate from zoology and explain sociology in its terms, as though human culture were a mere aspect of biology. Viewed from this perspective, all social phenomena—war, religion, music, industry, literature—require to be strictly explained in terms of biological needs and drives. But this is a reductionist position which is unwarranted by the evidence we possess. While the facts of social biology—population pressure, hunger, ecological balances and imbalances—go a long way towards explaining the social behaviour of man, the latter cannot be reduced to the former; man's ancestors developed culture to a degree where it ceased to be explainable as a mere secretion of biology and living conditions. What is more, as soon as it appeared, culture itself began to impinge upon early man's biology, and has been moulding it ever since in an unceasing process of feedback. The result is that today, man's mind depends as much on the soundness of the organism as on the existence of a cultural system.[4] Man is now genetically in need of a culture. His neurological system and his organic growth requires a uniquely slow and delicate process of mental maturation and learning that is only provided by culture. Thus its absence would not only impair the mind of men but would threaten the species with extinction.

*The definition of culture*

The classic definition of culture, in its sociological sense, is still that of Sir Edward Tylor, who first attempted to develop a unitary concept for what appeared to be a disparate congeries of phenomena. Culture, he said, is 'that complex whole which includes knowledge, belief, art, morals, law, custom, and any other capabilities and habits acquired by man as a member of society'.[5] Most definitions emphasise aspects of Tylor's seminal statement. Two social scientists, Kroeber and Kluckhohn, surveyed the many definitions to be found in the literature and concluded that in their light culture could be defined as consisting of 'patterns, explicit or implicit, and of behaviour acquired and transmitted by symbols, constituting the distinctive achievements of human groups, including their embodiments in artifacts,'; they added that, 'the essential core of culture consists of tradition (i.e. historically derived and selected) ideas and especially their attached values'.[6] Although this is the more sophisticated way of defining culture it is easy to see why Tylor's definition is still with us for, however unsystematic it may be, it is very simple. The fact is that although the notion of culture is perhaps not too difficult to grasp, it does not easily lend itself to brief and precise description.

Culture can be understood as a relatively integrated set of ideas, values, attitudes and norms of life which possess a certain amount of stability in a given society, and are seen in its structure and in the social behaviour of its members.[7] All that which man is and does, and which cannot be exclusively traced to his biological equipment and inheritance, is related to culture. That this page is written in English is not determined by anybody's original chromosomes; language is therefore culture. That the reader of this page belongs to, say, the middle class cannot be entirely explained by biological inheritance; social class divisions, which are part of social structure, are tied up with a vast value system that is part of culture.

Culture consists of models or patterns of thinking, feeling and behaviour which have been socially learnt. This means that culture entails a learning process (IV, 3) which takes place through human interaction, and also that culture is shared by groups, collectivities and members of institutions. Shared cultural patterns, however, are *abstract*. We detect them through both concrete behaviour and its results, which are themselves tangible.[8] Behaviour and its effects are the basis for our inductive inference of the norms, beliefs, ideological tenets, political values, moral principles, aesthetic rules, and the like that are the abstract—and very real—patterns of any culture. Their abstraction does not mean that they possess some quality that puts them beyond the world of human nature, although men have believed precisely this for a very long time; it means only that they are in our minds and that we can collect evidence for them only in social action or in its results. Some Hindus believe that certain white cows are sacred; as such, this belief is abstract and intangible, yet it is embodied in a system of regularities of behaviour, of reverence, protection and avoidance of this animal. The social scientist can map the geographical spread of this phenomenon over the Indian subcontinent, recording its relation to the social structure and discerning which groups uphold the belief, and can also attempt to uncover its history. He may then be able to tell us something of the nature of a belief that obliges one man of one culture to starve in the very shadow of a beast regarded as highly edible by members of other cultures, and as an object to be used for ritual entertainment by yet a third group. In Lima or Granada, the male of the same species is killed before the crowds, in accordance with the intricate rules of the bullfight. These are cultural patterns.

Such patterns are very complex, not only in the sense that they include many items but also in that they imply different ways of approaching the world. In the first place, they all entail natural *cognition*, that is to say, a degree of 'objective' knowledge about organic and physical phenomena—otherwise men would perish. First, no matter what a people's beliefs are about the world, the afterlife, the gods, the powers of men and so forth, they must have a series of patterns of objective information about their conditions of life and how to solve the continuous problems they present. Next to these we find *beliefs* of whose truth or falsity we say nothing, since they are usually beyond the reach of empirical test (VIII, 2). Connected with them in many ways are *norms*, *values* and *attitudes*. Something has already been said of the first (III, 4) and more will be said of the last elsewhere in this book (IV, 3). Values can be defined as principles of positive orientation towards a commonly felt good. They may be about morality (such as honour), about aesthetics (the social definition of what is beautiful and what is ugly —for instance, a particular fashion in dress) and about truth (and, indirectly, about falsity). These three dimensions of value often appear intertwined, and show different degrees of prominence in each particular culture.[9] The difference between values and attitudes is not easy to define. Attitudes are the practical embodiment of values, and can be equated to behaviour. If racial prejudice against the Chinese is part of the value system of certain Indonesian communities this will be shown up by a series of actual predispositions to act in a given way (attitudes) when Indonesians come into contact with Chinese. This, in turn, takes place in accordance with a definite normative pattern: the Indonesian may not mind buying commodities from the Chinese, but he will object to having his daughter marry one, or to letting him enter national politics. The three phenomena—values, attitudes and norms—are thus closely interdependent. *Signs* are also part of culture. They are a form of communication, and it is through them that all the other elements of culture are held together and become capable of transmission. Among humans, the most elaborate form of communication takes place through *symbols*, which are conventional signs.

## Communication and language

Communication is the sharing of information. Strictly speaking this can only happen between organisms, although one can use it allegorically for other entities. Communication in its most sophisticated form takes place between human beings. The process of communication has been described thus by semiotics (the science of signs): 'A issues $x$ as a sign of $y$, and B receives $x$ as a sign of $y$, in which process $y$ is communicated from A to B'.[10] Communication occurs, therefore, through signs and symbols; it is not an exchange of objects, but a transmission of information. Now this needs to be understood in a larger sense. Objects may be involved in the process, but if they are they stand for something else. The gift is the best example of this. When a man gives a bunch of flowers to a woman, the flowers themselves are only a means he uses to tell her how much he cares for her. Information may convey precisely the opposite to the truth—may 'misinform' in fact: members of a poor family may squander what little money they have left on clothes, thereby 'informing' their neighbours about the supposedly sound state of their economy.

The highest form of communication is *language*. Language is a communication system based on speech symbols (although one can talk figuratively of a language made up of other symbols). These speech symbols may be transformed into written form or some other kind of speech representation, but language will remain essentially an oral means for the transmission of meanings between humans. Although non-linguistic codes of communication are much older than our species, language is unique to it and, as Noam Chomsky stresses, 'without significant analogue in the animal world',[11] in spite of the quite sophisticated 'languages' of bees, monkeys and birds. This, as George Steiner says, must be made clear:

> at a time when it is the fashion to describe man as a 'naked ape' or a biological species whose main motives of conduct are territorial in the animal sense. . . We are, as Hesiod and Xenophon may have been among the first to say, 'an animal, a life-form that speaks'. Or, as Herder put it, *ein Geschöpf der Sprache*—a 'language creature'. . . [Man] alone speaks language, and, as Chomsky formulates it, does not select 'a signal from a finite behavioural repertoire, innate or learned. . .'
>
> Man's capacity to articulate a future tense—in itself a metaphysical and logical scandal—his ability and need to 'dream forward', to hope, make him unique. Such capacity is inseparable from grammar, from the conventional power of language to exist in advance of that which it designates.[12]

The importance of understanding the preeminence of language as the chief form of symbolic interaction among men is based on the fact that it is through language that we transfer meanings—and meanings, as we saw, are the chief criterion for the definition of social action, as distinct from other forms of activity (III, 3). Animal societies are held together by their instinctive languages. Human societies are also held together by language, but their idiom is more than an unchanging code; it is something men themselves constantly transform and which reflects with fine sensitivity nearly all the nuances of the human condition. In making this point one is not only referring to man's achievements in poetry, philosophy or science, but also very especially to other social phenomena such as class, politics, privilege and kinship networks. In a sense all sociologists must be sociologists of language: totalitarian ideologies messianic movements, sacred books, mining communities, parliaments, slum dwellers, armies—every conceivable social formation has a language of its own that must be accounted for and explained if a minimally acceptable picture of them is to be drawn. This leads to the difficult question of establishing the causal relationships between language (and communication generally) and social structure. For a long time it was taken for granted that language expressed basic human needs and that if each language showed different styles and nuances it was because they reflected the specific situations of either the speaker or the matter described. Thus the genius of Arabic was a reflection of the Arab way of life, and the richness of English was a consequence of successive cultural invasions and cultural mixtures; the specific wealth of each language would then be the consequence of a long historical experience, which would make it an especially good medium for the expression of one or several kinds of activity such as mathematics, diplomacy, jurisprudence, or business. Two linguists, Edward Sapir and Benjamin Whorf, have questioned this time-honoured assumption. They began to feel that the relationship ought to be reversed—it was language, they decided, that shaped human action. If, for instance, the language we speak has no concept for 'time', 'speed', 'snow', 'skyscraper', and other words, but has another set of words which other languages do not possess, it is quite obvious that our visualisation of the universe is bound to be restricted (or extended) accordingly. Consider these comments by Whorf on the language of a North-American Indian people:

> I find it gratuitous to assume that a Hopi who knows only the Hopi language and the cultural ideas of his own society has the same notions, often supposed to be intuitions, of time and space that we have, and that are generally assumed to be universal. In particular, he has no notion or intuition of TIME as a smooth-flowing continuum in which everything in the universe proceeds at an equal rate, out of a future, through a present, into a past; or in which, to reverse the picture, the observer is being carried in the stream of duration continuously away from a past and into a future...
>
> The metaphysics underlying our own language, thinking and modern culture . . . imposes upon the universe two grand COSMIC FORMS, space and time; static three-dimensional infinite space, and kinetic one-dimensional uniformly and perpetually flowing time—two utterly separate and unconnected aspects of reality...
>
> The Hopi metaphysics also has its cosmic forms comparable to these in scale and scope. . . It imposes upon the universe two grand cosmic forms, which as a first approximation in terminology we may call MANIFESTED or MANIFESTING . . . or, again OBJECTIVE and SUBJECTIVE. The objective or manifested comprises all that is or has been accessible to the senses. . . The subjective or manifesting comprises all that we call future [and] it includes equally . . . all that we call mental.[13]

While English, in common with all Indo-European languages, divides speech into verbs and nouns, with adjectives to qualify them, other languages fail to make such distinction. The Nootkas (another North American tribe, on the Pacific coast) do not say 'a house' but 'it houses' or 'a house occurs'. In Hopi there is no word for 'a flame', but several expressions such as 'it gives a flash', 'it flames up', 'it is sparkling'.[14] From this it becomes apparent that in a very large measure thought is fashioned by language. Aristotle developed his logic and laws of thought in accordance with the structure of Greek, which was an Indo-Germanic language. Newtonian physics can be equally related to language patterns. Now, the Sapir-Whorf hypothesis (that the structure of language determines the way reality is perceived) must not be understood to say, as is often thought, that everything, including the social structure, depends on the language itself. Ferdinand de Saussure regards language and social structure as reciprocal systems of influences.[15] In some areas language may become decisive, as is the case in national feelings and most nationalist movements. In others, its role as determinant of other phenomena is more problematic, as for instance in economic development or industrialisation processes.

However, the resolution of this question of priority between language and social structure is less important than the fact that their patterns coincide. (It is for this reason that social systems are more accurately described as sociocultural systems, although it seems more practical to use the shorter word.) Flows of communication in society, sources of information, leaders of belief and opinion, creators of art, ideology or entertainment are often hardly distinguishable from the social structure itself. Social structure is maintained, and manifests itself, through communication. This has been classically illustrated by Marcel Mauss' study of the gift relationship. Friendship, mutual visits and invitations, presents, obligations to give or to accept tokens, are not only ways of communication but also (as Mauss shows in his comparative study of these phenomena as they occur in some Polynesian, Melanesian and North-West American Indian societies) the actual expression of social equality and inequality, hierarchy, order and power, as much as the expression of liberality, honour, love, help and that consciousness of kind which, for humans, can only be expressed through culture.[16]

*NOTES on Chapter IV, Section 1*

1. Cf. K. Davies *Human Society* (New York: Macmillan, 1958) p. 29.
2. W. M. S. Russell 'Signals and Shibboleths' *The Listener* (August 9, 1962) pp. 207–13.
3. R. Fox 'The Cultural Animal' *Encounter* Vol. xxxv, no. 1 (July, 1970) pp. 31–45; D. Bidney *Theoretical Anthropology* (New York: Schocken, 1967) pp. 124–55.
4. Cf. special issue on 'Human Biology and the Social Sciences' *Social Research*, Vol. 36, no. 4 (Winter 1969).
5. E. B. Tylor *Primitive Culture* (London: Murray, 1871) Vol. I, p. 1.
6. A. L. Kroeber and C. Kluckhon 'Culture: a Critical Review of Concepts and Definitions' *Papers* (Peabody Museum, Harvard University 1952) Vol. XLVII, no. 1.

7. Cf. P. G. Grasso *Personalità giovanile in transizione* (Zurich: Pas Verlag, 1964) pp. 1–189.
8. H. Johnson *Sociology, a Systematic Introduction* (New York: Harcourt, Brace, 1960) p. 82.
9. D. Bidney *op. cit.* pp. 400–1.
10. A. Kuhn *The Study of Society* (London: Tavistock, 1966) pp. 154–55.
11. Quoted by G. Steiner 'The Language Animal' *Encounter* August 1969, p. 8.
12. G. Steiner *ibid.* p. 8.
13. B. L. Whorf *Language, Thought and Reality* (Boston: M.I.T., 1956) pp. 57–59.
14. *Ibid.* p. 55.
15. F. de Saussure *Cours de linguistique générale* (Paris: Payot, 1955, after course notes of 1906–11) p. 40. Cf. also A. Sommerfelt 'Strutture linguistiche e strutture dei gruppi sociali' in E. Beneviste *et alii, Problemi attuali dell a linguistica* (Milan: Bompiani, 1968) pp. 221–28 and R. Burling *Man's Many Voices* (New York: Holt, Rinehart, Winston, 1970).
16. M. Mauss 'Essai sur le Don' (1923, 1934) in *Sociologie et Anthropologie* (Paris: P.U.F., 1966) pp. 143–279. Cf. also R. M. Titmuss *The Gift Relationship* (London: Allen & Unwin 1971).

# 2    THE SYSTEM AND DYNAMICS OF CULTURE

*Cultural traits, complexes and areas*

Every culture must be studied as a whole or as a system since, no matter how many tensions and contradictory elements may exist in its midst, some degree of mutual integration and dependence must obtain for it to exist. But before approaching this question it is useful to define some basic concepts of cultural phenomena.

The smallest units of any culture are called *traits*. Traits are only isolated for purposes of analysis as they usually only make sense as parts of greater cultural patterns. A weapon, a way of greeting, an incantation, a tool, are all examples of traits. Normally they appear in functionally integrated wholes, which tend to persist in space and in time; these are called cultural *complexes*.[1] A type of habitation, together with the behaviour patterns it implies, is one such complex; the Russian *dacha*, the Catalan *masia* or manor, the French HLM (*habitation à loyer modéré*, roughly equivalent to the British council house) all represent economic, familistic and community complexes of traits. Totemism, the horse-drawn carriage, the aeroplane, the gramophone, the primary school, are also complexes; some of them are also social institutions, while others are artifacts, but they all encompass sets of cultural traits.

All these phenomena occur in definite cultural areas, with geographical boundaries. By virtue of this elementary fact entire cultures are often defined by their geographical location. When we speak of the Basque, Irish, French and Lapp cultures we also refer to certain parts of the world. Culture is in many ways territorial, which helps to explain why even the more dispersed peoples seek to satisfy the need for location by reference to some real or imaginary land. Zion has been for ages the hope and obsession of Jews of the Diaspora. Gypsies, however, seem to be an exception in this respect, and a satisfactory sociological explanation of their attitude is still wanting. Next to these geographical divisions made by laymen and specialists alike we find the more scientific ones, which map cultural systems of complexes over geographical expanses. Thus, American cultures north of the Rio Grande are usually divided into nine areas: Plains: Plateau, California, North Pacific Coast, Eskimo, Mackenzie, Eastern Woodland, Southeastern and Southwestern. Each of these areas covers many tribal units and cultures, but they each 'belong to one type, so that area defines the range of the culture type'.[2] Needless to say, the notion of culture area is a sociographic device which is essentially static. But areas change in size with time; they grow, shrink or disappear entirely. Cultural change occurs continuously, and affects the extension of areas. This extension also depends on which of the elements and criteria the observer takes into account. If he considers only language, together with a few other traits (perhaps quite peripheral ones) he may be justified in speaking of the Scots, New Zealanders, white Americans and Rhodesians as belonging to the same 'area'. One may carry generalisation a bit farther and, using a similar set of criteria, state that Filipinos, Argentinians, Mexicans and Spaniards belong to another such 'area'—the Spanish-speaking world. Politicians and ideologists certainly refer to wide and vague cultural affinities such as these when it suits their purposes. Provided one is aware of the limitations of using cultural areas of this size they can be useful to the sociologist. This is particularly evident with an area like Islam, which possesses a strong character and vigour of its own which cannot be dismissed as merely the artificial creation of the ideologist (VIII, 4).

## The levels of cultural reality

So far the intrinsic quality of traits, complexes and areas has not been mentioned. It is evident that a tool, a concept, a belief, a word, are all cultural traits of a widely differing nature. Further distinctions are, then, necessary. Yet such distinctions must inevitably be about the cultural *level* at which we look at the phenomenon rather than about the phenomenon itself, since cultural items often incorporate several dimensions. As Pitirim Sorokin points out, all sociocultural phenomena comprise three components: (1) meanings, values and norms; (2) biophysical means that objectivise them; and (3) conscious human beings who create, use or handle them in their interrelationships.[3] Components of each kind require the presence of the other elements. Take a tool such as the whip; it is an instrument (a physical means) which is the cultural expression of a system of economic and political exploitation (a system of norms) with which rowing slaves are kept at their task as members of a galley crew (a social group). This example illustrates the three chief levels of cultural reality. The first is the *symbolic-ideal* level. It includes beliefs, central notions, norms and values of social reality. In our example, certain main assumptions about the legitimacy of the galley system and slave labour must exist if it is to operate. The second is the level of *social action*, which is an expression of the first, albeit never its mirror image. Thus, a group may hold certain beliefs, yet in practice act in a way which is not entirely consistent with those beliefs. The compromise between central values, moral principles, individual motivations and circumstances is too common to need examples. But this phenomenon must be kept in mind, for it is a permanent source of tension in societies. Many political and religious movements begin with the rejection of such worldly compromises. The third cultural level is the *material*: the physical projection of the ideal and action levels. Houses, tools, artifacts, paintings, temples, books, belong to this level. They are not, as some have called them 'material culture'. Culture cannot be material, although it is reflected in material objects. When an object ceases to be culturally interpreted it becomes meaningless. The pyramid becomes just a hill in the landscape when the civilisation that built it dies. The descendants of the Mayas in present-day Yucatan and Guatemala live among the ruins of Chichen Itza and Mayapan, which to them are religiously and politically meaningless. In fact, archaeological expeditions have had to clear the jungle and vegetation that completely covered most Mayan monuments. Paradoxically, they have now become again objects of culture, though other systems of values have been attached to them—modern aesthetic values for the lovers of art, nationalistic values for some Mexicans and Guatemalans, and lucrative values for traders and tour operators.

A further distinction must be drawn in the realm of culture, namely the differentiation between *culture* proper and *subculture*. This distinction parallels that of groups and subgroups made above. Each subgroup tends to develop a subculture which is either complementary to the general culture of the group or at variance with it, while in certain circumstances it may partly complement and partly oppose it. In every society women, men, children and adolescents possess their own language, customs and folkways. The same can be said of social institutions (universities, armies, convents) and social classes and occupational groups (doctors, dockers, people in show business). Frequently the dividing line between culture and subculture is difficult to draw. Some subcultures are so different from the prevalent cultural system that they cannot strictly be considered as such, but in most cases a constant cultural exchange between the several sections of society takes place, blurring distinctions. American negro culture may be very different from that of white America but, in many ways, through jazz, slang, art, literature and politics, this subculture has vigorously contributed to the reshaping of the general culture that surrounds it, as much as it has itself been affected by its 'white' environment. In Great Britain the expansion of English culture has gone a long way towards eroding the cultures of the peripheral nationalities—Wales and Scotland. Cornish culture has been largely reduced to some folkloric remains. Only in Ireland anglicisation has been far from perfect. In another European political unit, Spain, the central expanding culture, Castile, has been less successful at cultural integration over the same historical period; Catalonia and the Basque country have not even become its subcultures. Yet Portugal, on the other hand, consolidated her political independence at an early stage and thus showed an apparently greater degree of differentiation from Castilian culture, though their differences may not be as deep. In spite of all this, an unprejudiced foreigner might find all these national differences imperceptible. To him both Hispanic and British culture could well appear remarkably homogeneous.

## Cultural integration

No known culture is a completely chaotic congeries of values, norms, attitudes, objects and means of communication. The different parts of any culture present a degree of mutual coherence which goes beyond mere coexistence in the same society. This vague but necessary notion is termed cultural integration. The least perceptive observer is aware that each culture has a distinctive 'style', and that it is in itself some sort of universe; and this applies not only to well-defined, isolated, tribal societies, but often to entire nations. The Japanese, the Dutch and the Americans possess such 'style', made up of equally vague yet often very real notions such as 'national character',[4] 'tradition', 'way of life'. It is far from easy to find more precise concepts for the measurement of integration, when we realise that very large, complex societies do not have to be culturally integrated in every sense of the word. In the classical Islamic empire, lack of religious integration was circumvented politically by allowing Christians and Jews to retain their religion and customs so long as they paid their tribute; the rationalisation behind this being that they were 'People of the Book', and their traditions part of Islam's own. It may also happen that one important kind of integration underpins an otherwise culturally non-integrated society. The political culture of countries such as Denmark, Switzerland and the United Kingdom permits a great variety of forms of political dissent and the free expression of the most varied ideologies. In such cases a high degree of consensus in some areas enables the peaceful coexistence of disparate cultural elements in others. This point bears on the question of the 'rigidity' and 'plasticity' of cultures, another phenomenon which is difficult to probe. 'Rigidity' is often a sign of vulnerability. The culture of Athens, which seemed to many observers to be weaker than that of Sparta, was the most lasting—in a sense it is not romantic rhetoric to say that it is not yet dead, centuries and centuries after it first flourished in Attica. The strength of Sparta was her total dedication to a narrow—if in some ways nobly unique—ideal and way of life. Athens' pragmatism and readiness for political compromise, her worldliness and relative tolerance of—even inclination for—certain forms of deviance, produced a culture which was not only more enduring but also remarkably universal and amenable to transfer to other sociocultural settings.

In order to understand the varieties of integration it is convenient to make systematic distinctions about the sense of this concept in its cultural context. Sorokin's observations are to the point here. For him there are four types of cultural integration: (1) *Spatial or mechanical adjacency* 'any conglomeration of cultural elements . . . in a given area of social or physical space, with spatial or mechanical concurrence as the only bond of union'. This, the lowest form of integration, is very common. Remnants and residues of several cultures often form heterogeneous, haphazard groups. (2)

*Indirect association through a common external factor.* This occurs when 'two or more culture elements, spatially adjacent but with no functional or logical connection, are also related to one another through the association of each with a common factor external to both of them'. Vodka, skis, stoves, timber houses and heavy felt boots, all typical of North Russian culture, are called for by climatic conditions. They do not require each other logically, but consistently appear together and complement each other in the way of life of the local population. (3) *Causal or functional integration.* Many cultural complexes belong to this category; it occurs when the presence of one trait requires that of the others. Conversely, the absence of one trait imposes severe modifications on the others. The stock-market system cannot be taken out of modern capitalism without changing the nature of the latter, for it is a functional element of its structure. (4) *Logico-meaningful integration.* This is the highest form of integration; it refers to the final sense of the cultural whole, and cannot be explained in merely functional terms. 'One cannot prove by mere words ... the inner consistency and supreme integration of the Cathedral of Chartres, or the Gregorian chant ... or the sculpture of Phidias, or the pictures of Dürer or Raphael or Rembrandt ...' but 'their supreme unity is felt by competent persons as certainly as if they could be analysed with mathematical or logical exactness'.[5]

The two last types provide the keys to the understanding and explanation of cultures. Functionally and causally united cultural phenomena show uniformities of relationship within social structures, while the inner meaningful unity of the culture provides the significance for the whole cultural system.[6] If these criteria are not accepted, then we must renounce the deep and rational interpretation of that intricate phenomenon which we call culture and limit our exertions to a shallow inventory of fragmented 'cultural' occurrences.

## Cultural systems

It is by concentrating on the logico-meaningful level of cultures that social scientists have attempted to order and classify their main types, as found in our species. Roughly there have been two approaches to this problem: either cultures have been classified according to evolutionary sequences in the social structures of human societies or they have been classified by their internal characteristics, quite apart from their place in such sequences. The first approach means that the social scientist starts by possessing a historical scheme, and regards cultures as stages. The roots of this approach are to be found in some of the theories of the Enlightenment period, such as those of Giambattista Vico and Johann Gottfried von Herder, and more especially in the Scottish Enlightenment; Adam Ferguson's *Essay on the History of Civil Society* (1767) offers a first classification of cultures in stages ('savage', 'barbarous' and 'polished') together with a highly sophisticated discussion of their internal structure and directions of change. Marx's sequence (primitive, oriental, ancient, feudal, bourgeois, communist) was built on this tradition, emphasising, though, above all else, the technological and economic aspects of culture (VI; VIII, 4; IX, 3; X, 2). Contemporary sociologists have seized upon the obvious advantages of sociocultural classification based on technology and the economy. As Sorokin himself recognises, the ultimate level of meaning can be expressed only with difficulty in rational, scientific language, so that the curt, laconic labels usually used for good classification are only partially adequate. Gerhard Lenski's typology is characteristic of this criterion; he classifies societies and cultures in a historical sequence, according to technological criteria: simple and advanced hunting and gathering societies; simple and advanced horticultural societies; simple and advanced agrarian societies; and industrial societies. Some adjacent subtypes (fishing, herding, and maritime societies) also enter his classification, which is backed by an impressive effort of erudition and sociological synthesis.[7] With the sole exception of the late-medieval Tunisian historian and sociologist, Ibn Khaldūn, however, writers in this tradition have tended to evade the issue of the central value structures and meanings as determinants of sociocultural systems. (Ibn Khaldūn not only explained the relationship between nomadic and sedentary life and their respective cultures and between polities and economies, but also went a long way towards grasping the role of mentalities, central beliefs and assumptions in shaping technology, art, science and the social structure generally. Yet his recognition by Western social scientists was unfortunately long delayed.[8]) By the same token authors who have mainly used the central criteria of meaning have tended to rely on excessively 'spiritualistic' and ahistorical classifications of cultures.

Some of these classifications, however, deserve to be taken into account, for they stress cultural elements often neglected by students of social structure. Once again in the present context, Pitirim Sorokin provides a good example. He has attempted to classify the major types of culture according to their logico-causal structures and their basic logico-meaningful integration. He distinguishes two profoundly distinct kinds of culture, each with its own world view, system of knowledge, mentality, moral standards, sense of the holy, and predominant forms of social relationships. These two extreme types are called by Sorokin 'ideational' and 'sensate'; a mixed series of types can be distinguished, among which the most important is the 'idealistic' type.

I. *Ideational culture* perceives nature as non-material—as an everlasting Being—and the needs of man basically as spiritual; man's highest needs must be attained by a minimisation of his physical needs. Ideational culture appears to have two main subclasses: (1) Ascetic ideationalism, which stresses the elimination of carnal needs, and takes the sensual world for a mere illusion; it strives towards the ultimate reality, which is conceived as super-sensory. Hinduism, Buddhism, Taoism, Sufism, Stoicism, and ascetic mystical Christianity belong to this subclass. (2) Active ideationalism, which is identical with the former in its major assumptions, but instead of entirely withdrawing from the carnal world it attempts to transform it. Reforming Christian movements belong to this subclass.

II. *Sensate culture* considers that reality is that which is perceived by the sense organs. The world beyond the senses is, if not actually denied, treated with agnosticism. Reality is not static being, but process, change, evolution, transformation. There are three main subclasses. (1) The active sensate, which seeks the consummation of its ends through criteria of sheer efficiency. It is the culture of empire builders, technologists, businessmen. (2) The passive sensate, which seeks parasitic exploitation of the external world and sensuous enjoyment. It is the culture of fun and entertainment. (3) The cynical sensate, which is the culture that achieves the satisfaction of sensuous needs through the mask of ideational ideals. Its representatives become monarchists, communists, capitalists or christians, as the circumstances of the situation may require.

III. *Idealistic culture* is the only one of the several possible mixed forms which appears as a balanced combination of the other two. Reality, for it, is many-sided, but the possibility of everlasting principles is admitted. Ideational values are considered supreme, but nevertheless this sensate world is not conceived as a mere illusion.

These obviously ideal types of culture indicate *culture mentalities* (VIII, 4). In a complex society it is generally possible to find them all present. The types and traits of culture mentality, says Sorokin, are not evenly distributed amongst collectivities and groups. And different mentalities dominate societies at different periods. It would be meaningless to state that Roman culture was of type $x$ or $y$, it would be much more accurate to say that at one stage sensate values came to predominate in Rome; for example, when the empire was first consolidated sensate values predominated. Nevertheless it is possible to speak of larger cultural systems as representing (or being dominated by) each type of mentality. Thus Buddhism, Jainism and Taoism represent ascetic ideational culture, while the modern industrialised world is basically 'active sensate'. 'Idealistic' cultural periods are hard to come by, and tend to be ephemeral. Confucianism, Sorokin says, seems to embody this culture type.[9] Numerous criteria of measurement, quantitative data and statistical tables allow him to illustrate types of culture and their fluctuations. For instance the portrayal of social classes in the plastic arts through the centuries, or that of the sexes and professions, allows for interesting quantifications which, combined with other indices and indicators of cultural reality (inventories of inventions, publications, political events), help to unveil the intricate causal relationships of complex cultures.

Some social scientists have been all too aware of the difficulties involved in such large-scale generalisations. Ruth Benedict believes that the large cultural configurations of civilisations must be understood as much as the small ones of tribal societies but stresses the relative ease with which the latter can be studied. She has herself studied the Zuñi tribe of the Pueblo Indians of New Mexico together with the Dobu of an island near New Guinea and the Kwakiutl of Vancouver Island, as three distinct different world views and solutions to human needs, among many others possible. Some of her general remarks about the wholeness and the structure of meaning of cultures are worth recording:

The three cultures of Zuñi, of Dobu and of the Kwakiutl are not merely heterogeneous assortments of acts and beliefs. They have each certain goals toward which their behaviour is directed and which their institutions further. They differ from one another not only because one trait is present here and absent there, and because another trait is found in two regions in two different forms. They differ still more because they are oriented as wholes in different directions. They are travelling along different roads in pursuit of different ends, and these ends and these means in one society cannot be judged in terms of those of another society, because essentially they are incommensurable.[10]

The cultural pattern of any civilization makes use of a certain segment of the great arc of potential human purposes and motivations, just as we have seen . . . that any culture makes use of certain selected material techniques or cultural traits. The great arc along which all possible human behaviours are distributed is far too immense and too full of contradictions for any one culture to utilise even any considerable portion of it. Selection is the first requirement. Without selection no culture could even achieve intelligibility, and the intentions it selects and makes its own are a much more important matter than the particular detail of technology or the marriage formality that it also selects in similar fashion.[11]

## Cultural change

Cultural change cannot be studied apart from social change in general. Although to affirm that culture shapes, as much as it is itself shaped by, social structure and people's life conditions may seem a platitude, yet to know the extent to which each of these levels of social reality is the cause of change in each instance is far from easy. The lineaments of this matter will be discussed later (X). Meanwhile reference can be made to some simple concepts in the field of cultural change.

Cultural change begins with *innovation*. This consists of the introduction of a new cultural trait, complex or pattern into a society. Its consequences vary enormously. Thus the seasonal innovations of fashion may be quite superficial, although this is not always the case.[11] But the introduction of an invention may transform the entire way of life of a people. We are all familiar with the consequences of the introduction of fire, the wheel, written law books and the motor car at different points in history; they helped change the social structure dramatically, and they changed culture itself still further. Innovations may simply be imported from other societies or transported from one society to the other. This is *diffusion*, a phenomenon by no means simple, as each society shows differing degrees of receptivity to new ideas. Resistances to change may be built into the culture itself, or may be created by the powers-that-be, frightened that it may threaten their preeminence or the moral and religious values of their subordinates.

## NOTES on Chapter IV, Section 2

1. Cf. A. R. King in J. Gould ed. *Dictionary of the Social Sciences* (London: Tavistock and UNESCO, 1964) p. 170.
2. C. Wissler *Man and Culture* (New York: Thomas Crowell, 1923) p. 50–57.

3. P. Sorokin *Sociological Theories of Today* (New York: Harper, 1966) p. 16.
4. J. Caro Baroja *El mito del carácter nacional* (Madrid: Seminarios y Ediciones, 1970).
5. P. A. Sorokin *Social and Cultural Dynamics* (New York: Bedminster Press, 1962) pp. 3–21.
6. *Ibid.* p. 23.
7. G. Lenski *Human Societies* (New York: McGraw Hill, 1970).
8. Ibn Khaldūn's *Muqadimmah* appeared in an English edition only in 1958, translated by F. Rosenthal (New York: Bollingen, 3 vols.). The full recognition of this sociological masterpiece is far from complete.
9. P. A. Sorokin *Social and Cultural . . . op. cit.* pp. 55–152.
10. R. Benedict *Patterns of Culture* (New York: Mantor, 1959; 1st ed. 1934) pp. 196 and 207.
11. R. König *Soziologie der Mode* (Zurich: Modebuch, 1961).

# 3   THE PROCESS OF SOCIALISATION

*Learning and socialisation*

Culture is transmitted and maintained by a learning process. *Learning* is the acquisition of knowledge, information, values, beliefs, norms and behaviour.[1] The process whereby individuals and groups learn cultural patterns and standards is called *socialisation*. In a certain sense, there is no difference whatsoever between them; all socialisation is learning, although the reverse is not always the case. The processes of learning and socialisation continue throughout the life of the individual and the life of the society. They imply a constant apprenticeship to the whole system of culture and social structure in which the individual exists, except in those areas to which he is denied access. The individual learns both the common denominator of his culture and the particular sections of that culture that belong with the role, status, privilege or social position that he is heir to or is expected to possess in the future. Part of this learning and socialisation implies *internalisation*, which is the intense acceptance by the individual of the values, beliefs, attitudes and norms of his groups. Strictly speaking, internalisation entails an identification of the person with these elements; they are taken for granted. From the meanings of words to the legitimate sources of authority in society men absorb a wide range of cultural traits and complexes which they come to take for granted and accept as part of their innermost self.[2] Next to this fully fledged internalisation, which implies much unconscious acceptance of the sociocultural world, we find the *instrumental* and the *critical* forms of internalisation—two kinds that often go hand in hand. The first is the acquisition of cultural patterns without belief in them, and their use and manipulation for the fulfilment of personal or group needs. This kind of internalisation appears in every society that shows a degree of complexity, and in which role and norm conflict provokes disbelief and gives rise to strategies of social action based on the assumption that cultural patterns are only conventions and do not possess any magic or mandatory power. In instrumental internalisation, patterns are learnt and mastered, and then used by some with corresponding although not apparent, disbelief. It is important to stress that only a section of a given population ever practises this at a given time and in a given area of social life. Critical internalisation also entails learning; it is not pervaded by amoral or even cynical instrumentality, but rather by a genuine desire to find the truth. Entire educational systems in complex societies are geared towards the development of this kind of internalisation especially in the field of natural science. Students must entirely accept the values that underlie scientific systematic scepticism, thus showing that some form of cultural dogmatism must always be present.

## Socialisation, culture and the social system

Slowly, right from his birth, through punishments and rewards (which include mild signs of approval and reproach), the child's groups—his family, neighbours, older children, adults in the village, the nursery school, the street—mould his personality. This moulding also occurs because there is an inborn desire in children to learn. The child, as Piaget has pointed out, wants 'logical and moral control'; he establishes a unilateral respect for the adult and lets him teach and guide him.[3] The result of this process, repeated for every generation, is the transmission of entire cultural configurations, thus ensuring not only the stability of social systems but also the development of specific patterns of change. (As was shown earlier, systems—as opposed to structures—allow for internal change (III, 7). Cultures that teach inventiveness, scientific research, and respect and deference for technological, philosophical, political, economic and artistic innovation, are thus systems producing their own change.)

From the standpoint of socialisation, the groups and institutions that surround the individual are seen as *socialisation agents*. Paramount amongst these is, of course, the family, although in modern societies other institutions are becoming increasingly more important, especially the nursery school (where it exists) and the primary school. This links socialisation directly with public policies and societal goals, the study of which is one of the most delicate areas of the sociology of education. More generalised agents of socialisation are churches, political parties, social movements, trade unions, the press, television and the universities. Some of these are obviously 'impersonal' means of socialisation, but are equally decisive in creating the cultural conditions in which people live. In a sense, however, they are not impersonal; behind a policy, a newspaper, or a television programme there are always people putting forward ideas, approving and supporting certain lines of information and thought, and eliminating or opposing others. Each one of these phenomena will be dealt with in turn as the groups that foster them come under scrutiny; what should be stressed here, however, is the permanent and universal dimension of socialisation.

It has just been seen that cultures do not cover the whole arc of human capacity for belief, value and action. Rather they are geared to the attainment of certain objectives and to the exclusion of others. The central orientations of culture mean that people in a given society must be trained to comply with them; they must internalise the 'right' set of attitudes and motivations. Parsons and Shils made an effort to classify these orientations in a general form and not according to given cultures, with the assumption that each one of them appears in varying degree and combination in each society; for this last reason they have called them 'pattern variables'. These pattern variables appear in dichotomic form, as alternatives of conduct on which an individual must make decisions in every given social situation. These authors suggest five possibilities (or disjunctives):

1. *Ascription-achievement.* Individuals have to decide how to act towards other persons depending upon either their 'quality' or their 'performance'—depending upon either their social position in terms of status or the nature of their activities.

2. *Affectivity-affective neutrality.* Action must be directed towards either the early satisfaction of emotional needs or the postponement of such satisfaction in the name of higher principles or other goals.

3. *Selforientation-collectivity orientation.* The individual has the choice of acting together in his own personal interests or in the interests of the community, as he sees them.

4. *Universalism-particularism*. Here the choice is between acting in accordance with standards that apply equally to all or in the light of personal circumstances, interests and inclinations.

5. *Diffuseness-specificity*. The dilemma here lies in whether or not the individual should concern himself with all aspects of the object, the other person or the situation, or with a limited number of these aspects.[4]

Although these dichotomic alternatives may not cover all possible alternatives in social action[5] they give a good indication as to how cultural patterns orient behaviour. It is said that the individual 'must choose' either of the criteria in each case; in fact, and as long as the situation does not appear confused to the actor (or even group or collectivity), the system of values and attitudes, and the norms into which he has been socialised, give him a guide for his action. Thus we speak of 'achievement-oriented' cultures, meaning that the prevalent values reward certain forms of individual excellence (attained through talent, effort and competition) by giving them a high status, while other forms (such as those which are inherited or derive from family background) are of less importance. Obviously the combination of several pattern variables gives us a much fuller picture of each culture. Both a capitalist and a socialist society are achievement oriented but collectivity orientation is, at least hypothetically, very low in the former and very high in the latter. Societies where favouritism, nepotism and personal likes and dislikes are important (particularistic societies) may also be virtually impartial towards certain prescribed types of individual achievement (III, 3).

## Personality

In Latin, *persona* meant a character in a play, a subject whose function was literally to play a role on the stage. The word has never lost its original connotation, although a much higher meaning—that of the person as a subject of moral rights and obligations —has been added to it. A person is said to possess a *personality*; that is, a configuration of individual attitudes, orientations and values, that set him apart from other human beings in the same group. Such characteristics may belong to his individual psychology, but nevertheless they are acquired as a result of his interaction with other people in the course of time and by his life experience. It follows, therefore, that personality is as important a sociological concept as it is a psychological one. The sociological assumption is that a given social environment breeds, by socialisation and learning, a given type of personality. Bureaucracies help create the 'bureaucratic mentality' or personality. Authoritarian patterns of education and family socialisation create 'authoritarian personalities' amongst the youngsters submitted to them. This is, in fact, a truism. Numerous social institutions are set up in every society for the sole purpose of moulding people, and especially the young, into the kind of personality required by the group. Spartan education of the young, Saint Ignatius' *Spiritual Exercises*, l'École Polytechnique in Paris, immediately suggest patently conscious efforts to create one kind of man specifically prepared for one style of life and action.

Does this contradict what has just been said about personality being a configuration of individual attitudes? In fact, there are two dimensions to personality: it is an individual characteristic, but at the same time each social milieu is made up of dominant personalities, or basic personality types, reflecting culture and socialisation processes. There is nothing to be gained by trying to decide which one of these two terms influences the other, for they are mutually dependent. Each individual is a unique configuration of characteristics, and is recognised as such by his fellow men and women; and yet social classes, nationalities, lineages, regions and institutions produce their own dominant personalities, and are in turn produced by them. The early United States of America was as much the result of the predominant personalities of her settlers (Puritan Protestants with a specific conception of work, property and the individual) as it was a consequence of the social structures and conflicts at hand (the recent struggle with the metropolis, abundant land, the 'savages'). The presence in a society of one predominant set of types of basic personality, together with the cultural system of which they are largely an expression, produces a specific number of results. Compare the dynamics of the same Protestant communities in North America with those of the French Catholic settlers, along the St Lawrence river nearby. For this is precisely one of the revealing aspects of personality: it is that variable that makes different individuals act differently when confronted with the same circumstances.[6] And this does not only apply to large social structures, such as the ones just mentioned, but to any situation—students in a classroom, people in public places, soldiers in battle.

Internalisation, socialisation, learning are all processes which show how culture is inculcated into man's mind and consciousness until it becomes part of his very nature. It would be wrong, however, to assume that this gives us the complete picture of what human nature is. And 'oversocialised conception of man' can only lead to a failure to understand the unpredictable new directions which his actions may often take, for, as Dennis Wrong says:

> 'Socialization' may mean two quite distinct things; when they are confused an oversocialized conception of man is the result. On the one hand socialization means the 'transmission of the culture', the particular culture of the society an individual enters at birth. On the other hand the term is used to mean the 'process of becoming human', of acquiring uniquely human attributes from interaction with others. All men have been socialized in the latter sense, but this does not mean that they have been completely molded by the particular norms and values of their culture.[7]

It has been said that when talking about the nature of social systems one has to take this unique disposition in human beings into account if one is to understand them adequately. All this does not mean that any form of prediction is completely out of the question in the human sciences. It means rather, that, apart from the many areas where prediction is feasible, a sociological interpretation of culture will indicate when and how the creative act—the consequences of which are not always foreseeable—is made possible.[8]

*NOTES on Chapter IV, Section 3*

1. For behaviourists learning is confined to behaviour. Cf. Th. Newcomb *Social Psychology* (New York: Dryden, 1950) p. 51. Also articles on 'learning' in *Int. Encyc. Soc. Sci.*, Vol. 9, pp. 114 ff.
2. For a description of this process G. H. Mead *Mind, Self and Society* (University of Chicago, 1934).
3. J. Piaget *The Moral Judgement of the Child* (London: Routledge, 1951) pp. 401–11. Anarchistic and extremely permissive theories of education tend to overlook Piaget's contributions in this respect.
4. T. Parsons and E. Shils *Towards . . . op. cit.* Chapter on 'Values, motives, and systems of actions'.
5. Other authors have added other pattern variables. Cf. S. M. Lipset *The First New Nation* (London: Heinemann, 1964) where he introduces: 'instrumental-consummatory', and 'egalitarian-elitist'.
6. A good collection of articles exploring these problems is to be found in B. Kaplan ed. *Studying Personality Cross-Culturally* (New York: Harper & Row, 1961).
7. D. H. Wrong, 'The Oversocialised Conception of Man' in *Am. Sociol. Rev.*, Vol. 26 (1961) pp. 183–93.
8. For personality studies in general cf. N. J. Smelser and W. T. Smelser eds. *Personality and Social Systems* (New York: Wiley & Sons, 1970, 2nd ed.).

# V The Community

## 1 COMMUNITY AND ASSOCIATION

The highest level of generality has been maintained so far in dealing with the themes, issues and notions of sociology. As we have seen earlier, social action, norms, functions, structure, conflict and the like are universal phenomena. The first step will now be taken in the direction of more circumscribed phenomena—those which appear in certain areas of social life and not in others, and under given circumstances. Perhaps not unexpectedly, we begin by approaching a theme that is still very broad: the division of all human groups into two general categories—communities and associations. This is a most elementary, seminal dichotomy, which has been incorporated into sociological thinking for a long time and is now well established. With this dichotomy *community* and *association* are seen as two basic modes of social order and structure, two elementary forms of interhuman bond and interaction, which must be regarded in terms of ideal types, since one can scarcely expect to find them in a pure state in real life (II, 1).

Although the assumption that there are two opposed modes of social action and structure is very old, its more precise sociological formulation is due to Ferdinand Tönnies, whose two concepts (*Gemeinschaft* for community and *Gesellschaft* for association) still tend to be referred to by their German designations, for corresponding words for them in other languages are not always entirely satisfactory. Tönnies' dichotomy was either assimilated by other sociologists (such as Weber, who explicitly acknowledged his debt to him) or was soon developed independently by them. Durkheim's idea of the 'mechanical' and 'organic' types of social bond, or solidarity, corresponds to the dichotomy, though the uninitiated should be warned that his use of the words 'mechanical' and 'organic' would be reversed by most other social theorists working on this theme, as will soon become apparent. Charles Cooley created a similar dichotomy when he distinguished between primary groups (communities) and the rest, which can be called secondary groups (associations). Through the efforts of Thomas and Znaniecki, in their classical study of Polish emigrants to America as they lived in their country of origin and, later, in Chicago, the dichotomy began to prove very useful in social research. Other theories or conceptual constructs such as the 'pattern variables' (IV, 3) can also be partially integrated into this distinction.[2] On the basis of these efforts the following summary of the two complementary and opposite notions can be formulated:

I. There are social formations which are based on emotional and affective bonds among their members. In them, individuals consider other individuals as ends in themselves, while they know each other personally, and mutually participate in each other's private lives. Members value the fact of belonging intrinsically to these formations. They may be referred to as *Gemeinschaften*, communities or primary groups. People are related to each other for what they are perceived to be worth in themselves, and action is based on a 'natural will' (*Wesenswille*, essential will, according to Tönnies) and on an emotional loyalty called by Durkheim the 'solidarity of similitude' (or 'mechanical solidarity'). On the other hand, we also encounter social formations of another kind based on utilitarian interests; in them the individual does not consider the other individuals as ends in themselves but as means to attain his own ends. Members of these formations know each other and interact impersonally. Members share the external or public life of other members, often on a contractual basis. Privacy[3] is not involved. Individuals value their membership extrinsically, instrumentally, through a 'rational will' (*Kürwille*). These social formations, so different from communities, are the secondary groups, *Gesellschaften*, or associations. In more than a merely allegoric way, then, it could said that communities are nearer the organic elements of man as a species, whereas associations are closer to the constructs of man's art, reason and culture generally. (Hence the misleading nature of Durkheim's labels for each type of group; modern industrial societies have many more 'artificial' or 'mechanical' bonds in them than pre-modern societies, whose structure was more 'organic' in the strict sense of this word. On the other hand, Durkheim used the term 'mechanical' to denote an unreflective, automatic response to social demands.) (IV, 2).

II. The criterion employed to distinguish between both kinds of group is to be found in the degree of prominence of the chief characteristics of either of them in each case. The distinction, then, is not an absolute one. (A) When sentiments and emotions are of paramount importance for the group and it can be said to be organised around them, the group is a community. The community is above all a community of life; life experiences are shared, the fate of its individual members is felt by the rest of the group and, conversely, the fortunes of the group have an immediate and direct emotional and personal effect upon each member. Such is the case of a family; it is an affective unit where sickness, joy, death, and the sharing of food and shelter find a unique and meaningful framework. (B) When the functional division of work and impersonal, complex cooperation are decisive for the existence of a group, and the group exists within the framework of a system of goals that transcend or escape those of primary groups, we are dealing with an association. A banking institution is an association. In it each employee deals with symbols: cheques, accounts, the figures of calculating machines, clients' letters, etc. Hypothetically no personal emotional contacts are needed for the good functioning of the bank; accordingly emotional ties are excluded from the explicit rules of interaction, which are all highly formalised. There also exist in a bank, however, friendships, gossip, likes and dislikes, struggles for promotion, feelings and expressions of comradeship, and acts of favouritism; but all these are 'officially ignored' and relegated to the background. And yet, as sociological research in the fields of industry and organisations has shown, the development and strength of 'informal groups' (primary groups) in the framework of factories, commercial enterprises, government departments and other institutions are vital for the understanding of their dynamics, efficiency and behaviour. This all goes to show that in many instances communities and associations may not be at all incompatible. In some cases underlying community relationships may even be vital for the fate of the formal organisation; in modern armies, platoon morale and effectivity in combat depend more often on its internal loyalties than on other more impersonal factors.

III. In most societies communities and associations are found together or side by side. The more primitive a society is, however, the more prominent its primary groups tend to be. Among paleolithic and mesolithic peoples (as well as in societies in Australia, the Amazon basin and Africa which have survived well into the twentieth century) society, tribe and primary group are one and the same thing. Community bonds are reinforced by the absence of formal organisation; or, more precisely, the entire social system precludes such organisation, although rudimentary forms of political and religious leadership are to be found in them.[4] At the opposite pole we encounter civilisations (complex societies, usually urban, with a very high cultural development); their social structure is based on a network of associations, where social action is channelled according to impersonal codes of behaviour and oriented towards the satisfaction of organisational goals rather than towards the goals of communities, although in some cases these may coincide; in fact existing communities will try to redirect organisational goals to their own benefit. Thus the cliques and elite groups—primary groups— at the top of a large political party—association—will usually do their best to serve the party's official programme while gearing its policies in their own private interests; if the second trend prevails rank and file supporters may say that the party 'has been betrayed'. In the light of all this, then, it looks as if mankind has undergone a vast historical process away from social systems which were exclusively based on the community bond and into social systems based on associational structures. None of the authors who first developed the dichotomy 'community-association' pretended that there was a simple and linear process from the first to the second kind of society, much less that in modern industrial societies primary groups were all doomed.[5] Nevertheless it is clear that a number of associational structures and systems have been irregularly but surely gaining ground over the last millennia: bureaucracies, state administrations, imperial systems, finance, factories, markets, and scientific academies and universities. Conversely, many groups based on affective ties and on a consciousness of kind—clans, extended families, tribes, peasant communities have been losing their original importance as the central structures of social cohesion and political, cultural, economic and demographic survival. This is particularly true of the most industrialised societies, but it does not mean that primary groups have all died in them. Some have succumbed to change and new ones have emerged, while others have readapted themselves to the new situation. What has disappeared in some industrialised countries is the traditional centrality of communities for many key functions of social life, since, in them, a great many economic, political and educational tasks have been taken over by associational institutions. This, however, has resulted in a deep transformation of the quality of community ties and life rather than its outright abolition (X).

If the above characteristics of communities and associations were generalised to whole societies, the following table, which contrasts them schematically, would result:

| Predominant Traits | Social Systems | |
| --- | --- | --- |
| | Communities | Associations |
| Nature of the social bond: | Natural will 'Mechanical' solidarity | Rational will 'Organic' solidarity |
| Orientation of social action: | End in itself Particularism Ascription | Means Universalism Achievement |
| Organisation: | Organic; clan-like; relatively small | Administrative; bureaucratic; large group |
| Economy: | Unit of production/ consumption; biological division of labour; cooperation | Capitalist market/ socialist economy; class; wage and/or profit; rationalisation of work |
| Position of individual and nature of his membership: | Natural member; communion; 'we'-feeling | Artificial member; manpower; anonymity; ego-feeling |
| Principal mode of conduct and nature of the behavioural relationships: | Personal; love-hate | Impersonal; contractual; through symbols (money, etc) |
| Sources of freedom: | Identification with social system | Choice of behaviour; privacy; legal guarantees; multiplication of life chances |
| Sources of constraint: | Tradition; mores; 'tribal' penal law | State; class; market fluctuations; alienation; political coercion |
| Thought: | Intuitive; conservative | Analytic; innovatory |
| Belief: | Religious and/or ideational | Ideological and/or sensate |

## NOTES on Chapter V, Section 1

1. Precedents can be found in Hesiod, Saint Augustine (in his distinction between the 'city of God' and 'the city of men') and Ibn Khaldūn amongst others.
2. The three basic statements of the dichotomy are F. Tönnies *Gemeinshaft und Gesellschaft* (Leipzig, 1935, 8th ed.; 1st ed. 1887); E. Durkheim *De la division du travail social* (Paris: Alcan, 1893); and Ch. Cooley *Social Organization* (Glencoe: Free Press, 1956; 1st ed. 1909). A first decisive refinement is that of H. Schmalenbach 'Die soziologische Kategorie des Bundes' in *Die Dioskuren* Vol. I, 1922. For a summary of some of the vicissitudes of these notions E. Shils 'Primordial, Personal, Sacred and Civil Ties' *Brit. Jnl. Soc.* Vol. XVIII, June 1957.
3. For a sociological analysis of privacy E. Shils 'Privacy' in *Law and Contemporary Problems* Vol. XXXI, Spring 1966 and G. Martinotti *Controllo delle informazioni personali e sistema politico* (Courmayeur: Olivetti Seminar, 1971), mimeographed.

4. E. Service *Primitive Social Organization* (New York: Random House, 1962).
5. This misinterpretation, however, is quite common. See my criticism of it in S. Giner, *Sociedad masa: ideología y conflicto social* (Madrid: Seminarios y Ediciones, 1971), and in *Mass Society* (London: Martin Robertson, 1976).

# 2  COMMUNITIES

If associational bonds are necessary for the establishment of civilisations, those of community can never be dispensed with. They are primordial human bonds, absolutely necessary for the normal development of the individual. As already stated they can be said to be nearer nature, as intimate emotional relationships and a consciousness of kind are the chief rallying points for the community. But primary groups cannot be classified and studied in as systematic a manner as secondary groups, for the very reason that they are very often informal. In many cases, especially in societies with a high degree of geographical and social mobility, primary groups emerge that are strictly based on what Goethe called 'elective affinities' (*Wahlverwandtschaften*), thus creating networks of friendship, 'personal contacts', and the like. Such primary groups, in spite of their often shifting borderlines are hinged on solid loyalties which fulfil the need for the personal solidarity, warmth and companionship once supplied by the tribe or the village community. In other cases primary groups are far more institutionalised, as is the case of the family. A high degree of institutionalisation, however, does not mean greater social importance; in all societies pervaded by a strong sense of individualistic values friendship bonds are extremely important, though also extremely difficult to pinpoint. (The poverty of quantitative sociological measurement is quite marked in this respect; sociographic tests cannot reflect the profound and eminently qualitative nature of genuine friendship, and yet a sociological treatment of the phenomenon of friendship is perfectly feasible by other means, especially those offered by the humanistic dimension of the discipline.)

Of the whole range of possible communities[1] two will now be looked into: kinship and family units, and territorial communities. While they will be occasionally mentioned later, other types of community will not be examined in detail. It is important, however, to stress that some of the latter are not precisely minor communities. In the great modern cities, for instance, the 'street-corner gang' is a primary group with vital functions for its members and often for the neighbourhood as a whole.[2] Teenage groups create socialisation by protecting their members from the greater society, training them in internal competitions, establishing hierarchies, and fulfilling emotional, erotic and friendship needs not available in other settings. Apart from these and similar types of community based, one way or another, on links of comradeship and friendship, family and territorial communities have distinctive sets of functions that make them stand out in the whole range of human primary groups.

*NOTES on Chapter V, Section 2*

1. On communities cf. R. M. Maciner's 1917 classical study *Community* (London: Frank Cass, 1970) and R. König *The Community* (London: Routledge, 1968), also R. M. French, ed., *The Community: A Comparative Perspective* (Itasca, Illinois: Peacock, 1969).
2. W. F. Whyte *Street Corner Society* (University of Chicago Press, 1954); cf. also T. R. Fyvel *The Insecure Offenders* (London: Chatto & Windus, 1961).

# 3 KINSHIP

## The Family

The family is a social system found in all societies. It is one of the chief agents of socialisation in most of them, as well as an institution that maintains social control and fulfils (in varying degrees) sexual, emotional, and economic functions; sometimes political and religious functions are also embodied in families. All this points to the difficulties involved in defining precisely what the family is. It is unsatisfactory to state that it regulates the sexual access of men to women (or vice versa), since in many societies 'lawful' sexual intercourse is not confined to the family. It is even less satisfactory to say that the family is a social unit for biological reproduction, as in some societies (for instance) the biological father is not the putative father, from whom the son or daughter inherits name, status and economic situation. After comparing a considerable number of societies, Murdock reached the conclusion that there are three chief characteristics of all families: common residence, economic co-operation, and reproduction—to which, in nearly all cases, a fourth can be added: socialisation.[1] Of course, taken by themselves these functions are also satisfied by other institutions and norms. Thus in many societies sexual play and even intercourse is admitted as a licit form of behaviour among the unmarried young, without necessarily implying future marriage. What distinguishes the family from other social systems is its capacity for integrating the four functions in one single formula for coexistence. In the light of all this the family can be defined as that group in which sexual intercourse is permitted between man and wife, and where the children born to women are accepted as legitimate offspring to both parents and are brought up within the family community (which is, besides, an economic unit—at least in the sense of economic consumption).[2]

*Marriage* The bond that makes families possible is marriage. This is a relatively stable relationship of sexual and home cohabitation between a woman and a man, which is recognised by society as a lawful institution for these purposes as well as for the domestic life and education of their children. By extension, marriage is also the rite whereby the majority of cultures formalise and solemnise the formation of such stable relationship. Stability may either be for life, as among Catholics, in which case matrimonial dissolution is forbidden on religious grounds, or it may be the intention only, in which case divorce is permitted under given circumstances. Basically, marriage possesses all or several of the following characteristics: (a) the satisfaction of erotic needs; (b) the establishment of a home; (c) the social division of labour on a *Gemeinshaft* basis; (d) the development of personal, community bonds of care, mutual help and communication; (e) the transmission of patrimony and the sharing of status, privilege and power—or lack of it; (f) the transmission of rights and patrimony amongst spouses (dowry, brideprice, mutual inheritance); (g) the creation of new links of reciprocity among two different families; and (h) the public and legal recognition of the institution.

Marriage appears in several forms; two are fundamental: *monogamy* (where the individual has only one spouse at any given moment) and *polygamy* (where the plurality of wives or husbands is recognised in their society). In turn polygamy may be *polygyny* (when the husbands may have two or more wives) or *polyandry* (where the wife may have two or more husbands). Of all these forms of marriage polygamy is the most frequently found, even though Western societies are relatively monogamous; and this monogamous pattern of marital arrangement is now spreading under the world influence of Western civilisation.[3] (We say that Western societies are 'relatively' monogamous because in most of them serial polygamy—a person having two or more legal mates, but not simultaneously—is very common.) However, polyandry is much rarer than polygyny, and the former, when admitted in a society, often occurs only with women of very high status. Polygamy in its strict, simultaneous form, often encounters economic barriers. This is particularly so in Islamic countries, where a man is permitted to have up to four wives (in addition to concubines) but must, by Koranic prescription, treat them all equally, at least in economic terms. As a result the number of men who can afford polygamous households is small. Census data for Islamic countries show figures often much lower than ten per cent of polygynists among all married men.[4] Although this can now be attributed to contemporary social change, the economic barrier to the expansion of this form of polygamy has always existed in those countries. On the other hand the growth of the divorce rate in many industrialised societies has resulted in an escalation of serial polygamy for both men and women.

With few exceptions, which are rare even in the most modern Western societies, marriage is not a relationship that affects only two people and their offspring; it is an institution that connects and relates their families of origin to each other, establishes new economic relationships, new rules of reciprocity among formerly unrelated individuals, and new juridical rights and duties. Not only exchanges of gifts, visiting patterns and rules of mutual help enter the picture here but also, in many societies, rules of residence: *matrilocality*, if the married couple must live where the wife's parental household is; *patrilocality* if it is at the husband's; and *neolocality* if it is a new, different one. Thus in many a sense marriage is a microcosm that faithfully mirrors much wider phenomena. This is especially true of the new social unit that appears once a marriage takes place—the nuclear family.

*The nuclear family* The family, in general, is a group made up of several sub-units, of which the most important is the nuclear or *conjugal* family. (The family in the wide sense is called the *extended* family, and its size and structure, as well as the intensity of the different kinship bonds, vary considerably from society to society.) The nuclear family is composed of husband, wife and their offspring. Its degree of dependence on the extended family of which it is a sub-group varies from a point of almost total identification with the wider unit on the one hand to extreme nuclear family isolation with ties practically severed from other members of the family on the other.

In spite of its relative simplicity its internal structure presents important variations. There are even cases where the conjugal family presents a hazy or problematic configuration. Thus the

Nayar of India do not seem to recognise marriage as an institution, although they possess a nuclear family composed of a brother, a sister and her children. A husband exists, with whom the sister has entered into matrimony and whom she has ritualistically divorced, but her children may have been sired by any of her lovers; one of these—not automatically the biological father—recognises them and confers a name on them.[5] This type of situation is not entirely unknown in the West, where the putative father is considered for all legal purposes as the biological father, and where extra-marital sexual relationships in most instances have no legal weight for inheritance. In all these cases the juridical system—or the mores, as the case may be—operates in the direction of social control, favouring the recognised kinship structures (and their patrimony) and ignoring the bonds of affection and passion, which are seen as feelings that may be disruptive to such structures. For the same reasons the law ignores internal quarrels, hostility or disruption. This public disregard for internal family conflict indicates the importance attributed in all societies to the nuclear family as a central institution of social order.

An important criterion for the study of the nuclear family is its authority patterns and the way it copes with the division of labour. Traditionally one distinguishes between 'patriarchal' and 'matri-archal' families, depending on who takes the major decisions. But this distinction is, for two reasons, somewhat equivocal. First, in patriarchal societies the authority is usually vested in the head of the extended family rather than in the heads of the nuclear families that are part of it, although the latter are usually given considerable leeway by the patriarch in matters relating to their households. Second, even in the most patriarchal societies, such as classical Rome, it was usual for the wife to wield considerable power within the household, and even influence all its external affairs. By and large, however, women in most societies have possessed lower status than men and have been subordinated to them in the family struc-ture. The causes for this situation cannot be spelled out here but must be sought in the many millennia in which the necessary social division of labour gave man power and prominence over house-bound, child-bearing and child-rearing women. Only a very com-plex series of events (which one could, with some diffidence, per-haps, group together under the heading of 'modernisation') has allowed for this age-old situation to be undermined (VI, 3). Yet to this day the family status tends to depend on the social status of the husband, although where they exist the high status of the wife, her wealth and high degree of education, enhance these same qualities in the husband's social position.[6] Too much of any of these three elements on the part of the wife, though, may be counterproductive for the husband's status, which fact serves to indicate the considerable bias towards male predominance found even in Western cultures. Thus, marrying beneath one's own social status is more acceptable for men; countless European aristocrats are married to former models, but countesses are not supposed to marry their hairdressers. By the same token, the ambassador's wife receives the same honours as are due to her husband, but not vice versa; the king's wife receives the title of 'queen', but the queen's husband only that of 'prince consort'. Jokes and scurrilous remarks about obscure husbands married to more intelligent, able, or prominent women only stress the apparent discrepancies between the innate worth of men and women, although a constant trend towards equality has been noticeable ever since the Enlightenment period in the West, and the nineteenth-century European expansion of influence over the rest of the world. Change in this direction has really been very fast; great strides have taken only a few generations, but people involved in it—especially women—have understandably perceived the process as a very slow one.

*Divorce* Divorce is the legal termination of matrimony during the life of both spouses. Technically it can be distinguished from mere separation and annulment, the latter being a legal declaration that marriage never existed, but sociologically the distinction is not always clear. In countries such as Italy until 1971 or Spain after 1939, annulments have been used as a means of divorce for those who could afford the high expenses charged by the Catholic Church. (The same Church has much more reasonable fees in other countries, such as the United States where high costs may incline Catholics to ignore cannon law and seek the help of a civil court.) Adherents to the Anglican Church cannot divorce either, though there are signs (1971) that its General Synod may change its marriage discipline; once again the lure of the civil court plays an important role in this matter. At the other extreme of the spectrum we find states such as Israel and Moslem countries where divorce may occur simply by mutual consent. Intermediate cases (divorce based on grounds of cruelty, adultery or desertion) are much more common, but a trend towards the recognition of divorce by consent is quite marked, at least in the public opinion of many different countries. Now, the mere stating of these facts is sociologically meaningless; the incidence of divorce is by itself no indicator—it tells and proves next to nothing. Let us see why.

The family is always considered as a central social institution, and marital dissolution is hardly ever ignored by religious, political or civic authorities. It is their interference that either invalidates the value of divorce rates as indicators of the state of families in a given collectivity or reduces it considerably. If and when divorce is introduced in Brazil, Ireland and Spain, marital dissolutions in those countries will not mean that the passing of a law has suddenly 'weakened' the family, but simply that a new solution has been found to a given social problem, previously merely ignored, not non-existent. In those countries the causes for the absence of divorce have to be sought in a combination of religious and political influence. In others it may be ideology and power. In the Soviet Union, in spite of early revolutionary steps for the automatic granting of divorce (in itself a measure which took place within the framework of a deliberate effort to disintegrate the family in the name of Marxism and communism), a very strong antidivorce drive was launched in the thirties, in an attempt to compensate for the apparent results of the free-love policy: a decrease in the birth rate, the dissolution of community ties, an increase in the number of illegitimate children and (so the communist authorities asserted) increased hooliganism. The pro-family campaign swung the pendulum as far in one direction as the former campaign had swung it in the other. Divorce became extremely difficult, and a stigma was attached to it; since 1935 involvement in a divorce has had to be recorded on passports and birth certificates.[7] Only when external pressures like these can be removed from a given country can divorce rates begin to be indicative of other factors, such as economic fluctuations, social mobility, migration of male workers, changes in moral values and the like.

In general divorce shows the highest frequencies in countries which are either very secularised (as in the West) or undergo intense industrialisation (as in Japan between 1887 and 1919) or both, and also in countries where religion has traditionally taken a tolerant attitude towards it, as in the Islamic lands. The more it is considered by the law (or those who made the law) as a remedy or a lesser evil and not as a 'social sickness', the more it is likely to occur frequently. It is interesting to note that states that forbid divorce (or make it extremely difficult) in the name of family stability are indirectly fostering marital desertion, neuroses, and delinquency. Thus, if it is true that children of divorced parents

show a higher incidence of emotional troubles and juvenile delinquency than those of unbroken families, the children of broken
families where divorce has never or could never take place are even
more prone to fall prey to such evils.

## Kinship systems

Nuclear families—even those that appear as 'independent'—are all
part of greater networks, or kinship systems. Strictly speaking only
husband and wife are conjugal members of a family, although their
respective blood relations enter into some sort of indirect kinship
through the fact of their marriage. The *consanguine family* is based
upon blood relationships of parents, children, aunts, uncles, cousins,
and grandparents, as well as second-cousins, great-grandparents,
and so on. If the consanguine family subordinates conjugal families
to its general structure we are faced with extended family systems;
otherwise, as occurs in several modern industrialised countries, it is
the nuclear families that subordinate, although they do not abolish,
consanguine ties. The belief that one system cancels out the other is
simply wrong. The widely held idea that the extended family has
literally disappeared in some Western countries has been shown by
several studies to be erroneous. Modern families are not large units
living under the same roof—if they ever were—but evidence of the
disintegration of the family is lacking. The contrary is very often
the case in the United States itself, where 'extended family get-
togethers and joint recreational activities with kin dominate the
leisure time pursuits of urban working class members' and where
'kinship-visiting is a primary activity of urban dwelling and out-
ranks visitation ... [of] friends, neighbours, or coworkers'.[8] In
England, as Colin Bell has shown, mutual aid among members of
the middle-class extended families is very common, and his references to other countries indicate that the phenomenon is quite
general.[9] All this is not to say, of course, that the modern extended
family possesses the same compact and quasi-tribal quality typical
of families in agrarian societies. What it does say is that, in any
society, families are structures that interpenetrate other institutions
and associations and communities. They criss-cross the social world,
and establish channels of communication, exchange and solidarity
that can never be created by other social formations. At this stage,
though, we must look at the key institution that makes such inter-
penetration (and indeed sociocultural, as opposed to merely natural,
life) possible among humans: the incest taboo.

*The incest taboo, and the consequences of exogamy*   In all known societies incest—sexual relationships amongst members of the same family, related by blood, and in varying degrees of kinship, depending on the society—is forbidden. Like the family itself the prohibition of incestuous relationships is virtually universal. Permitted incest seems to occur in isolated cases, not in collectivities, and is not a genuine exception to the rule, for incest in such cases is not just allowed but rather prescribed, and highly ritualised, as in Egypt among the pharaonic family, where it was intended to preserve the blood purity of the ruling dynasty. The universality of the prohibition (which because of its sternness has received the name of taboo) has led some students to think that it might possess some biological basis. Although the negative genetic results of close and continued inbreeding for humans (and some other animals) are clear for those who follow them up over a period or series of generations,[10] this by itself does not suffice to explain it. Some sociologists have believed in the past that the incest taboo was a sociocultural norm oriented towards the avoidance of the negative biological results of consanguine intermarriage. But such clear-sightedness in primitive peoples cannot be proved at all. And as Lévi-Strauss points out, eugenistic rationalisations only begin to appear towards the sixteenth century.[11]

Durkheim's approach to the question of incest opens a way to understanding it for what it is—a necessary regulation for any society endowed with culture. In primitive peoples marriage within the clan (*endogamy*) implies for him violation of one's own totem, since there is a substantial identity between totem and clan. Therefore, members of one clan must seek their mates among members of other clans (often prescribed), within or without the same tribe. This explanation, Lévi-Strauss remarks, has the weakness of presenting incest as a mere residue of primeval rules of avoidance of endogamy, the rules which prescribe *exogamy*, or the seeking of marriage or sexual mate outside one's own family of origin. And yet it has the advantage that it relates the incest taboo to the social structure and the world of culture. As we saw earlier, culture is communication, interchange of goods, behaviour, symbols; and communication is what makes human social systems possible. The incest taboo imposes patterns of family interchange (very clear-cut and strict in tribal societies, and not so rigid but equally detectable in industrial societies) which maintain a necessary degree of circulation of individuals. If this were not the case men would never have left a state of semicultural hominid bands. That the incest taboo is first and foremost connected with the necessity for some form of exogamy in every society which maintains a differentiated universe of culturally defined socio-structural rules is proved by the fact that it is not always expressed in terms of real biological kinship but in that of kin as defined by the language of the group.[12] (Names given to kinsmen are of enormous importance here, and vary considerably from culture to culture; often terms of kinship are untranslatable into the languages of the Indo-European peoples, who in turn possess their own distinct vocabulary[13]). Relatives' roles are defined, often regardless of their true biological relationship. In some Hispanic cultures *compadres* (both the father and the godfather of a child) stand to each other in a special relationship (*compadrazgo*) which implies kinship; and the godfather's duties towards his god-child are in some countries stronger than those of, say, an uncle. Also, in any society, a member of the extended family—a grand-parent, an unmarried aunt—living permanently under the same roof with the nuclear family ought to be considered an integral part of the latter. As always what counts is how individuals and their groups define and feel their own life situation and the roles others play in it.

Both centrifugal and centripetal forces, exogamous and endo-gamous tendencies, are found in every kinship *Gemeinschaft*. Endogamy strengthens the group and maintains its cultural, econ-omic and political identity; it is not Gentile discrimination against the Jews that has kept them from intermarrying with other peoples as much as the stern sanctions—often in the form of strong family pressures and prohibitions—of the Jews themselves against the mar-riage of their children to Gentiles. (This is, of course, ethnic, not clan, endogamy.) On the other hand exogamous prescriptions tend to remain within an area safe enough for the preservation of com-munity identity, especially if the possible exogamous marriage might otherwise demote it in the social scale. 'Unbecoming marriages' are one of the perennial sources of tension and open conflict in every known society. The prearranging of marriages by bargaining be-tween the families of potential spouses, or the 'going steady' and 'dating' of potential grooms or brides one's own parents are likely to approve, are different ways of bridging the gap between the imperative of endogamy (marrying within certain groups) and that of exogamy (finding a spouse outside one's own closest group); the phenomenon that results often entails what is called *homogamy* —'like marries like'. As William Goode says. 'all mate-selection systems press towards homogamous marriages'.[14] This statement is

true of every known society, including highly urbanised and industrialised societies. Contrary to common belief in these societies even
people who are socially very mobile tend towards homogamous
marriages; and region, neighbourhood and a common cultural
background play a decisive part in their mate-selection. Perhaps the
small minority that practice extreme heterogamy most frequently
—artists, intellectuals, and certain types of businessmen—are more
noticeable than other people, and thus contribute to the popular
misapprehension that marriages across race, country or class barriers
are more common and typical of the cosmopolitan world in which
we are supposed to live than they actually are.

### Kinship and society

It follows from what has been said above that family and kin cannot
be understood solely in their own terms or in those of our biological
species. Economic values, political attitudes, religious taboos, racial
prejudices, national loyalties—all have a part to play. After a long
period devoted by most sociologists to the isolated study of family
structures, this has now become the 'central proposition of contemporary family theory'. But as Goode says, 'the structure and work-
ings of the family do not materially help to explain the rest of the
social structure'.[15] Societal characteristics and social value systems,
on the other hand, do explain family structures and changes. It is
by looking at these that real understanding of the family will be
achieved. (The sociological tradition for this approach already
exists. Friedrich Engels attempted to understand family structures
as dependent on the stages of economic development; in the same
epoch Frederic Le Play studied the ecological setting of families as
the determining factor.)[16] Today fertility rates, sexual mores and
folkways, parental authority and the like are studied in their wider
context, as reflections of societal trends. Not surprisingly the wealth
of data thus obtained is casting new light on how the family unit
itself and the kinship systems which predominate in each country
react upon their social environment and try to mould it to their
needs.[17] The maintenance of this double perspective when looking
at the family avoids the pitfalls of either seeing it as a mere variable
of other social phenomena (for instance, the economic system) or
idealising it, as if it were the 'basic cell' of society, on which everything else depended.

*NOTES on Chapter 5, Section 3*

1. G. P. Murdock *Social Structure* (New York: Macmillan, 1949) pp. 1–11.
2. Cf. M. Zelditch 'Family, Marriage and Kinship' in R. L. Faris ed. *Handbook of Modern Sociology* (Chicago: Rand MacNally, 1968) p. 681.
3. W. J. Goode *World Revolution and Family Patterns* (New York: Free Press, 1963).
4. *Ibid.* p. 103.
5. E. K. Gouch 'The Nayars and the Definition of Marriage' *Jnl. Royal Anthrop. Inst.* 1959, no. 89, pp. 23–34.
6. M. Zelditch *op. cit.* p. 707. For a discussion of the role and status problems of women in modern societies see A. Myrdal and V. Klein *Women's Two Roles* (London: Routledge & Kegan Paul, 1968 ed.).
7. N. S. Timasheff 'The Attempt to Abolish the Family in Russia' in N. W. Bell and E. F. Vogel *A Modern Introduction to The Family* (New York: Free Press, 1960) pp. 55–63.
8. M. B. Sussman and L. Burchinal 'Kin Family Network' in W. J. Goode *Readings on the Family and Society* (Englewood Cliffs: Prentice Hall, 1964) pp. 170–75.
9. C. Bell *Middle-Class Families* (London: Routledge, 1968).
10. D. F. Aberle *et alii* 'The Incest Taboo and the Mating Patterns of Animals' in W. J. Goode *Readings ... op. cit.* pp. 11–20.
11. C. Lévi-Strauss *Les structures élémentaires de la parenté* (The Hague: Mouton, 1967 ed.) p. 15.
12. *Ibid.* pp. 34–35.
13. *Ibid.* and G. S. Ghurye *Family and Kin in Indo-European Culture* (Bombay: Popular Books, 1962 ed.).
14. W. J. Goode *The Family* (Englewood Cliffs: Prentice-Hall, 1964) p. 33.
15. Quoted by G. Lewis 'The American Family, Social Values and Socio-cultural Change' mimeographed paper (the University of Reading, England, and the University of Vermont, USA, 1971) p. 2.
16. F. Engels *The Origin of The Family, Private Property and the State* Eng. trans. *Der Ursprung der Familie*, etc. 1884; F. Le Play's monographs on Families and *Les ouvriers européens* (1855).
17. Cf. among others, G. Hawthorn *The Sociology of Fertility* (London: Macmillan, 1970); G. P. Homans *English Villagers of the Thirteenth Century* (Harvard University, 1942); A. Sauvy *Théorie générale de la population* (Paris: P.U.F., 1952–54); R. Fletcher *The Family and Marriage* (Harmondsworth: Penguin, 1962); N. Bell and E. Vogel *op. cit.*; W. J. Goode *World Revolution and Family Patterns* (New York: Free Press, 1963).

# 4 TERRITORIAL COMMUNITIES

*From locality to nation*

The physical living space is one of the chief determinants of the structuring of societies. Though influenced by their habitat and their physical setting generally, societies also react upon that environment and reshape it. This phenomenon, which can be studied from many angles, from ecology and human geography to geopolitics and regional economics, can also be considered from the standpoint of the *Gemeinschaft*, for the fact that a collectivity of people permanently share a common area means that a whole way of life is also shared by them. This is especially true of peoples not living in cities, as cities are designed for people living together, where social differentiation—and therefore greatly differing ways of life—is made possible within relatively narrow bounds. It is in the rural setting that the traits of the community, based on a genuine sharing of the same space for living, are most conspicuous. In it people interact practically always on a face-to-face, personal basis; they tend to be economically self-sufficient; there is a high degree of overlap between their community and the kinship network of the whole population; and they share common ends and norms (although serious rifts and social tensions are often also present, e.g. between the haves and have-nots, and between the political rural bosses and the uninfluential labourers). Above all, numbers of these communities are conscious of belonging to the place, of forming a local unit, unique in every sense.[1] For all these reasons, as Robert Redfield affirmed, the small rural community is one of the prevailing forms in which humanity comes to our notice. The little territorial community (a much older form of settlement than the city) is a self-contained whole—an ecological system, a social structure, an outlook, a history and even, because of its internal tensions, a combination of opposites.[2] We have only to consider the tribes, villages, settlements that come to mind—the medieval English village, the small neolithic town around its temple in Mesopotamian Sumer, the Norwegian fishing village of today, the small community in the North American prairie or in the Siberian steppe—to realise that they all meet these requirements in their very different ways. Some rural communities are scattered over the hills, and some on the plains; some specialise in one type of agriculture, hunting, gathering, or fishing; others are politically sovereign units, while still others toil under feudal shackles. But it is their unity within their diversity that allows sociologists and anthropologists to approach them as entities which tell us something basic about the human condition—man's need to live in an ordered world, which he can comprehend and which is the proper place for his emotions and loyalties.[3]

A series of historical developments—the growth of city life, the emergence of the state, the creation of political empires—broke, at a point in history, the total isolation of primeval communities. In consequence, and with varying degrees of collective awareness, local communities in many areas of the world are now conscious of belonging to wider ethnic, or 'national', communities, and are aware also that they are united by this fact. Now this apparently trivial point is one of the most equivocal in the whole spectrum of social issues and one that causes endless confusion, especially since the rise of the modern nation and the so-called nation-state. The problem of nationalism is a matter for political sociology and political science, but it is important that it should be mentioned at the present stage, for nations are, above all, communities—*Gemeinschaften.*

Sociologically, a nation is neither a society whose borders necessarily coincide with those of political units nor a nation in the very modern sense of the word, such as developed in Europe after the French Revolution. It must be defined somewhat obliquely as a collectivity of people feeling themselves united in nationhood, and wanting to achieve at least a degree of political autonomy. (Linguistic, racial, religious considerations alone will not do for this definition; there are too many exceptions.) If an ethnic collectivity does not want or does not press for political unity it is not a nation: the Kurdish people or the Irish people became nations only at the moment that their 'national consciousness' was born. The fact that the Kurds do not possess a unitary political organisation while the Irish have gone a very long way towards one is another problem. Moreover, if some local leaders press for nationalism alone, their collectivity does not for that reason become a nation. Many past wars have been regarded as 'wars of national liberation' when they were not; they were led by particular groups who wanted to secede from a state or an empire to carve out a political unit for themselves —often of course taking advantage of the previously existing discontent of wide sectors of the local population. In the long run, though, the new unit, by its sheer permanence—by continued socialisation—may create bonds of nationhood among the peoples living in it. This is the way in which European nations painfully grew out of the feudal world. Contemporary African states are an excellent example of the 'artificiality' of the state. Yet those same governments that recognise the fact that African frontiers are 'anti-natural' because they disregard tribe, ethnic group and nation, zealously stick to them, whether it is in Sudan, Nigeria or Zaïre —and this regardless of cost to human life and suffering. The conclusion is that the state owes as much to the nation as the nation to the state. The nation calls forth a political unit; the state tends to hammer its several territorial communities into one single nation offering the least possible resistance to it (VII, 3). What is interesting in this context is the re-emergence of the polarity community-association at the widest possible level—the societal level. Societies are not idyllic collectivities; in them some people are rich and others are poor, some are powerful and others powerless, but, without glossing over this, it is true that in some complex societies people are 'united by common sympathies'—to use John Stuart Mill's expression— and thus desire to live apart, as 'one people'. This 'popular will' (if one is still allowed to use this Rousseauian expression) and this consciousness of kind are essentially *Gemeinschaft*like. The state by contrast must needs be a *Gesellschaft*, a 'state apparatus', and the modern state is the secondary group par excellence (VIII, 6). This dichotomy is nowhere more clearly illustrated than in cases of national crisis, when politicians appeal to 'patriotism', 'defence of the fatherland', and other similar community symbols of that widest of primary groups—the nation.[4] Emotional attachment to the state alone is simply inconceivable.

## The urban community

Among the several intermediate territorial communities which stand between village and nation the city is the most important and, indeed, the most complex, for the city is paradoxically the entity that has made *Gesellschaften* possible in the first place. Although the inhabitants of a town, city or metropolis may feel certain bonds of affinity, and even solidarity, it is the city that has historically been the framework of universality, civilisation, citizenship, and the nucleus whence science, the greatest art and the most elaborate political systems have irradiated. For this reason, perhaps, some students of city life have preferred to look at the city as a mosaic of social worlds rather than as a unit; it is true that, because of its size, its internal differentiation of labour and the immense variety of human experience that a city can encompass in a few square miles of space, it is very difficult to see it as one single community. Yet this is precisely what Robert Park and the University of Chicago school of urban sociologists tried to prove, and also that the city was not 'merely a physical mechanism and an artificial construction' but that it was 'involved in the vital process of the people' who composed it.[5] Starting with this last postulate, urban sociologists have attempted to understand the structure of cities, the location of neighbourhoods, the processes of segregation, the urban geography of social success and failure, and the moral and cultural map of our cities.

The results achieved by several decades of intense work in urban sociology are quite impressive, but beyond our scope here. Sociologists soon became aware that the city hid the secret of an entirely new mentality, as Fustel de Coulanges' classic statement on *The Ancient City* (1864) had first explained. The industrial revolution could also be interpreted in terms of a process of urbanisation affecting every part of the countryside and which would, later, transform the entire world. Meanwhile urban zones, with their business districts, slum areas, political quarters, residential neighbourhoods, and 'vice' districts, remained as apparently easy-to-grasp units, where all sorts of relevant social indicators, indices and correlations —sizes of dwellings, geographical mobility, family networks, occupational structures—could be found. Consequently a great deal of sociological work was channelled in this direction.[6] It soon became apparent, also, that this field was one of the most 'useful' aspects of the discipline, for disorderly urbanisation was one of the most serious problems mankind had to face. City, and regional planners can no longer ignore the work of sociologists in this field, and the help of the latter is now frequently sought—often as a matter of course. Yet the resulting situation is not entirely satisfactory. Very little work has been done on the ideology underlying much of today's urban sociology, on the reasons that lie behind those decisions of politicians that affect our cities and urban areas, or on the motivations of economists, geographers and statisticians engaged in such projects.[7] This is certainly a field which is as delicate as it is important since the continuous expansion of the urban way of life has meant a deep transformation in the meaning and aims of urban sociology itself. It does not study isolated urban communities any longer, and it cannot take cities as independent variables, as it were, for they have fused with modern society itself in all its dimensions. Thus urban sociology cannot limit itself to establishing correlations between poverty and slums, crime and residential areas, and the like, but must also look for more complex processes, such as political power and slum clearance, land speculation and electoral constituencies, the ecology of scientific knowledge, the social commitments of planning authorities, and similar problems. Such a shift of interest is already occurring; large-scale social change in highly industrialised societies has given such pre-eminence to urban and regional planning—to the programmed transformation and construction of our urbanised environment—that urban sociology has increasingly become the sociology of planning. As such it must keep asking itself certain basic questions about its own fundamental values, and about the morality and rationality of the goals to be achieved, in addition to examining the technical efficiency of the job to be carried out under issued instructions. The instructions themselves— that may transform people's lives—must always remain under sociological scrutiny. That this may not always endear sociologists to the powers that be is another matter, but the critique of society which is an element of the sociologists' task cannot be abandoned.

*NOTES on Chapter V, Section 4*

1. R. T. Havighurst and A. J. Janse 'Community Research' in *Current Sociology* (Vol. XV, no. 2, 1967) pp. 7–9.
2. R. Redfield *The Little Community* (The University of Chicago, 1955). Cf. also R. Koenig *Sociologie der Gemeinde* (Cologne: Westdeutscher Verlag, 1962).
3. It is impossible to give even a short list of small community studies; for one thing almost all anthropological research is based on such techniques. The student is referred to the ample bibliography contained in the *Current Sociology* issue mentioned above. Redfield's *Little Community* (*op. cit.*) is a short masterpiece, and refers critically to much work on small communities.
4. On nation and nationality: A. Smith, *Theories of Nationalism* (London: Duckworth, 1971); E. Renan *Qu'est-ce qu'une nation?* (Paris: Calmann-Lévy, 1947); R. Laffont *La révolution régionaliste* (Paris: Gallimard, 1967); F. Hertz *Nationality in History and Politics* (London: Routledge, 1957), 4th ed.); J. S. Mill *Considerations on Representative Government* (New York: Liberal Arts, 1958, 1st ed. 1861), ch. xvi. On contemporary European nations which do not possess a state J. Solé Tura *Catalanisme i revolució burgesa* (Barcelona: Edicions 62, 1968). On the relationship between ethnic character and nationalism O. Pi-Sunyer, ed. *The Limits of Integration: Ethnicity and Nationalism in Modern Europe* (University of Massachussets, Anthropology Research Report no. 9, 1971).
5. R. Park 'The City: Suggestions for the Investigation of Human Behaviour in the Urban Environment' (*Am. Jnl. Soc.* 1916); reprinted in R. Sennett *Classical Essays on the Culture of Cities* (New York: Appleton Century, 1969) p. 91.
6. R. Sennet *op. cit.* reproduces some of the chief statements on the city by sociologists (M. Weber, G. Simmel, R. Park, L. Wirth) but omits Fustel de Coulanges. N. D. Fustel de Coulanges *La cité antique* (Paris: Hachette, 1900, 17th ed.) and others. Cf. also G. S. Ghurye *Cities and Civilization* (Bombay: Popular Prakashan, 1962); J. Caro Baroja *La ciudad y el campo* (Madrid: Alfaguara, 1966); P. H. Chombart de Lauwe *Paris: Essais de Sociologie* (Paris: Editions ouvrières, 1965); K. Lynch *The Image of the City* (Cambridge, Mass.; M.I.T., 1960). In general, for USA, P. K. Hatt and A. J. Reiss *Cities and Society* (Glencoe: Free Press,

1957), a reader in urban sociology; for Britain R. E. Pahl *Readings in Urban Sociology* (London, Pergamon, 1968) and studies such as M. Stacey, *Tradition and Change: A Study of Banbury* (Oxford University, 1960).

7. However, see M. Castells and F. Godard *Monopolville* (The Hague: Mouton, 1974) where the authors study the urban region of Dunkirk, correlating the economy, the political system and the urban system to its industrial growth.

# VI The Economy, the Social Division of Labour and Stratification

## 1 ECONOMY AND SOCIETY

What is known as the economy is made up of the patterns of social action whereby a population satisfies its needs of consumption and production of scarce goods. Scarce goods are any objects or services whose output needs the use of human labour, machinery, technology and knowledge, that is, goods that are not readily and abundantly available. Since commodities and services are vital for the survival and prosperity of societies, it is obvious that all must possess an economic dimension. This dimension presents definite patterns in any given society and can be called a system. (If the society itself is taken as the system, the economy can be understood as one of its general subsystems.[1]) The nature of the economic system around which a society is organised is a decisive factor in shaping every other sphere of social life. In fact societies can be classified according to the criteria of their chief economic pursuits: hunting and gathering, horticultural, pastoral, trading, capitalist, socialist, nomadic, and the like. It follows that the effect of the implantation of a given economic system—or institution—in a society is bound to be felt throughout that society, and in consequence the whole social system will have to adapt itself to it; conversely, the establishment of a given social structure in a country will have decisive effects on its economy. Indeed, the investigation of this obvious mutual relationship between the economic sphere and the other areas of social reality is the chief preoccupation of economic sociology, as distinguished from the science of economics in the strict sense of the expression. While economists will treat the more quantifiable and impersonal concepts of the economy (such as 'manpower resources', 'liquidity', 'budgetary control') sociologists will relate economic phenomena to real people and their attitudes, problems, and position within the processes under scrutiny.[2]

Sociologists must ask themselves why the highest proportion of a state's budget goes into the armed forces, why the rich are less taxed in some countries than in others, why factories are erected in one part of a country and not in another, where the economic conditions seem more favourable, and countless other questions whose answer partly lies beyond the strict economic realm—in ideology, political power, social class, international relations, religious attitudes. In the process, the sociologist is also forced to go into the meaning of such concepts as economic 'needs' and 'wants', and why they arise.[3] The rise in consumption of bubble-bath soap in a given town may not be caused by people suddenly becoming cleaner; more probably commercial television campaigns have created the 'need' to buy such soap well beyond the amount objectively required, if at all, by purposes of hygiene. Although economic rationality[4] is a strong force in human behaviour, extravagance, waste and parasitism are no less common. Yet not all economic actions which appear as artificial needs can be simply called irrational. To be sure, there is an element of irrationality in the futile waste of excess soap, as there is in buying cars just because they are new models and one's own car is already over one year old. But these processes of collective overconsumption, typical only of the richest societies, are highly 'rational' in keeping a given social structure going for a considerable period. Slavery is an economic system of production which has been highly functional and 'rational' for the people who have lived off its economic surplus, even though it may be repugnant to the moral principles of the observer and deemed irrational by him. Hence, Pareto's distinction between 'logical' and 'non-logical' action should always be seen from the viewpoint of the motives of all the actors involved (III, 3).

A fruitful approach to these questions may consist in first looking into the cultural and political variables that are the setting of economic life. Why is a technique used differently by each culture? The compass was an Eastern invention, but in spite of China's high degree of civilisation it was never found necessary to use it in the way Europeans later employed it; their seaborne empires and expansion cannot be understood without the magnetised needle. The Greeks and Romans did not make use of the very high potentialities of their knowledge to start the industrial revolution, which actually began centuries later. Today we are constantly told that

Argentina is 'potentially a very rich country' and yet it seems entangled in endless economic trouble; Japan, on the other hand, historically much farther removed from the impact of Western influence, joined in the industrial revolution and has become one of the greatest economic centres in the world. All these questions seem to possess a particular fascination for social scientists and laymen alike.

One example of a sociological interpretation of the dynamics of economic systems as they relate to the rest of the society in a network of mutual causal links is the theory of the 'Asiatic mode of production' (thus labelled by Marx), where the sovereign of the country is supposed to be the absolute landlord as well. According to economic determinists the existence of a system of production generates a sociopolitical and religious system, in this case the great despotic empire. Karl Wittfogel and other orientalists have tested the hypothesis in depth and shown that the development of a large-scale irrigation economy, in early civilisations, called for political centralisation, bureaucratic control, *corvée* labour and specific forms of despotism and worship—and this not only in Asia, but wherever a similar situation obtained (as with the Incas).[5] Loopholes in their theory can be found, for centralised despotic government was not only the consequence of the internal economic structure of these early empires but also of the perennial threat of barbarian invasion from the areas surrounding the coveted islands of urban wealth and civilisation: permanent well-disciplined armies living off the economic surplus of the enslaved peasantry were essential. However, in this instance, on the whole technological and economic causation of other social features fits neatly into place. Yet in other situations the sequences of social causality can be reversed. There is much evidence that the Calvinist Protestant ethic and the mentality of economic self-interest that it fostered among the faithful became in some countries a spur for the consolidation of capitalism as an economic system.[6] There is also evidence that Japanese feudalism and, especially, religion were the basis for the readiness of that society to embrace Western patterns of capitalist production[7] and embark on an economic mutation that thus far remains unique among non-European countries (VIII, 3).

In trying to resolve these questions, sociology must eventually look into the meaning of 'goods' and 'needs' in a situation. It must discover why some kinds of object or behaviour are selected and others ignored, and by whom. For instance, why have some peoples preferred extermination to slavery, when others have accepted it? Which socialisation patterns enter this economically decisive cultural attitude? Or take a key economic notion, such as 'property'. When is it not only a right over things (*ius in rem*) but also a right over persons, a *ius in personam*? What are the consequences of such distinction for the social structure? And what are the effects of 'public' property being also sacred? Do all societies admit private property? If so, how does each society define it? Some of the answers can be found by approaching these economic problems from the angle of the social division of labour, the study of social inequality and the observation of the consequences of economic surplus in human societies. Let us look at each of them in turn.

*NOTES on Chapter VI, Section 1*

1. Cf. N. J. Smelser *The Sociology of Economic Life* (Englewood Cliffs: Prentice Hall, 1963) pp. 36–38. The acceptance of this postulate does not necessarily imply an identification with Parsons' and Smelser's theories on this question.
2. This approach is also characteristic of the tradition represented by political economy—men such as Ricardo, Marx, Veblen, never isolated economic facts from the people involved, and it is just as well that political economy is coming back into favour. All this must not be taken to mean that economics 'forgets people' and is therefore a sort of degenerate science; on the contrary the isolation of economic facts is essential for proper analysis, and it is this that has made the growth and success of contemporary economics possible.
3. G. Bouthoul *Variations et mutations sociales* (Paris: Payot, 1968) pp. 127–66.
4. Cf. S. Ackroyd 'Economic Rationality and the Relevance of Weberian Sociology to Industrial Relations' *Brit Jnl. Ind. Rels.* Vol XII, No. 2, 1974, pp. 236–48.
5. This conception has had curious ramifications amongst certain contemporary communists who denied its existence in the work of Marx, against all evidence to the contrary. Cf. G. Sofri *Il modo di produzione asiatico* (Turin: Einaudi, 1969); K. Wittfogel *op. cit.*
6. M. Weber *Die protestantische Ethik und der Geist des Kapitalismus* (1904) Eng. trans. *The Protestant Ethic and the Spirit of Capitalism* (London: Allen & Unwin, 1948).
7. R. N. Bellah *Tokugawa Religion* (Glencoe: Free Press, 1957).

# 2 THE SOCIAL DIVISION OF LABOUR

*The nature and evolution of the phenomenon*

Even in the simplest, most primitive, societies tasks are not the same for every individual. Since leadership and social hierarchies exist in non-human primate societies, it is clear that sex and age were not the only criteria for the social distribution of tasks in the earliest societies. The more complex a society was, the greater also was the differentiation in the division of tasks and labour among its members. In turn, the social division of tasks was a basis for the structure of the whole society.

Over the last millennia the multiplication of tasks, and the concomitant development of an increasingly complex system of social division of labour, have posed several important questions. These have received only very general answers, which are perhaps not entirely satisfactory and are doubtlessly tinged with different underlying philosophies of history. Durkheim's effort to come to grips with the nature and evolution of the social division of labour may be cited as one of the most significant of such attempts.[1] For him the division of labour in society is more a consequence than a cause of the evolution of mankind. Social order first appeared in the form of what he called *segmentary societies*, or primeval human bands. In them social cohesion was maintained through 'mechanical solidarity' (V, 1), a form of cooperation that requires that each individual recognises that the very same operations and tasks are performed by others, with a negligible degree of differentiation, based only on physical strength, age and sex. In a sense, there is in these societies no sociocultural division of labour. Such division is typical of more complex societies, which cohere internally through the bonds of 'organic solidarity' (V, 1). How did men come to accept specialisation and tolerate a variety of roles? How did they come to accept that other men were different by virtue of their work, and yet an integral part of their group? The causes for the emergence of this form of solidarity that admits—and encourages—differentiation are several, Durkheim thinks. First, we encounter two primary causes: (1) the breakdown of the segmental type of society caused by a growth of what he calls 'material density' and the subsequent increase in its 'moral density'. Material density is the physical density, or increase in proximity, of the population in a given area, as a result of its growth. The increase in the size of a population in turn increases its moral density by complicating the patterns of social interaction and fostering the specialisation of tasks. (2) A growth in the volume of the societies accompanied by an increase in population density. (Growth in size without a population splitting up into several new societies must imply diversification, if only because the greater the extension covered by it, the greater the differences in habitat and ecological needs become, thus increasing the number of distinct tasks to be performed.) Next we encounter two other causes, which are secondary but nevertheless very important: (1) the progressive indeterminacy of collective consciousness, that is, its progressively smaller dependence on the physical environment, and the consequently richer contents of such consciousness; and (2) the breakdown of the 'hereditary principle' in social groups, which is the faithful and invariable reproduction of the social pattern—the substitution of attitudes more favourable to change and innovation for sheer repetitive tradition. Once these processes began, new principles of human interdependence and interaction modified the social order. At our end of the historical transformation 'organic solidarity' embodies these principles, while the homogeneous and 'mechanical' solidarity of primeval societies has diminished very substantially. One of the important features of 'organic solidarity' is specialisation—the performance of tasks that apparently separate us from each other. Actually the more specialised our function, the more dependent we are socially upon others. As in any society, the individual is a microcosm of the 'collective type' of society to which he belongs. The bricklayer implies the architect, the student implies the teacher, the political prisoner the dictator.

The conceptual scheme for interpreting the social bond in complex and, especially, modern societies in terms of 'organic solidarity' presents some difficulties. Georges Friedmann has shown that, from the point of view of the sociology of work, Durkheim's notions are inadequate in certain situations in industrial societies. 'Mechanical solidarity', for all its primeval roots, has not disappeared from the modern factory; it is easy to detect its presence in the method of production typical of modern manufacture—the conveyor-belt production line.[2] Also, political sociologists and students of collective behaviour have noted important similarities between the solidarity of the primeval horde and that of certain contemporary mass movements.[3] In modern society contractual, *Gesellschaft*like relationships may be important, as we saw earlier (V, 1), and ties of complete subordination of the individual to his group are often very strong, as the behaviour of workers under conditions of industrial unrest constantly reminds us. Yet, the Durkheimian legacy has fostered a conception of the social division of tasks which sees this division as part of a vast historical process—a process by no means linear and even, which has arrived at its present extreme form of minute specialisation, whether it be in manual labour or in technological and scientific work. Latterly, though, electronic computing, automation, cybernetics and other techniques have permeated the world of production, trade and information and have raised the question of the social division of labour to another level. The very logic of the process that once led to the atomisation of work and tasks, together with the increasing complexity of the knowledge and the society based on it, has finally given rise to these techniques, which in turn are producing a metamorphosis in the modern world, by reducing or abolishing the monotonous chores of early industrialism (X, 3).

In a different, non-historical sense, the social division of labour is simply the structural distribution of tasks amongst the members of a group. This has two meanings: (1) the *social* division of labour, which, strictly speaking, appears embodied in the occupational structure of any society, and which is related to the economy (to the individual's roles in the relationships of property, production, consumption) and to power and authority; and (2) the *technical* division of labour, which refers to the distribution of tasks within any enterprise or institution—in industry, administration, trade, politics, etc.[4] The several correlations between the two are one of the chief subjects in the field of social stratification, since the role and status of individuals are largely the expression of the position they occupy within a general structure of division of tasks. This is particularly evident if we understand this phenomenon in the Durkheimian sense, as not only covering the economy but also the moral and cultural tasks to be carried out by individuals, groups and institutions.

## Alienation and the division of labour

It is just possible that sometime in the mists of our remotest past men and women distributed the tasks among themselves according to talent, strength and natural disposition. But this is only a hypothesis which, in spite of its powerful attractiveness in the field of social thought (where it has haunted the minds of many men) is not confirmed by the societies that have been studied. In them labour is divided with varying degrees of justice, and performed by people with equally varying degrees of willingness. Sometimes people are fairly free in their lives and content with their work, but very often they are bound by necessity. This is not always a natural necessity but one that frequently stems from social coercion. Man has an unique ability to enslave and exploit man, or to use, manipulate and delude him into performing services which are never fairly rewarded. That this is a situation which must be improved is another matter; the dispassionate recognition of its existence implies neither approval nor resigned acceptance; in fact it may imply just the opposite—the hope that social science may helps towards the diminution of these evils through the exercise of an objective and systematic study of the phenomenon.

One of the chief effects of this state of affairs in the realm of the social division of labour is alienation. Alienation is a form of un-freedom consisting in the separation of our activities from the control of our own will; subjectively this separation, when felt, is a sense of powerlessness, estrangement from our activities, and en-slavement to forces outside our control. Although this phenomenon is universal in social life—we can speak of political, cultural, educa-tional, or any other sort of alienation—historically it has been first approached from the standpoint of work; it is perhaps in this con-text that it can be tackled most fruitfully.[5] Starting from an idea originally developed by Hegel, Karl Marx was the first social scientist to spell out the nature and dynamics of alienated labour. It was clear that once man had begun to free himself from the shackles of natural necessity he had sunk into those of a social order based on several degrees of slavery. To be a slave is to be possessed by somebody else, not to be oneself—that is, to be estranged or alienated. The immense majority of mankind have lived in this situation ever since the dawn of civilisation. In modern times, though, serfdom and slavery have been legally abolished. Yet, as Marx saw it, the majority still continued subject to, and enslaved by, the minority, for, if the worker was now nominally free, he was in actual fact still restricted in his political rights, he was denied property, education and welfare and was at the mercy of market fluctuations, since all he owned was his ability to sell his capacity to work. The worker thus becomes a commodity, a unit of man-power, whose market price is the wage. When he is hired, he is estranged from the objects he produces, from the tools with which he produces them, and from his own activity. In Marx's own words:

> The object produced by labour, its product now stands opposed to to it as an *alien being*, as a *power independent* of the producer. The product of labour is labour which has been embodied in a thing, and turned into a physical thing; this product is an objectification of labour. The performance of work is at the same time its objectification. This performance appears . . . as a *vitiation* of the worker, objectification as a *loss* and as *servitude to the object*, and appropriation as alienation.[6]

After being estranged or alienated from the fruits of his labour and from his labour itself, the worker is also alienated from his employer, who sees him only as a source of labour and income and not as a human being, and also from his fellow-workers—privatised and atomised in their deadly struggle for jobs. This culminates in self-estrangement and alienation from himself when the worker realises that he is not any longer the master of his own actions.

Marx's notion implies that this process, which he sees as embodied in work and reaching its most intense form under capitalism, is also, as Raymond Aron says, 'a sociological process by means of which men or societies construct collective organisations in which they become lost'.[7] Certainly both the Marxist and non-Marxist heirs of this conception have tended to generalise it across the whole of modern societies.[8] Although this certainly has the advantage that alienation is seen as a consequence of any modern form of exploitation (especially by means of impersonal manipulation)—as something possibly existing in China, the Soviet Union, or Czechoslovakia as much as it may exist in West Germany or Switzerland—it has the serious inconvenience that the concept is stretched to include every form of malaise which can be attributed to industrial society, whether capitalist or communist. No other concept has arisen, however, to convey so well the feeling of powerlessness, purposelessness and estrangement from one's own groups or institutions as does alienation. It is for this reason perhaps that the notion is found as frequently in contemporary social philosophy as it is in empirical social research, especially in the field of industrial and occupational sociology and in the sociology of bureaucracy (VII, 6). As a notion it is now used by social scientists subscribing to the most disparate schools of thought. It is probably as well that it should be retained, for it vividly expresses the predicament of men who cannot control their own lives in the impersonal situations generated by many modern institutions. But it should be used prudently, for we have now reached a time when the word has been degraded by its own popularity, especially by those who think that merely pronouncing it exorcises and explains every modern social problem. The sources of alienation, its direction, its victims' reactions to it and its relationship to other phenomena which are akin to it, must also always be made explicit.

NOTES on Chapter VI, Section 2

1. E. Durkheim *De lo division du travail social* (Paris: Alcan, 1893) pp. 282–9, 445, 467–68.
2. G. Friedmann *Le travail en miettes* (Paris: Gallimard, 1958, 1st ed. 1956) pp. 133–40.
3. S. Giner *Sociedad masa: ideología y conflicto social* (Madrid: Seminarios y Ediciones, 1971); E. Canetti, *Crowds and Power* (London: Gollancz, 1962).
4. J. L. A. van Loon *Het sociale leven* (Assen, 1959) Vol. III, p. 1450.
5. S. Giner 'De la alienación y el pensamiento social' in *Rev. de Est. Pol.* July–August, 1962, pp. 47–63.
6. Quoted by R. A. Nisbet *Sociological Tradition op. cit.* p. 290.
7. R. Aron *Les étapes de la pensée sociologique* (1965); Eng. trans. *Main Currents of Sociological Thought* (Penguin, Harmondsworth, 1968) Vol. I, p. 148.
8. Cf. E. Mandel *Traité d'économie marxiste* (1962); Eng. trans. *Marxist Economic Theory* (London: Merlin Press, 1968) Vol. I, p. 173; also L. Feuer 'What is Alienation?' in *New Politics* (Spring, 1962) Vol. I, no. 3, pp. 116–34. For a comparison of anomy and alienation in industrial societies, see J. E. T. Eldridge *Sociology and Industrial Life* (London: Michael Joseph, 1971).

# 3 SOCIAL STRATIFICATION

## Social inequality: its nature and dimensions

I understand that there are, in the human race, two sorts of inequality: one, which I call natural or physical, because it is established by nature, consists of the difference of ages, health, the forces of the body, and the qualities of mind and soul; the other, which one can call moral or political inequality, because, it depends on some sort of convention, is established, or at least authorised, by the consent of men. The latter consists of the different privileges enjoyed by some in detriment of others, such as being richer, more honoured, more powerful than they, or simply by commanding their obedience.[1]

Even the greatest champions of equality, such as Rousseau, who wrote this at the beginning of his *Discourse on the Origin of Inequality amongst Men* (1754), have begun by recognising this elementary fact. In the animal kingdom natural inequality is the basis for social inequality; in that of men, this causal link breaks down. Yet—and here lies one of the most interesting aspects of the problem —it does not collapse entirely. Among the most primitive human societies ever recorded by ethnological research, age, sex and individual talent and characteristics often become the decisive factors in the degree of prominence accorded to individuals. And in all other societies they are all, in varying degrees of intensity, at least factors in the competition for status, privilege, authority and power. Natural characteristics are nearly always very important for the establishment of patterns of inequality among human beings, but they are first culturally redefined before they become elements in our systems of inequality.[2] Descent from a lineage, colour of skin, talent for oratory, mathematical ability, are all natural capacities; yet they must be assigned values by one cultural system before they can have weight in the distribution of rewards in a given society.

The existence of systems of social inequality is usually referred to as social stratification. In fact 'social stratification' is a misnomer, for the term, with its geological and stratigraphic echoes, only points to the existence of one of the elements of social inequality, that is the existence of *strata* or collectivities of men and women possessing a similar degree of status, privilege, power and wealth in a society. In this sense stratification can refer either to the process whereby a society is so divided, or to the resulting system itself. However we shall not quarrel with this name, so long as it is clear that it is not only with strata that the study of social stratification is concerned, but also with a set of closely interrelated phenomena—power, social mobility, status, privilege, occupation—which pertain to the central issue of social inequality.

Of these aspects of social stratification, three stand out: 'stratum', 'status' and 'power'. They are conceptually different: the first refers to the aggregate of people who find themselves in the same economic, political and cultural area of a society; the second to the amount of deference a person receives by virtue of his social position and occupation; and the third to the degree of control a person or a collectivity of people exercises over the actions of others. They are even empirically different, as social research has often been able to demonstrate. Yet they are not separate. They are essentially distinct dimensions of the one single complex phenomenon of social inequality. Are these three, however, its *only* dimensions? The answer is probably 'no'.[3] But ever since Ferdinand Tönnies and (especially) Max Weber began to treat stratification as a three-dimensional phenomenon[4] there has been a tendency to admit, first, that most aspects of social inequality could be subsumed into one or the other of these three dimensions (for instance, honour under status, wealth under stratum, and so forth) and, second, that as dimensions they are not only mutually dependent on each other but also in some sense manifestations of the same thing. Some socio-logists, however, do not accept this, and prefer to reduce the whole affair to one element. Thus an economic reductionist will say that economic position determines everything else, while a political reductionist will say that power is the decisive factor. We shall adopt a less simplistic attitude, by admitting that each stratificational element generates effects in the other dimension. A poor man who climbs to a position of political eminence will perhaps then be able to amass a fortune; in turn, a fortune is often a great help in political advancement; the cultural imprint left by belonging to a group of low status in a society is a barrier for people who wish to become influential and powerful, even when they have the requisite financial means. In addition it is clear from the comparative study of stratification that all elements which go to make up social in-equality in each society or subsection of it, are of potentially equal importance. Depending on the culture as much as on the economy and the political system, in some places people will strive for honour more than anything else; in others, business success will be seen as the principal source of both wealth and status, while in yet others political office may be the overriding desire. And each sub-culture has its own status system and its own ways of attaining status. The writer may renounce wealth in order to be esteemed by the positive reference group he has chosen—a small select reader-ship; the footballer, the bullfighter and the movie-star may want both wealth and popularity (a form of status) but ignore power.

Not only do stratum, status and power present differing degrees of prominence in each case, but elements within these dimensions may differ. Especially in pre-industrial societies, the degree of con-gruity of the chief three dimensions of social stratification often tended to be high. The poor peasant ranked low in power, in status, and in the position of his stratum—the peasantry. As for elements within the main dimensions, consistency has also varied historically and from society to society. *Status consistency* and *inconsistency* is perhaps one of the clearest cases for observation, closely associated with question of the varieties of role and status a person may possess (III, 4). A West Indian doctor in England will possess a low status among white people who are racially prejudiced in that country, but will be accorded the high status of the physician in the hospital where he works; white unskilled manual workers in the United States have a higher status in most groups than very skilled or even middle-class Negroes. A professional criminal, with the lowest status possible in a society, may be highly regarded and admired in the underworld.[5] All these examples are only possible in complex societies, where several social 'worlds' intermingle and coexist.

All these dimensions and varieties of stratification indicate, in so many ways, the existence of a phenomenon that is peculiar to man in the civilised stages of his history, and which can be stated as the lack of positive correlation between human excellence and the functional importance of an individual's position in the social structure. Though this seems rather obvious, some sociologists have come close to asserting the opposite. It is thus that the 'functional theory of stratification' has arisen. The best known statement on the point is that of Kingsley Davies and Wilbert Moore:

> . . . the main functional necessity explaining the universal presence of stratification is . . . the requirement faced by any society of placing and motivating individuals in the social structure. As a functioning mechanism a society must somehow distribute its members in social positions and induce them to perform the duties of these positions. . . Social innequality is thus an unconsciously evolved device by which societies insure that the most important positions are conscientiously filled by the most qualified persons. Hence every society, no matter how simple or complex, must differentiate persons in terms of both prestige and esteem, and must therefore possess a certain amount of institutionalised inequality.[6]

These unorthodox assertions have had the virtue of originating a fruitful debate on the nature and possible necessity of social inequality in any society. Although a conservative attitude is possibly detectable here, the important fact is that Davis-Moore hypothesis is based on an assumption which can be easily verified by experience, namely that in societies there are systematic rewards for those who fill their 'important' posts, especially those which are inevitably scarce, with sophisticated systems of incentives provided to encourage people to strive towards those posts. Such rewards have the desired effect for, although the individuals and groups already possessing these positions of power, influence or social eminence spend a great deal of their energy trying to preserve their position, social mobility and displacement occur continually under the unrelenting pressure of those who feel themselves to be (and, indeed, may be) more suitable for the coveted positions. An answer to this important theoretical matter can only be attempted by a further inquiry into the known varieties of social inequality. These processes of upward and downward movement require more detailed study.

*Systems of social stratification*

When referring to social inequality we always speak of 'systems'. This is because stratification always possesses features of definite shape and profile and exhibits a definite pattern of relationships of power, rank, economic reward and position, and status, all mutually interdependent. It is far from easy to establish a rigorous taxonomy of stratification systems. One can be attempted by looking into the type of stratum which is predominant in each society, and excluding from this classification all preliterate societies, for their stratification systems present a bewildering variety of types, where often political, lineage, and tribal ties are more important for inequality than strata.[7] Apart from these, we can distinguish four broad systems of inequality:

I *Despotic agrarian stratification* This is a characteristic of the great empires based on the management of irrigation by a small stratum of officers (often identified with a priestly order), extremely privileged, but entirely at the service of an absolute king, emperor or pharaoh. (The latter, in these societies, tends to be the incarnation of a god, and this may curtail, by ritualisation, his powers of arbitrary decision, which may then be exercised by grand viziers.) In these societies status is measured by degrees of proximity to the centre of absolute power. There are, as Wittfogel has indicated,[8] two basic strata: the men in the political system, including soldiers, administrators, priests, and the rest, peasantry tilling land that is more than nominally owned by the king. The populace has an obligation to provide service, whether it is for the erection of palaces, castles, highways and dams, or in the direct operations of cultivation and harvest. The ruling stratum in these societies, for all their prominence, lacks guarantees of personal safety; the will of the despot or that of his viziers is paramount. With varying characteristics, Sumer, Akkad, Egypt, Aztec Mexico, the Inca Empire, the Chinese Empire, are examples of this type of stratification. It must be stressed that the most complex of these societies, such as Imperial Rome or classical Islam, developed to such a point of complexity that many specialised communities and strata appeared (merchants, artisans, independent farmers) that do not fit the harsher traits of the 'pure type' of despotic agrarian stratification. These new developments were accompanied by powerful cultural and religious movements fostering a more humane treatment of men, and even to a large extent, preaching equality as a godly virtue. Some doctrines of the Hellenistic period—Stoicism, above all—and the Islamic and Christian religions are examples of such movements (VII, 3).

II *Caste stratification* This is formed by closed sections of the population, ranked into a gradation of statuses. The social hierarchy of the caste system shows a very high degree of endogamy and hereditary rigidity, and is very closely linked with the occupational structure of the society. A person's caste (or rather, sub-caste) determines his place in the social division of labour; thus often sub-castes are named by the job assigned to its members. In its most clearcut forms, caste is thoroughly sanctioned by a religion which explains and legitimises the central concept of pollution; pollution is the act whereby individuals belonging to a caste deemed 'unclean' and ranking lower in the system of inequality come into contact with a higher caste, thus violating its 'purity'. This 'coming into contact' must also be interpreted in religious terms, as a profanation of the rituals of social distance, e.g. drinking from a well reserved to the higher castes. Accordingly, a caste system exists when the belief of pollution exists. The Indian subcontinent presents the most developed case of caste stratification. Although theoretically the chief castes in India are four, the unit is the *jati* or sub-caste, of which there are more than two thousand. Yet, the Brahmins, the Rajputs (who replaced the old Kshatriyas), the Vaishyias and the Sudras—'priests', 'warriors', 'commoners' and 'slaves'—are still the chief points of reference in the mental map of the Hindu. The *jati*, though, allows for extreme refinement in the intricacies of social distance: locality, tribe, profession, lineage, and the like.[9] In the Southern region of the United States and in South Africa castelike formations are also to be found: the belief in pollution is also present but it either appears in disguise or is maintained only by some important sectors of the white population. Next to these systems that affect the whole society we find instances of one single pariah caste, isolated within a non-caste society. Such is the case of the Danish *Rakkerfolk* (nomads) or *Natmandsfolk* (nightpeople) and Japanese *Burakumin* (ghetto residents), both untouchables. While the despotic agrarian system has shown very little resilience before the onslaught of industrialisation, the caste system has proved more resistant. It has certainly been eroded in urban India, and, in the United States, the caste features of Southern society have been replaced by the less blatant and more subtle patterns of racial discrimination of the North, although these are, in turn, under attack throughout the country. In Denmark, the Rakkerfolk disappeared after the First World War by integration into the larger society; yet their Japanese counterparts, the two million Burakumin, are still suffering from 'outcaste' segregation, in the midst of their country's advanced economic and technological development.[10]

III *Feudal stratification* is based on the legal sanction of a series of strata, called *estates*. Although religious backing for the system is often present, this is less prominent for legitimation than in the case of caste society. The gaps between the strata are very narrow, especially once the system is well established, and intermarriage and individual mobility between estates is possible. Thus in medieval Europe instances of the ennoblement of rich burghers and merchants, as well as of the marriage of the poor nobleman to the rich commoner's daughter, are common enough. In more than one sense, though, such phenomena enforce rather than undermine estate society, for its lower ranks aspire rather to ennoblement for themselves than the abolition of the system. Feudal society consists of a general system of vassalage in which a varying degree of human freedom is often possible: the ceremony of homage, whereby the feudal social bond is established between lord and vassal, prescribes duties and rights and is—hypothetically at least—entered into freely. This contractual relationship has helped to create a very complicated social structure, with numerous cases of infeudation and subinfeudation, a requirement for bills of rights, guarantees of freedom and the like (such as the *Usatges* of Barcelona or, later, the Magna Carta in England), that created the legal bases of other more open social systems. Estate or feudal society has been very dynamic and changeable; double vassalage constantly created ambiguity in property, law and political alliances and allegiances, and estates themselves were subdivided into many fine distinctions of rank. Basically there were either three estates (the nobility, the clergy, and the commoners or third estate) or four (the nobility, the clergy, the bourgeoisie, and the peasantry), and several sub-estates such as the *noblesse d'épée* and the *noblesse de robe* in France. Divisions are also clearly identifiable at the top of the authority structures of the feudal world: Emperor, Pope and King in Europe—Shogun and Emperor in Japan. Except in these two areas feudal societies have not existed in a 'pure form', but semi-feudal structures and cases of historically arrested feudalism exist in many areas of the world.[11]

IV *Class stratification* is entirely lacking in legal or religious sanction. Its origin is linked to the development of capitalism; this economic system fostered the view that status could be largely based on economic power, while hypothetically through a system of competition, the acquisition of wealth became possible for anyone. Other systems of competition for status—through study, skill, personal talents—became part of the class system. As a system, it is far more open than all others previously discussed. However, it has itself many degrees of variation and rigidity as well as differences in the direction of social change. This type of stratification system deserves special attention.

All these systems are far from homogeneous over any single territory. In feudal Europe some areas (such as Castile) had a social structure that was hardly feudal—in fact most historians agree that no real feudalism ever existed there. By contrast Catalonia, a country bordering Castile, presented one of the highest forms of feudalism and, like Normandy and England, of an almost 'pure type'. Furthermore the historical processes of stratification systems are haphazard. While the entire feudal system in Western Europe was crumbling, Poland and other areas of Eastern Europe went into a process of intense feudalisation. And Tokugawa Japan (the last historical phase before modernisation) was a clear case of feudalism being deliberately crystallised by political means. In the contemporary world nothing is more common than the uneasy coexistence of several stratification systems, India and Hispanic America being the obvious examples. In several South American countries the differences between urban and rural society are such that a rural-urban continuum—the smooth gradation between the social structure of the great cities and that of the most isolated areas in the countryside —is virtually non-existent. This is accentuated by the existence in the rural areas of a native Indian and *mestizo* (racially mixed) population. Thus in Peru Indians constitute forty per cent and *mestizos* thirty-two per cent of the entire population. Certainly until the early 1970s these people had no access to the centres of power and privilege, which were traditionally monopolised by the urban upper and middle classes of Spanish descent. In Peru, Ecuador and Bolivia rural society is Indian society. The existence of great absentee landowners or *latifundios* serves to aggravate the situation. In addition the existence of a 'dual society' in these countries has been accentuated by the fact that, throughout South America, urbanisation has frequently not been the consequence of industrialisation; indeed it is industrialisation that has the deepest, most marked effects on the rural hinterland, and that is why in South America rural stratification has remained untouched by non-industrial urbanisation. Hence in those areas one must not carry the dichotomy urban society/rural society too far, for, as Aldo Solari remarks when commenting on these developments, there are traits in South American social structures that cut across entire countries and are found both in the cities and in the countryside. Because of the type of agricultural exploitation prevalent in the latter, the cities are filled with unskilled labour which is, in turn, employed and exploited in a similar fashion, although in an urban or industrial setting.[12] Cultural patterns and political structures may give a certain unity to societies which actually possess several, and not one, stratificational systems. However, the long-range tendency for all systems found in one single political and economic area under conditions of modernity is to converge towards one single system of inequality. (This must not be taken to mean that all modern societies are converging into one single type, rather that the varieties of stratification, power and culture within one state are now under very strong pressures to integrate into single systems, though the process of integration itself may be extremely slow and uneven.) However varied its concrete forms, one can now speak of a vast urbanised, industrial society whose steady expansion, in contrast with that of other historical types of stratification, has resulted in the parallel decline in the size and importance of the other systems, as the following table shows:

*Degree of Urbanisation in the Countries of the World,*
*Classified by Degree of Agriculturalism (around 1953)*

| Percentage of gainfully active males in non-agricultural occupations | No. of countries | Percentage of population in cities of 100,000 or over |
|---|---|---|
| 80–100 | 11 | 32·3 |
| 70–79 | 11 | 23·6 |
| 60–69 | 7 | 23·2 |
| 50–59 | 7 | 21·9 |
| 40–49 | 16 | 17·7 |
| 30–39 | 17 | 8·9 |
| Less than 30 | 86 | 6·3 |

Adapted by N. P. Gist and S. F. Fava *Urban Society* (New York: Thomas Cromwell, 1967, 1st printing 1964), p. 36, from K. Davies and H. H. Golden 'Urbanisation and the Development of Preindustrial Areas' (*Econ. Dvpt. and Cultural Change*, Oct. 1954, no. 3).

*Social classes*

A large aggregate of individuals of similar status, income and culture, and broadly sharing the same position in the general division of labour in a given society, is a social class.[13] A number of people are said to belong to the same class when they share a similar set of life chances, that is, the same degree of likelihood that they will enjoy a certain type of education, income, status, standard of living, private property, position in the political structure, and the like. All these traits are essentially true of strata other than classes, in other stratification systems, such as those mentioned above. The difference is that a proper definition of class must include a historical element; classes are the specific large stratificational units of the societies which have been affected by modernisation. In the West they constitute the system that emerged as a consequence of the breakdown of feudalism, with the rise of the bourgeoisie, the growth of a proletariat, the diminution of the rural population, capitalist, industrial, and technological expansion, and the transformation of the traditional political system (X, 3; VIII, 4). A single, concise definition is misleading.[14]

Some confusion is added by the fact that the public and sociologists alike tend to use the term 'social class' either to indicate any large stratum in any society, pre-industrial or otherwise, or to refer to subsections of a social class, as in expressions such as 'the managerial class', 'the political class', 'the intellectual class'. These expressions lack precision but they are not unduly misleading when used in their usual context.

In order to overcome these and other difficulties, sociologists have made an effort to discover whether there exists a central unit of social class which could be isolated. A whole school of thought has seized upon the family as just such a unit. Families, even in the most industrialised societies are units of economic consumption, sharing the same status, power, and privilege of the head of the household, while possessing a common residence and, frequently, dependent offspring.[15] This has evident advantages for research, and for the counting of large numbers of people, as exemplified by the procedures followed by most national censuses carried out on the basis of households (i.e. families) and not of single individuals. However, no matter how important both family upbringing and inheritance, and research convenience, may be in the elaboration of a 'family' concept of social class, excessive emphasis on this unit would cause us to lose sight of the real sources of class inequality as well as of the factors that determine their respective size, internal structure and mutual conflicts.

Classes, as the celebrated expression of Marcel Mauss puts it, are 'total social phenomena', for they include all the possible dimensions of the social: the religious, economic, ideological, psychological and political dimensions. For this reason an enumeration of traits has frequently been substituted for a proper definition of social class. This approach is acceptable if it is regarded merely as a preliminary step towards a deeper grasp of the phenomenon being considered. It is in this spirit that classes can be defined as collectivities possessing the following characteristics:

(1) Legally classes are open, but in the realm which is outside the law, they are actually semi-closed. Legally, access to a class is not barred, especially since the complete spread of the franchise. But many extra-legal mechanisms operate in the attempt to maintain classes as closed and exclusive social areas. Class endogamy is one good example of this; in the overwhelming majority of cases marriage partners are chosen from the same class—even within one's subsection of that class, or at most within the nearest subsection. Upper-middle-class people are more likely to marry members of the lower-upper class or of the lower-middle class than members of the lower, unskilled-labour class.

(2) Classes are collectivities in which egalitarian interaction occurs. People within a given class feel equal to each other, and constantly recognise the other as such. Social interaction by itself does not imply such recognition. Egalitarian interaction, on the other hand, entails specific forms of communal reciprocity that overtly show social equality: conviviality, commensality, mutual visiting, special use of first names and a familiar form of behaviour. This phenomenon is usually accentuated among the members of an occupational group with the same status (soldiers, teachers, dockers, nurses), but it is also a vital part of class culture. Egalitarian interaction is also used for class-discrimination purposes: people who are invited to a 'social occasion' may be carefully screened from the angle of class.

(3) Classes are mutually antagonistic. If classes are by definition expressions of an unequal system of social rewards, perceived as unjust in varying degree, they must inevitably create cleavages and arouse hostility. Whether this hostility will in some instances be submerged by certain forms of consensus and in others explode in revolutionary outbursts must depend on the circumstances.

(4) Classes show internal solidarity, especially when individual

opportunities for getting out of them by moving to a higher rank or to another class are poor.

(5) Classes are not organised, or at least not formally so. Trade unions, upper-class circles or political parties may be the expression of 'classness' and class interests, but they never entirely coincide with a class, in spite of frequent ideological statements to the contrary.

(6) Members of a class are conscious of belonging to it.

(7) Classes are closely related both to the economic system of production and consumption and to the entire occupational structure of a society, the latter including the educational system whereby they are maintained and whence they evolve.

(8) Classes possess a life style, a subculture. There is a middle-class 'way of life', the life of 'high society', the language and lore of the working class, and so on. This life style is to an extent a by-product of other elements, especially political and economic power, but once established it acts as an independent variable as a conservative force in the ongoing processes of class stratification.[16]

Let us now look at some of these characteristics in greater detail.

## Class consciousness

Social classes are usually measured and quantified by several objective indices—income levels, patterns of expenditure, consumption of goods, cultural behaviour, voting patterns, and the like. Yet next to these criteria with whose help an 'objective' profile of social classes may be obtained there are other elements, of a psychological nature, that represent the subjective dimension of this social phenomenon. This dimension consists chiefly of the perception members have of their own class, of its position *vis-à-vis* the other classes, and of the nature of the class system in which they live.

According to Karl Marx, class consciousness is not simply to 'know' that one is working class, or a member of the petty bourgeoisie, or a labourer; it is rather the transformation of the objective interests of a class into subjective interests. If this phenomenon does not occur all we possess is a certain class awareness. When a class 'knows what it wants' within the system of inequality, it acts accordingly. If this awareness is lacking, Marx thinks, we are actually faced with an incomplete class. Accordingly, it is by virtue of class consciousness that classes cease to be 'classes in themselves' to become 'classes for themselves', or fully-fledged social classes. Thus understood, class consciousness is a vital element in the development of class conflict and class struggles. Every ruling class possesses, by definition, a class consciousness; they direct their efforts towards the maximisation of their privileged position; they skilfully divert the attention of the ruled and exploited classes towards matters that will distract them from attaining full consciousness— hence Marx's popular dictum that religion is the 'opium of the people'. (In this context, it was Machiavelli who, centuries earlier, developed a whole theory of popular ideological distraction, mainly through religion, as a further refinement on the Roman policy of bread and circuses.) The non-ruling classes, according to Marx, may or may not possess such class consciousness, and this depends on various economic and historical circumstances; thus the economic crises of capitalism, he thought, were bound to raise the level of the class consciousness of the proletariat to such revolutionary heights that the whole capitalist system would finally collapse. That this has not happened in the way foreseen by him does not invalidate the sociological value of his notion of class consciousness, especially if one takes into account the fact that most classes generate organisations which cater for some of their interests. Trade unions, although often representing a minority of workers, are the tools of the working class, or of the middle-class professionals. Depending on the historical moment, such unions may have a revolutionary 'class-struggle'-oriented policy (as during the Popular Fronts of the 1930s in Europe), or a conservative policy (as the AFL–CIO in the United States today) but in many cases they genuinely represent the class consciousness of their members. That either type of union may be 'misguided' is a political question which does not invalidate the fact that the union members may share the same aims as their elected leaders. In doing this they may, of course, be misguided and be exhibiting in Marx's phrase a 'false consciousness' (VIII, 4) of the genuine interests of their class. If this could at all be proved to be so it is a form of class alienation and, in so far as this leads union members to avoid revolutionary activity, it aids the smooth functioning of the political and economic systems of a given class society.

Class consciousness does not find expression solely in acts of collective solidarity. Individual class consciousness is an important factor in the orientation of action of single individuals, especially among those who want to make good—to 'get on in life'—and who identify these processes with ascending in social rank. Under these circumstances a person's awareness that his class is too low for his aspirations and merits is also class consciousness, although of a kind very different from collective class consciousness. In this context reference-group identifications and rejections play a decisive role (III, 2). In the main though, class consciousness is connected with class cohesion and closeness—with a continuing process of class discrimination which seems to be universal in human societies. This process is intense in borderline situations; for example, snobbery is a very important phenomenon which occurs among people who have not been admitted to the inner circle of higher groups (established high bourgeoisies, or aristocracies) but harbour high hopes that, by several social strategies of imitation, expenditure and social connections, as well as by 'avoiding getting caught' in any unworthy situation, they will succeed in gaining entry to them.[17] The worlds of snobbery are many, and they extend to would-be artists, intellectuals, and people in show-business, in addition to the typical case of wealthy people trying to penetrate high society.

Another essential element of class cohesion and consciousness is class morality and the particular method each class uses to punish transgressors to its moral code. Svend Ranulf's study of the relationships between moral indignation and the psychology of the middle classes in several countries and historical periods has shed much light on this matter. He carried out a content analysis of Calvinistic, Catholic and Jewish middle-class documents, Puritan preaching and war propaganda, and Nazi and Bolshevik evidence, apart from other materials drawn from African and Asian countries, and reached the conclusion that

> ... the disinterested [unrevengeful] tendency to inflict punishment is a distinctive characteristic of the lower middle class, that is, a social class living under conditions which force its members to an extraordinarily high degree of self-restraint and subject them to much frustration of natural desires.[18]

Although the rise of the so-called 'affluent society' might seem partially to have invalidated such an assertion for the contemporary lower middle classes in some countries, Ranulf's investigations, starting with an earlier classical work of his on the emergence of a criminal code in fifth-century Athens and its connections with the new social class that came to rule Athenian society, have opened the way for a novel examination of the nature of class consciousness and psychology and their consequences for morality and law.

Class consciousness, finally, implies a way of perceiving the social structure, the true map of the social world. Stanislav Ossowski has shown how people's perception of their own society as dichotomic (two opposed social classes), functional (mutually necessary and complementary classes), or based on schemes of gradation (multiple ranking orders) has decisive effects on the directions taken by the processes of social change occurring within the different systems of inequality.[19] Frequently the secret of consensus to a manifestly unjust social order may lie not in sheer terror and repression but in the way a majority of people have internalised a certain view of inequality and accepted it as legitimate and bearable.

## The dynamics of class: mobility, elites and conflict

When an individual exchanges his social position in a given group for another in another group without gaining or losing in status we say that horizontal social mobility has taken place. An unskilled worker who goes from one similar job to another, perhaps in a different town, is an example of such mobility. Pure horizontal mobility is rare, though; if people seek new jobs it is because they expect at least some gain in income or status. Most social mobility is *vertical*, which indicates changes in social position that imply changes in status; vertical social mobility can be either *upward* or *downward*. The rate, the direction, and the volume of social mobility in a given society depend on a great variety of factors. Many are to be found in the social structure; parents' income, educational facilities, government policies, discriminatory practices, patterns of favouritism and the like—these either favour, or set up barriers to, mobility in every given group and institution.

Next to these structural elements which canalise mobility along the prescribed norms of political power, economic privilege, racial prejudice and so forth, we encounter personality structures. These are developed through socialisation in each culture and play a very important role in determining mobility and other stratificational phenomena. In Italy, for example, children in Piedmont and Lombardy are socialised in a different way from those in Sicily. Sicilian society possesses a social structure which is more traditionalistic and static than the very modern North, but the values that are inculcated in the middle-class Northern child are certainly far less fatalistic than those taught to the Sicilian child. Individualism, self-reliance, a certain confidence in legality and fair-play, and a desire to 'get on in life' by hard work, are explicitly taught in industrial, secularised Turin and Milan. The opposite characteristics are true of Sicily. The same comparisons could be made between England and Ireland, Catalonia and Andalusia. (We must bear in mind, of course, that there is oversimplification in these statements, for if Sicilian, Irish or Andalusian societies show very high rates of emigration it must be that the idea of getting on and improving one's lot by one's own work has penetrated very deeply. Besides socialisation patterns, then, the local social structure must also be taken into account, for it probably offers lesser opportunities for individual advancement there than elsewhere.) Certain subcultures, such as early Calvinism or modern Jewry, have been notably success-ful in this kind of individualistic socialisation and have helped break barriers that, at the beginning of the historical process, must have looked pretty formidable. Today the values of competitive individualism have been enthroned in the educational, political, and intellectual economic systems of several countries, it is precisely at this juncture, though, that they seem to be undergoing a crisis. (VII, 6; X, 3).

Among the structural elements that canalise, favour or put a brake on upward social mobility, one of the most important is the nature of the society's *ruling classes*. Although this term has suffered from much confused use since it was first introduced by Gaetano Mosca, we may accept Aron's definition of it, as referring to 'those people who, without exercising actual political functions, influence those who govern and those who obey, either because of the moral authority which they hold or because of the economic or financial power they possess'.[20] They are the top stratum of modern class society, and must be distinguished from the *political class*, which is very largely recruited from among the ruling class itself and formed by the minority who hold some form of political office in political parties, in the organs of the state, or through other institu-tions. There are several means the ruling classes use in their efforts to maintain privilege—exclusive schools, private wealth, exclusive clubs, careful family ties, and every other conceivable method. In this, however, they must strike a balance between the exigencies of social change and their own desire to remain at the top. Thus the demands of industrialised society impose a more open educational system and the award of high status to technological and scientific professions which have now been thrown open to a great number of people—at least to the vast middle-class student population. In communist countries, party membership may be the gateway to the ruling class, but the professions must also command full status if the needs of economic, military and scientific development are to be met by the state; the result is that increasing numbers of scientists, technologists and professors apply for party membership as an almost ritualistic step towards success.[21]

The notion of the ruling class cannot be fully understood without the parallel but very different concept of the *elite*. This is a very necessary but unfortunately misleading word, for elite in common speech might refer to a decadent group of reactionary leaders, and the noun has inevitably been linked to the adjective 'elitist'. Sociologically, though, an elite, as first defined by Pareto, is simply a set of 'people who have the highest indices in their branch of activity'. This way of defining it has two corollaries: first, that every branch of human endeavour, and every sufficiently broad social institution, will possess its own elite or elites and, second, that elites do not necessarily have to be in command in order to be elites. Thus, talking about government, Pareto distinguishes between governing elites ('individuals who directly or indirectly play some considerable part in government') and the non-governing elites (the rest).[22] But each stratum or large enough group will also possess an elite. The leadership of a revolutionary trade union, even if that union is outlawed, will be such an elite, just as a government is the central political elite. But there will also be one or more artistic, intellectual and scientific elites in each complex society. Of all these elites some will be more egalitarian, some more oligarchic, than others. However, as both Pareto and Michels indicated, elites tend to perpetuate themselves in power or influence; Roberto Michels went so far as to speak of an 'iron law of oligarchy', whereby power in the political realm under any regime eventually concentrates in a small group of people, and has to be wrung from them at a later stage.[23] However, age, conspiracies and institutionalised channels for the renewal of social positions (prescriptive retirement, elections, terms of contract) and many other methods of change, prevent the perpetuation of the elites in power and ensure they are renewed. This is what Pareto called the circulation of elites. In very rigid stratification systems, elite circulation at the highest levels of responsibility is obviously restricted to the ruling classes from which they are exclusively recruited.

Elite circulation does not occur without conflict, but it is not necessarily *class conflict*, although conversely this last phenomenon often entails a confrontation between the respective elites of each social class, which is most apparent if there is insufficient circulation of the elites of non-ruling classes. Thus the degree of social capillarity—the capacity of a class to permit members of lower classes to seep through into it, making room for them even at the price of concessions in privilege and status—is a very important variable in determining the acuteness of class conflict. Dahrendorf is largely correct when he affirms that, 'if an individual can improve his position by moving up in terms of status, he does not need to ally with others to achieve this end'.[24] The fact is that the question of class barriers and the social frustration of ambitious elites is always present in situations of class conflict. And this is further complicated by ethnic or cultural diversity. A given religion, as Catholicism in Ulster, or Coptic Christianity in Egypt, may be a pretext for the maintenance of a given pattern of class dominance. The use of racial criteria to enforce class patterns of inequality is familiar to everybody. In all these cases, certain collective physical or cultural characteristics are a pretext, and not a proper cause, of class inequality. Once prejudice of this kind has been internalised, it can be considered as an immediate cause of conflict provided the observer does not lose sight of the fact that the true origin of the whole situation is mostly to be found in class inequality and not in the *a posteriori* rationalisations ingrained in the culture and ideology of each contending party. In its most acute form class conflict becomes a class struggle, and in so far as it tends towards a reversal of the prevailing societal structure, it becomes a chapter in the sociology of revolutions (IX, 3).

*NOTES on Chapter VI, Section 3*

1. J. J. Rousseau *Discours sur l'origine et les fondements de l'inégalité parmi les hommes* (Paris: Editions Sociales, 1954, –1754) p. 67.
2. R. Bastide *Les formes élémentaires de la stratification sociale* (Paris: Sorbonne, C.D.U. mimeograph, 1965) pp. 16–25.
3. W. G. Runciman 'Class, Status and Power?' in *op. cit.*, pp. 102–40.
4. F. Tönnies 'Stände und Klassen' and M. Weber *Wirtschaft und Gesellschaft* (Part III, ch. 4) reprinted and trans. in R. Bendix and S. M. Lipset eds. *Class, Status and Power* (London: Routledge, 1967 rev. ed.) pp. 12–28.
5. A. Malewski 'The Degree of Status Incongruence and its Effects' (1963, *Polish Sociol. Bull.*), reprinted in R. Bendix and S. M. Lipset *op. cit.*, pp. 303–8.
6. K. Davies and W. E. Moore 'Some Principles of Stratification' (1945) reprinted in R. Bendix and S. M. Lipset *op. cit.*, pp. 47 and 48, together with M. Tumin's criticism (pp. 53–58) and further material on the subject by other sociologists.
7. Cf. for an initial contact with the 'primitive' systems of stratification, R. Bastide *op. cit.* and G. Lenski *Power and Privilege* pp. 94–116 and *Human Societies op. cit.* pp. 118–236. For slavery: J. Elkins *Slavery* (The University of Chicago, 1959).
8. K. Wittfogel *op. cit.* pp. 301–68.
9. For an initial contact with caste stratification cf. E. Bergel *Social Stratification* (New York: McGraw Hill, 1962) pp. 35–67; G. K. Pillai *The Origin and Development of Caste* (Allahabad: Kitab Mahal, 1959); O. C. Cox *Caste, Class and Race* (New York: Monthly Review, 1959); and L. Dumont *Homo Hierarchicus* (London: Weidenfeld, 1970).

10. G. de Vos *Japan's Outcastes, the Problem of the Burakumin* (London: Minority Rights Group, 1971).
11. For initial information about estate society, E. Bergel *op. cit.* pp. 80–161; R. Coulborn *Feudalism in History* (Princeton University, 1956); and M. Bloch *Feudalism* (London: Routledge, 1961 2 Vols.).
12. A. E. Solari *Sociología rural latinoamericana* (Buenos Aires: Paidos, 1968) pp. 1–46. For a portrayal of social class in *latifundio* society in the Iberian Peninsula, see J. Cutileiro *A Portuguese Rural Society* (Oxford: Clarendon, 1971).
13. For the second part of this definition cf. K. Marx *Das Kapital* (Moscow: Marx-Engels-Lenin Institute; Volkausgabe, 1932) Vol. III, pp. 941–42.
14. G. Gurvitch *Le concept des classes sociales* (Paris: Sorbonne, CDU, mimeograph, 1966) includes and analyses some of the chief definitions and their implications.
15. Cf. B. Barber *Social Stratification* (New York: Harcourt Brace, 1957) p. 73.
16. This is a modified version of P. A. Sorokin's enumeration of class traits; cf. his 'What is a social class?' in R. Bendix and S. M. Lipset *op. cit.* 1st ed. (Glencoe: Free Press, 1953) pp. 87–88.
17. Ph. du Puy de Clinchamps *Le snobisme* (Paris: PUF, 1966).
18. Svend Ranulf *Moral Indignation and Middle Class Psychology* (Eng. trans. of 1938 Danish ed., New York: Schocken, 1964) p. 198.
19. S. Ossowski *Class Structure in the Social Consciousness* (London: Routledge, 1963).
20. R. Aron 'Social Class, Political Class, Ruling Class' *Europ. Jnl. Soc.* (1960) reprinted in R. Bendix and S. M. Lipset *op. cit.* p. 204.
21. F. Parkin, *Class Inequality and Political Order* (London: MacGibbon and Kee, 1971).
22. V. Pareto *op. cit.*; as rendered by T. B. Bottomore *Elites and Society* (Harmondsworth: Penguin, 1966) pp. 7–8.
23. R. Michels *Political Parties* (Glencoe: Free Press, 1949, 1st ed., 1911).
24. R. Dahrendorf *Conflict after Class* (University of Essex, 1967) p. 19.

# 4 THE SPAN OF INEQUALITY: A NOTE ON ECONOMIC SURPLUS

With the sole exception of some isolated and ephemeral communities the entire history of civilised man has taken place within social systems pervaded by and based on inequality. For many a hopeful mortal this may not be sufficient evidence to assert that social inequality will forever remain a feature of human society, and we shall remain silent on this score, for sociology has thus far gathered very little evidence either for or against this assumption. It has not even produced enough evidence on the most serious issue of all, which is simply the question: why social, as opposed to natural, inequality? The answer probably lies in increased knowledge about human nature, a knowledge which could perhaps disclose why greed, rapaciousness, and an unquenchable thirst for power are so common among us, and why they so often cast a shadow over other desires such as peaceful emulation and legitimate ambition. These last characteristics, one would surmise, ought not to be incompatible with a more equal *and* free society. Yet as an acquaintance with anthropological philosophy makes abundantly clear, this answer is not readily available and social science is left alone with its own meagre findings.

A first, primordial question that these findings have helped to answer is the issue of the existence of different types and degrees of inequality. Once the fact of inequality has been stated—to put it again in Rousseauian language, once it has been established by common sense that man may have been born free, but humanity is everywhere in chains—the first thing that springs to mind is the immense variety of social inequality. This is shown above all by the varying *span* of social inequality in different societies, that is, by the total social distance that separates the highest post in the structure of authority and power from the lowest in the same society. This last fact is one of the principal factors shaping the life experience of the men and women who happen to live at a given time in a given place. As much as any other sociocultural differences, this overall extent of inequality is what makes the status, dignity and freedom of, say, 'the same' middle-class urban wife so different in Mexico, Bombay, Glasgow, Leningrad and Naples; or what makes the Bavarian and Brazilian peasants two different persons—the former being a citizen, the latter a mere underling of the rural boss.

A completely plausible general theory of social inequality has yet to be produced, but several approximations are familiar. After the notable efforts made by the social thinkers of the Scottish Enlightenment, such as Adam Ferguson (*History of Civil Society*, 1767) and John Millar (*The Origin of the Distinction of Ranks*, 1771) other scientists pursued their own lines of thought, which entailed, among other things, correlating technology and the economy with inequality. Marx explained how, 'in the social production of their own existence', men develop economic systems which create fixed relationships among them, and which are independent of their free will. These relationships, he thought, directly depend on the material productive forces at their disposal.[1] Without falling into a simplistic interpretation of such a postulate, it is evident that scientific and technological culture has far-reaching consequences in the realm of inequality, and that these are worth pursuing. The 'oriental despotism' hypothesis we have come across earlier is, after all, thoroughly grounded in assumptions of this nature. And the parallel development between technology and increased inequality amongst primitive cultures reinforces many a suspicion about the hypothesis of the economic and technological causation of inequality. Simply put, up to the expansion of the industrial revolution the volume of economic surplus was a decisive factor in the span and degree of harshness of the prevalent systems of social inequality.[2] Simple correlations are nearly always absent, but the fact remains that, historically, the multiplication of economic efficiency only meant further hoarding and control of goods by the sovereign, the oligarchy and their immediate officers, with the populace forcibly kept, for thousands of years, on a bare subsistence level, with an appalling rate of disease, starvation, and death through direct exploitation by the ruling classes. By the same token the 'leisure class' created by this economic surplus was a precondition of the further development of science and technology necessary for the industrial revolution.[3]

The immense surplus created by early technology and the first stages of the industrial revolution, under the aegis of the bourgeoisie and the capitalist market and system of production, created a novel situation where oligarchies could not keep a tight and complete control of wealth; wealth began to spill over, so to speak, to people hitherto systematically barred from it. Subsequently a class society began to form, and this put an end to the perennial situation of oligarchic rule and the enforced scarcity of goods for the many. One must hasten to say that the expression 'put an end' must be taken as meaning that class society, with its explicit denial of religious, legal, or political barriers to inequality, with its basic individualistic cultural assumptions about personal worth, status and achievement, has presented mankind with the possibility of breaking the long-standing vicious circle of serfdom and oligarchy, and opened the way to democracy (VII, 5). The alienations of modern man may be many but, at least from the point of view of inequality, many modern societies are more humane than any previously known. The growth of an industrial world has sometimes been connected with new forms of *corvée* work and slavery (such as forced mass labour and concentration camps); imperialist wars and invasion are still waged in many areas. But the fact remains that ever since the Puritan and the French revolutions men have over and over again either risen or acted directly against the prevailing class system with the explicit intention of further eroding inequality.

This has been so because—for a complex series of reasons, some of which will be examined later (X, 2, 3)—the value system of most contemporary societies has come to include an acute enmity against inequality. People have for ages been aware of family privilege, educational advantages, political favouritism and, above all, of the appropriation by the few of the economic surplus produced by the toil of the many,[4] but only in modern times has the practical reduction or abolition of such patterns of domination become ingrained in the ethos of some parties, social movements and in the social sciences themselves.[5]

Yet the crisis in economic growth created by an increasing scarcity of economic resources and energy stuffs—combined with the enormous increase in population which the economic surplus itself made possible together with the industrial and scientific revolutions —has been already affecting, since 1973, the patterns of surplus of recent times. The new scarcity is stiffening international and class conflicts to the point that no optimistic prediction can be made about the continuation of the erosion of social inequality in the near future. Equality and freedom may not depend only on general economic wealth but, as the study of ancient despotism teaches us, excess population and stagnant wealth[6] are not precisely the factors that work in their favour.

## NOTES on Chapter VI, Section 4

1. K. Marx Foreword to his *Capital: A Critical Analysis of Capitalist Production* (London: Allen & Unwin, 1938).
2. For a development of this notion, G. Lenski *Power and Privilege, op. cit.*
3. Cf. Th. Veblen *The Theory of the Leisure Class* (1899).
4. D. Caplovitz *The Poor Pay More*, for the persistence of this phenomenon in contemporary America (New York: Free Press, 1967).
5. For the latter, cf. J. Urry and J. Wakeford eds. *Power in Britain* (London: Heinemann, 1973) and A. Pichierri ed. *Le classi Sociali in Italia* (Turin: Loescher, 1974).
6. Club of Rome *The Limits of Growth*, 1973.

# VII The Polity

## 1 POWER AND AUTHORITY

The political dimension of a society is known as the polity. This notion is more comprehensive than that of state or party; it refers to the entire universe of the political in which men move. In each society, the polity presents certain patterns, regularities and detectable trends, and hence it can sometimes be identified with the concept of political system.

To achieve a proper understanding of the political universe one must first understand the two notions or elements that constitute the polity—power and authority. The polity, and particularly government, is concerned with 'getting things done' in the wider society. In large societies governments serve this purpose by gearing and coordinating the action of many people towards established goals, and in accordance with certain set priorities; this is done by means of power and authority. Power and authority bring about social order by imposing patterns of behaviour on great numbers of people. Not without reason are the dictates of those in command also called orders; their constant flow shapes and structures social life, while giving it a sense of direction.

*Power* is the capacity that individuals or groups have to influence the behaviour of others to accord with their requirements. Such capacity takes many forms, including physical force, the superiority of one mind over another, domination by giving explicit commands which are then followed, and more subtle influence by implicit manipulation—that is, the ability of somebody to create the conditions which will incline others to act in accordance with his will. Often this is attempted through propaganda.[1] Except in the case of physical coercion, power is possible in society because of the existence of a related, though different, phenomenon: *authority*. Although physical force is common enough, it cannot by itself account for the maintenance of political and stratification systems:

for such systems to become ongoing concerns a high degree of obedience, deference to and confidence in authority must also exist among a large number of the people affected. Yet what is authority? The notion is elusive because it perhaps denotes one of the central facts in social life; people respect, esteem and have a regard for certain other people and institutions, and this fact prompts them to bestow status and rank upon them and to obey them. Hence authority is not by definition brute force. This does not mean, however, that physical coercion cannot be used in a given society in combination with authority. In Rome, non-domestic slaves, such as those who worked in the mines in vast numbers, were kept to their chores by brute force, while full citizens and other people accepted consular and senatorial authority by virtue of consensus. That political consensus and deference to authority have always existed in varying degrees in every society and are, under given circumstances, the basis of a well-ordered, free and worthy polity, proves that, as Sebastian de Grazia has pointed out, authority is not mysterious, necessarily undemocratic, despotic, or irrational.[2] Under certain circumstances it can, of course, become these and more, but there is no shorthand formula to determine when this is so. A high degree of consensus may not mean democracy, as the infatuation of the German people with the Nazi regime and its psychotic leadership sufficiently proves. It is precisely one of the tasks of political sociology, together with social psychology, to explain the fluctuations of authority between reason and folly, and between the reasonable consensus of a civilised majority and the collective alienation of the many to the whims of the few.

Authority, then, is power that is acknowledged, widely accepted and institutionalised in a society. When this occurs we say that it is legitimate, or at least regarded as such by a large proportion of the people. Thus legitimacy is an essential part of authority, political or otherwise. For some people authority is always legitimate whatever others may think. This can be seen during periods of extreme social conflict, such as civil wars. During the American War of Secession there were two states and two sociologically legitimate political systems, even if on constitutional, moral or 'popular will' grounds each camp considered the other as illegitimate. On similar grounds the Spanish Republican Government represented the legitimate state when, in 1936, a considerable section of the Army, backed by right-wing and fascist groups, rose against it; yet the rebels soon had to create their own system of legitimate power, a whole network of consensual relationships. More than thirty years later terror and repression still played a very important part in the functioning of the state born of the Republican defeat in Spain in 1939, but processes of consensus and legitimation have been at least equally important in maintaining the regime. The trial and execution of the English King Charles I in 1640 shows how strong a hold this notion of 'legitimate authority' had taken on seventeenth-century society for both contending parties made elaborate efforts to justify it and explain its meaning. All civil wars are crises of legitimacy, and it is by studying them that we understand how, in the last resort, authority derives from the willingness of various groups to sink their differences for a common good. It is useful to make some analytical distinctions between kinds of authority and their processes of legitimation. Such distinctions are especially possible in the more complex societies since, in the tribal world, religious, moral, political and legal authority tends to be fused and vested in the same people, in spite of some specialisation such as that represented by witchdoctors and shamans. Analysing the 'natural basis' of authority in each polity, Weber identified three pure or ideal types of legitimate power, or authority:[3]

I *Charismatic authority*, 'resting on devotion to the specific and exceptional sanctity, heroism and exemplary character of an individual person and of the normative patterns or order ordained by him'. Social movements that upset and change an established order and create a new one are often led by individuals who possess such charisma. Charismatic leadership, however, does not necessarily apply to vast social movements, nor is it always revolutionary. Moreover, examples of individuals possessing charismatic qualities are found in all types of political, religious and military movements. One thinks of Mohammed and Jesus, but one also thinks of Hernán Cortés, who conquered the Aztecs; Adolf Hitler; the British liberal leader Lloyd George; Che Guevara. They were all different men who stood for very different values. Yet they shared this charismatic power over their followers, the capacity to embody with their persons a unified version of many strands of thought and feeling. Often, the political and religious auras surrounding such figures are inextricably intertwined. Mohammed developed a political system that expressed his religious teaching; Hitler used cults to justify political means.

II *Traditional authority* rests on 'an established belief in the sanctity of immemorial traditions and the legitimacy of the status of those exercising authority under them'. Here authority is based on norms that have allegedly 'always existed'. Persons born to positions of authority do not have to achieve charisma in order to command loyalty. The political structure finds its legitimation in hereditary laws and appeals to religious sanction ('By the grace of God . . .', or 'defender of the Faith', etc.). In traditional polities rights, duties, and patterns of status and obedience, are not expressed in codes and constitutions, though legal precedents may be established in the course of time. Yet these patterns create limits to power so that each person in the polity knows what 'can be done' and what 'cannot be done' in each case. There is a pragmatic knowledge of power and authority. Such limitations of powers and curtailment of arbitrariness by tradition are, nevertheless, very varied. The powers of an Ottoman sultan were certainly not the same as those of a coetaneous European monarch; they were far wider. On the other hand, in Western Europe only the nobility could reach high office, while in the Ottoman empire until the seventeenth century, Christian slaves trained in the Sultan's official household could reach a very high office.

III *Rational-legal authority* rests on 'a belief in the "legality" of patterns of normative rules and the right of those elevated to authority under such rules to issue commands'. Such authority appears clothed in rationalistic justifications, and wears the claim that the law is the expression of popular sovereignty, which, in turn, is the ultimate source of legitimacy. Under such circumstances it is the law that is sovereign, and not the several groups. Hypothetically it applies equally to all. This system was first developed by the ancient Greeks, who went a long way towards translating it into an actual polity, and it has been revived with varied fortunes by several modern peoples. Basically it is a system of explicit guarantees, based on the notion of citizenship (the opposite of that of vassalage) and on the participation of citizens in political life.

As with any ideal type, these three kinds of authority—and their corresponding polities—are nowhere to be found in a pure state. A great polity based on rational-legal authority, such as Great Britain, possesses a monarch whose title is merely traditional. Other sovereigns, such as the King of the Belgians, owe their position to an explicit incorporation of their office into a written (rational-legal) constitution. Conversely medieval bills of rights granted by kings may be considered as the historical origin of modern rational-legal authority. Totalitarian systems, which are extremely irrational from many a standpoint, often possess detailed constitutions that guarantee every conceivable right of opinion, political office, religious worship and peaceful demonstration. There are, besides, countless states which do not seem to fit either of the three systems. What is one to make of the Greek regime born out of the military coup of 1967? To say that Greece was, until 1974, a 'semi-fascist, militaristic, dictatorship' does not answer the present question about the three types of authority. Yet the classification remains enlightening, because it is not a taxonomy of regimes but a lucid attempt to isolate three main dimensions of authority which are everywhere present, although often one of the three tends to be more prominent than the others.

The more permanent forms of authority are the traditional and rational-legal: charismatic authority, whose creative forces are historically very important tends to lose impetus with time. The leaders of successful political movements, precisely because of their success, have to cope with the day-to-day routines of government and administration. Inevitably what Weber called the process of *routinisation of charisma* sets in. Commemorations and revival ceremonies are established and monuments to the great deeds of the past are erected, but the original charisma becomes harder to recapture as time goes by. The history of the modern communist parties provides several examples. The Chinese 'cultural revolution' instigated by Chairman Mao in the late 1960s was, among other things, a vast exercise in the maintenance of the 'revolutionary spirit' against the odds of routinisation.[4] In consequence the fate of charisma— whether in the realm of politics or religion—is central to the explanation of the structure and evolution of old and new factions, orthodoxies, parties and sects. (VIII, 3.)

*NOTES on Chapter VII, Section 1*

1. H. Goldhamer and E. A. Shils 'Types of Power and Status' in *Am. Jnl. Soc.* Vol. XLV, Sept. 1939, p. 171.
2. S. de Grazia 'What Authority is *not*' in *Am. Pol. Sci. Rev., LIII*, June 1959, pp. 321–31.
3. M. Weber *Staatssoziologie* (Berlin: Dunckner und Humboldt, 1966 ed.) pp. 99–110; Eng. source M. Weber *The Theory of Social* etc., *op. cit.*, pp. 324–423. The following quotations are from this text.
4. S. Karol *Guerrillas in Power* (London: Cape, 1971).

## 2 SOCIAL STRUCTURE, CULTURE, AND THE POLITY

*The social structure of politics*

Political sociology studies the social effects of political power and authority distributions among people and between societies, and the conflicts which accompany these phenomena, as well as the reverse process, the effects of the other levels of social reality upon the political realm.

In the last chapter two features of stratification were mentioned which have a decisive effect upon the nature of the polity: class and elite. The relationship between these two and political power is far from simple, however. In some cases it may be true to say that 'the state is the property of the upper class', of which it is merely the tool, but in most cases the state is much more than that. It may so happen that different classes have different degrees of access to the several institutions of the state, or that while a well-entrenched ruling class is present it is on the defensive, constantly influenced by the ruled and the oppressed. Thus political sociology primarily directs its attention to the modes in which each section of a given society enters the political arena, or is kept away from it. Some concrete examples of this approach will be examined below (VII, 3, 4). The chief assumption in all cases is that the polity is a reflection of the actual power relationships found in the social structure, and not something independent of it.

From an analytical point of view it is possible to conceive of the polity as a system of activities related to power and authority, separated from the rest of social activities. In this vein David Easton has proposed that the political system ought to be conceived as a relatively closed universe of political units interacting with the rest of the social world. This interaction takes place through a flow of decisions (policies) which can be called 'outputs'. Simultaneously the political system responds to flows of 'inputs', i.e. demands, from some sections of the society, and support for its policies from others. Such demands cover different matters: higher salaries, the granting of certain freedoms of assembly, the release of political prisoners, the calling of elections, the resignation of ministers, and so forth. To the extent that a system (or government) can prevent a demand becoming an issue the demand is likely to be met or ignored or to result in compromise. Whether issues can be solved or ignored, or compromises can be reached, depends on the quantity and scope of the support received. Finally, as in every system, the response of the actors creates new conditions, and transforms the political environment, creating, through a process of feedback, a new set of political relationships.[1]

This conception, for all its simplicity, is illuminating and helps to put the political process in the right perspective, since it can be integrated with other aspects of political life, such as conflict. This is especially true if the system is not conceived in the last resort as an entity separate from the economic and class cleavages, tensions and needs of societies, or from the religious, educational or other cultural problems of the people living in a polity.

## Political culture and socialisation

The nature of the polity and the kind of political decisions that are taken by the political units at every step of the political process are not only the consequence of occupational structures, the relative sizes of the social classes, economic inflation, invading armies, and other similar major 'objective' phenomena, but are also the result of attitudes, values, outlooks, ideologies and patterns of behaviour previously established in the society. In other words, culture also shapes political life. One of the conditions for the success of a democratic, representative government based on elections is a large majority of people with confidence in the state and in the fairness of the political process. In societies where elections have been un-known or have consistently been rigged by political bosses and political machines people have attitudes that are unfavourable to them, and pave the way to self-appointed dictators. Religious alle-giances, regional loyalties, commitments to other values or institu-tions, all play an important part in colouring the final political behaviour of each individual. They can be described as cross-pressures, and this bias sometimes radically changes people's orienta-tions.[2] The influence of religion in the voting patterns of Germany and Italy, and its tragic effects on the course of events in India after its independence and the subsequent creation of the state of Pakistan, are all well known. The degree of tolerance of beliefs other than one's own is also a cultural element which has decisive political effects. Taken together all these cultural factors add up to a political culture. Gabriel Almond and Sidney Verba have been able to show how this culture must be included in the province of political sociology for it to achieve a fuller understanding of political phenomena.[3]

If culture is a vital part of politics it is obvious that a process of socialisation into the political culture, or political socialisation, must be a part of the life of the polity. By means of families, schools, newspapers, television sets, political campaigns and their occupations, people are always learning progressively about their own roles in the political realm, as well as about those of the state, local officials, magistrates, army officers, and every institution connected with authority. The life experiences of vast numbers of people in a given society—especially those in the same class—resemble each other, and as a consequence so do their beliefs, or political culture, and the ideologies to which they have been exposed and may have internalised (VIII, 4). Thus in some countries with a long experience of oligarchic rule, where attempts at introducing democracy may have been violently defeated, children are consistently taught by their frightened parents 'not to meddle in politics', which of course is a private reinforcement of a public attitude which cannot but please the government. In others they are taught the opposite, or at least they do not constantly hear disparaging remarks about rigged elections, corrupt officials and police repression. Through these processes the varieties of personality one finds in any given population are reshaped according to prevailing cultural patterns.

By combining types of political expectations Lowell separated people into those contented with their current lot and political situation and those discontented with them. He then separated those who were sanguine about the future—who believed things could be improved—and those who were not. The result can be exemplified thus:[4]

```
                          contented
              liberals       |       conservatives
sanguine ─────────────────────┼───────────────────── non-sanguine
              radicals        |       reactionaries
                        discontented
```

For his part, Eysenck, feeling unhappy about the oversimplifications of the right-wing/left-wing dichotomy, used William James' classification between 'tender-minded' and 'tough-minded' characters to draw a similar diagram:[5]

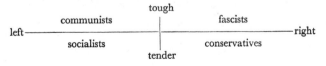

```
                          tough
            communists       |       fascists
left ────────────────────────┼───────────────────── right
            socialists       |       conservatives
                          tender
```

Admittedly, these are only crude models or points of departure on which to base a satisfactory psychology of politics. For one thing they themselves must be subjected to cross-cultural analysis. Thus Maurice Duverger seems to be right when he partially objects to Eysenck's paradigm on the grounds that it hardly holds for the 'non-Anglo-Saxon' countries, where the pair 'tough-tender' cannot be readily assimilated by the 'authoritian-democratic' dichotomy.[6] Nevertheless, in our context these schemes shed some further light on people's proneness to act in given political directions. The true sociological question, though, is not whether 'authoritarian', 'democratic', 'progressive' and other types of personalities exist, but why, in what numbers, which social conditions and institutions foster them, and what are the chances in each case of certain people attaining power or significant political office on the basis of their personality. Other things being equal, by the laws of probability each type of political personality ought to be equally represented in each large population; in fact, however, people's groups, traditions and fortunes in the historical process favour the success of one or another type of political man.

In spite of his use of colourful and 'unscientific' vocabulary, Pareto's analysis of character types and their presence in each kind of political elite opened the way for the exploration of this matter, for he related them to differing phases of political life. He spoke of 'speculators' and 'rentiers' as predominant personality types in different elites, the first being 'innovatory' and the second 'conservative' characters. Pareto's 'speculators' and 'rentiers', as Bottomore points out, bear a close resemblance to Machiavelli's classic distinction between the 'foxes' and the 'lions' in politics.[7] During the early stages of the fascist movements Wilhelm Reich produced a penetrating study on the family sources of what he called the 'mass psychology of fascism', in which he related German authoritarianism in the training of children to their later subservience to any kind of public power, and their inclination to blind obedience and extreme discipline within the framework of the Nazi movement.[8] Today there are many studies of working-class psychology (especially working-class conservatism), middle-class radicalism and activism, the role of given types of religious education in political life, the development and nature of the nazi, communist and democratic mentalities, and of many similar issues.[9] In the majority of these studies the concept of political socialisation and culture has rightly been expanded to cover the entire life experience of the people concerned, including a picture of the intimate subculture of which they are a part.

*NOTES on Chapter VII, Section 2*

1. D. Easton 'An Approach to the Analysis of Political Systems' in *World Politics* (Vol. IX, April 1957) pp. 383–400.
2. Cf. S. M. Lipset *Political Man* (London: Mercury, 1964, 1st ed. 1959) p. 101.
3. G. A. Almond and S. Verba *The Civic Culture* (Princeton: University Press, 1963).
4. A. L. Lowell *Public Opinion in War and·Peace* quoted by H. D. Lasswell *Power and Personality* (New York: Viking, 1962, 1st ed. 1948) p. 60.
5. H. J. Eysenck *The Psychology of Politics* (London: Routledge, 1954).
6. M. Duverger *Sociologie politique* (Paris: PUF, 1968) pp. 186–89.
7. T. B. Bottomore *Elites . . . op. cit.* p. 51.
8. W. Reich *Die Massenpsychologie des Fascismus* (Copenhagen: 1933); Eng. trans. *The Mass Psychology of Fascism* (New York: Orgone Institute Press, 1946).
9. S. M. Lipset *op. cit.* on 'Working Class Authoritarianism' and 'American Intellectuals: their Politics and Status', pp. 97–130, 310–43; R. Parkin *Middle Class Radicalism* (Manchester University Press, 1968); F. Murillo *Estudios de sociología política* (Madrid: Tecnos, 1963) pp. 37–90; Z. Barbu *Democracy and Dictatorship* (London: Routledge, 1956).

# 3 THE STATE

Within any complex polity the most distinctive and at the same time the most comprehensive unit is the state. The state is a political institution that monopolises sovereignty over a territory, as well as the legitimate use of force within its boundaries, while claiming authority over all the people in it. Every state possesses a central agency, called government, which coordinates its entire political and administrative complex, dictates policies, gives orders and raises taxes from the population under its control. A government, in the strict sense of the word, is the executive nucleus of the state, and is always made up of a relatively small number of people.

Although there is some substance in the view that the state is an invention of modern times, born in the Europe of the Renaissance and coming to full development after the French Revolution, the kind of political organisation just defined has existed since much earlier times. The question of the exact origin of this institution is a matter that has puzzled social scientists ever since the old theory of a primeval political compact was long ago discarded as fanciful. Lewis Henry Morgan's early comparative studies of government and the state among Iroquois, Aztecs, Romans and Greeks led Friedrich Engels to develop the notion that the state is the inevitable product of the unequal distribution of political and economic power in any complex, stratified society. The ruling class needs a political structure to maintain the kind of social order it wants, and this is the state; the state, then, is merely the tool of the upper class, and government 'the executive committee of the ruling class'.[1] (This view has been incorporated into the Marxist ideology and is one of its main tenets.[2]) Without thereby fully contradicting the notion of the state as an institution at the service of the dominant stratum, some sociologists then developed the 'conquest theory of the state'. Although originating in the work of Ludwig Gumplowicz, it was Franz Oppenheimer who gave it a more convincing form. According to him (and to several other social scientists of his day) the state originated in the needs of conquest. The people who occupy a territory and pacify it are immediately thereafter confronted with the question of administration, taxation and control of the economic surplus; they must create a permanent apparatus of control, or remain in a barbarous state of continued plunder. The fact that the history of every state shows an element of conquest in it strengthens this theory considerably. Great Britain's institutions owe much to the Norman conquest; the Austrian state—with its Czechs, Magyars, Italians, Slovenes and other peoples—was held together by a central conquering Germanic power; the more rudimentary East African states south of the Sahara, as Richard Thurnwald has shown, were carved out by tribal warfare and subsequent conquest; so was the Inca empire. The examples are endless.[3]

Although some marginal objections can be levelled against this hypothesis[4] historical evidence seems to be overwhelmingly in its favour, especially if it is understood to mean not only conquest of one people by another, but also of several communities or tribes by another, perhaps with the same ethnic and cultural background. Egypt is a clear example of this last case, for the unification of the Nilotic clans, first into the Lower and Upper states and, later, into a single Egyptian state, was carried out internally by the final victory of a Southern faction, which installed its own priestly aristocracy and a single head—a supernatural pharoah— in the new capital of Memphis. (In well-developed states capitals are as necessary as governments. As the history of the great Tartar empires—the Turkish and the Mongol—shows, when tribal ties begin to weaken only a geographically centralised and city-based administration can keep the new state from rapid disintegration.) The expansion of the

Duchy of Muscovy into the Russian state and the unification of
Italy by Piedmontese invasion are further examples of state formation by internal conquest.

The characteristic of lasting states, however, is that once they
have sufficiently institutionalised the early phases conquest fades
into the past: a consciousness of kind develops among the inhabitants
of the territory, access to the higher posts of state administration
begins to be possible for people outside the old conquering groups,
which themselves begin to dissolve through sustained intermarriage.
Although integration is often slow, and memories and ethno-
political groups die hard (as events in Northern Ireland constantly
remind us), a transformation may then take place, especially under
conditions of modernity: the state may become a political arena for
every class, pressure group and party in the land, ceasing to be the
outright monopoly of a small ruling caste-like collectivity. Although
patterns of inequality persist and some groups have greater amounts
of control than others, certain states, based on the notion and value
of citizenship, develop; instead of remaining structures of oppression they become polities for freedom. To establish precisely under
which conditions this process can take place is one of the chief tasks
of political sociology.

## NOTES on Chapter VII, Section 3

1. L. Krader *Formation of the State* (Englewood Cliffs: Prentice Hall, 1968)
p. 23; F. Engels *The Origin of the Family, Private Property and the
State*, many editions.
2. R. Miliband *The State in Capitalist Society* (London: Weidenfeld, 1969);
N. Poulantzas *Pouvoir Politique et Classes Sociales* (Paris: Maspéro, 1968).
These left-wing critics have made conscious efforts to show that this
situation is not a simple one, and that there are several degrees of control
of the state apparatus depending on social class and occupational group;
the power elite though, remains for them in ultimate control of the entire
state. See also C. W. Mills *The Power Elite* (New York: Oxford University Press, 1963).
3. F. Oppenheimer *The State* (New York: Vanguard Press, 1926). R. Thurnwald Vol. 4 of *Die menschliche Gesellschaft* (Berlin & Leipzig: Gruyter,
1932).
4. H. Kammler *Der Ursprung des Staates* (Cologne: Westdeutscher Verlag,
1966).

## 4   ON THE VARIETIES OF POLITICAL OPPRESSION

It would be tempting to classify all polities as either 'coercive' or 'democratic', but tyrannies often include many consensual elements, while democracies, generally based on consensus, cannot do without some degree of coercion. The Athenian Republic was democratic at home, but imperialist and interventionist abroad. The United States—also a democracy—has conquered entire countries—for instance, the Philippines, after 1898—or has briefly invaded them to suit its own interests (as in the Dominican Republic in 1965). It is with these important qualifications in mind that we can make some observations about coercive political systems.

Although coercive polities—especially those based on traditional authority—do not exclude large consensual elements, they are systems in which open oppression is clearly institutionalised. To a large extent they may be said to be 'absolutist', that is to say that in them power is conceived as concentrated totally in the hands of a ruling class, an elite, a monarch, or a single political party. This 'absolutism' or monopoly of power by a limited number of people is based in a 'zero-sum' conception of power. In other words, when any individual or group outside the sphere of rulers increases its power and status, that of the rulers is reduced proportionately. It follows, therefore, that whenever possible steps are taken to prevent the rise of such a group or individual, to crush it if it has arisen. Groups outside the rulers which possess some power or influence are often 'tolerated' just so long as they are needed—as in the case of the Jews in medieval Europe. Early repression of trade unions in England was an example of reaction to this 'zero-sum' conception of power; the ruling classes were frightened of new structures of power arising outside their traditional control of the entire polity. 'Absolutist' control, though, is very often hypothetical, for there are fissures and built-in institutions within the system that preclude a perfect monopoly of power. In the Chinese empire the greatest despot could not ignore the established and age-old patterns of nepotism, favouritism, corruption, and local loyalties. Revolt or stubborn opposition has often caused ruthless governments to give in or make concessions to entire regions or social strata. Even the modern totalitarian state, the most elaborate of all absolutist states, has frequently had to act in this way.

There are several types of polity based fundamentally on coercion. Three can be mentioned. *Tyrannies*, in the strict sense of the word, are monarchies of traditional legitimacy, where a despot, often aided by his favourites, has transgressed the discretional limits established by custom. As Plato and Aristotle indicated, tyrannies are degenerate monarchies. Ivan the Terrible in Russia and Nero in Rome are notorious examples of tyrants. Yet the name has been extended colloquially to many types of political expression. *Dictatorships*, by contrast, are typical of the modern world, although they tend to occur in countries such as Greece, Portugal, Venezuela, the Argentine, Paraguay and Brazil where modernisation itself has not been an even or general process. (The classical type of dictatorship is, of course, very different; it is the emergency dictatorship, legally established in Rome by Senatorial will, for a specific period of time.) Dictatorial regimes possess an absolute control of the state and do not admit the existence of opposition groups, save in disguise. In the Portugal of the Salazar regime (1932–1974), because of international pressures, a degree of electioneering and opposition was sometimes allowed, but the omnipresence of the political police guaranteed the continued rule of the oligarchy. These regimes also tend to embrace ideologies of different types—in the Portuguese case a vague corporatism and semi-fascism, in the Ghana of the Redeemer (*Osagyefo*) Nkrumah (1949–1966), 'African' socialism—but these ideologies remain secondary to the absolute and personal power of the ruling cliques. Extensive use of other cultural sources of support is also common. Pope Pius XII pronounced the war against the democratic Republic in Spain a Crusade and blessed the victorious forces without reservation when it ended (1939). 'Papa Doc' Duvalier had a keen interest in the voodoo religion of Haiti and used it vigorously as a means of practically deifying himself in the eyes of the terrified populace. Thus, in spite of their numbers and their evident interest, it is very difficult to generalise about dictatorships, whether they be conservative authoritarian regimes or semi-socialist, 'left-wing' ones. Perhaps their relative lack of popularity among political scientists and sociologists[1] is due to the more spectacular features of outright totalitarian regimes.

The *totalitarian state* is, of all coercive political systems, the most clearly definable, and is historically unique, for it strives to leave no area of society uncovered or outside its reach and control. An official ideology and a 'party line' are its invariable characteristics; equally, the totalitarian state entails a very detailed, bureaucratic and paramilitary domination of the society by one single political party. This is achieved, as in other systems, by extensive use of terror and the political police, but here these elements do not operate haphazardly or through personal whim, as other coercive polities typically do. And totalitarian states are, of course, highly paranoid—they are all based on a theory of international conspiracy. A highly developed propaganda apparatus combined with a total monopoly of the mass media of communication is another fundamental trait of these regimes. For all these reasons totalitarian regimes can be defined as those in which there is almost complete identification of the state with the entire polity. This is not true of every other regime. Democracies leave large areas of the polity outside the direct (and even indirect) control of the state—unions, parties, political associations, groups of citizens who engage in spontaneous demonstrations. And many 'old-fashioned' semi-military dictatorships allow the existence of certain factions in the opposition so long as they do not attempt to mobilise diverse voluntary associations politically.

Social scientists have explored totalitarianism mainly from two different points of view: its genesis and its internal structure. The first view finds its modern origin in the classic work of de Tocqueville, who explored the possibility that modern polities, based on universal participation in the state and emerging from egalitarian currents, may by their own internal dynamics degenerate into a new kind of tyranny. Tocqueville thinks that under the new conditions of modern life

> Men, not being attached to each other any longer by the ties of caste, class, association, and family, are only inclined to busy themselves with their personal interests, always envisaging solely themselves and closing themselves up in a narrow individualism where all public virtue is suffocated. Despotism, far from fighting against this tendency, renders it irresistible, for it takes from the citizens all communal passion, all mutual need, all need to understand each other, all occasion of acting together; so to speak, it walls them within their private lives. They already tended to be alone: it now isolates them; they already cooled each other: it now freezes them.[2]

The fragmentation of the social web under the pressures of capitalist competition, individualist values and a struggle against aristocracy may thus erode a sense of hierarchy based on genuine human excellence. The time may then be ripe for totalitarian elites to seize power and impose the despotism which is bound to 'freeze' men. But the process is infinitely complex. Tocqueville himself distinguished two main paths towards this modern tyranny for which he could not find a satisfactory name; one was through universal competition, as in America, leading towards a complete alienation of individuals torn between egalitarian conformity and a senseless rat-race for status; the other path led through outright serfdom and a state-run regimentation of society, as in Russia.[3] This prediction appeared couched in prophetic terms, but it was the fruit of a careful study of the chief structural trends of large societies in their recent history. Contemporary students of totalitarianism have followed in Tocqueville's steps and have also traced its origins with a view to explaining its nature. Some, like Barrington Moore, have explored the very beginning of the process, in the original breakdown of traditional patterns of lordship and vassalage; others like Talmon, have looked into the historical birth of modern messianic mass politics, for instance in Jacobinism and Bavouism during the French Revolution; still others, like Hannah Arendt,[4] have examined its most recent precedents.

No general picture arises capable of expression in a single formula or in a few words. But this is not to say that no generalisations can be made about the social origins of totalitarianism, the conditions of political terror, the role of the secret police, the internal structure of the single party and all the other related problems, for scholarship in these matters has been reasonably successful. The effect of this scholarship upon the contemporary struggle against totalitarian tendencies in our societies can only be positive, and one hopes that as many minds as possible will be trained in the sociological discipline and become aware of its findings. 'Without knowledge democracy will surely fall. With knowledge, democracy may succeed.'[5]

## NOTES on Chapter VII, Section 4

1. Cf. however J. Linz 'An Authoritarian Regime: Spain' in E. Allardt *et alii Cleavages, Ideologies and Party Systems* (Helsinki: Academic Bookstore, 1964) pp. 291–341.
2. A. de Tocqueville *L'ancien regime et la Révolution* (Paris: Gallimard, 1952) pp. 73–74.
3. A. de Tocqueville *De la démocratie en Amérique* (Paris: Gallimard, 1951) Vol. II, pp. 430–31.
4. B. Moore, Jr. *op. cit.*; J. L. Talmon *The Origins of Totalitarian Democracy* (London: Secker & Warburg, 1952); H. Arendt *The Origins of Totalitarianism* (London: Allen & Unwin, 1951, 1858); S. J. Woolf ed. *European Fascism* (London: Weidenfeld, 1968).
5. H. D. Lasswell *The Analysis of Political Behaviour* (London: Routledge, 1948).

## 5 THE DEMOCRATIC POLITY

### Democracy as a social system

Democracy means government by the people, and, accordingly, countries in which the government is based on varying degrees of popular participation and control are called democracies. Yet sociologically democracy can be defined not as just one more type of state but rather as a particular mode of organising political life at all social levels. Democracy in this sense consists of a set of enacted values about each individual's right to participate in the political process by standing for office in an election, by electing his or her representatives, or by taking part in a varied series of public activities, which range from serving as a member of a jury to demonstrating freely in the streets on any issue. But as a social system democracy does not stop here. It has vital cultural underpinnings which are just as important as the inventory of legal rights and duties whose aim is to guarantee freedom and avoid tyranny. One of them is the acceptance by a large majority of the population of the existence of divergent opinions, and their recognition of the right of other people to exist and organise themselves politically under the same common system. This includes the active recognition of the right to dissent from majority opinions and from the chief policies of those in authority. All this presupposes that large sections of the population have internalised the notion that

> mankind are not infallible; that their truths, for the most part, are only half-truths; that unity of opinion, unless resulting from the fullest and freest comparison of opposite opinions, is not desirable, and diversity not an evil, but a good, until mankind are much more capable than at present of recognising all sides of the truth [These] are principles applicable to men's modes of action no less than to their opinions.[1]

The fact that most people in democratic societies may not be as articulate as John Stuart Mill, the author of these words, is not entirely relevant; what counts is that the political culture of democracy requires the practical and unreserved acceptance of pluralism, together with a notable degree of undogmatic attitudes towards ultimate 'truths' as they relate to matters of human coexistence.

Another basic cultural underpinning is communication. Democracy is the political system of public communication. The actions of government in democracies are publicly discussed in the press, among people, in open forums. Verbatim parliamentary debates are made available to the public. The administration of justice is also open. Public debates and even referenda often precede important decisions. In the midst of this system, though, varying degrees of secrecy are necessary for the proper functioning of government, but even their mere presence is a constant source of tension and turmoil.[2] Secrecy and democracy are, in the end, incompatible concepts, just as secrecy—a secret police, permanent conspiracy, control of the mass media, censorship and the crushing of all open criticism —is the essence of the opposite system, totalitarianism.

So much for the ideal type of democracy. Actual democracies are all so divergent from it in one or several respects that a ruthlessly analytical mind might even contend that democracies do not exist. In the first place, as in other fields in the world of social affairs, the very word 'democracy' possesses a great number of meanings. For some there can be no democracy under a capitalist system; for others democracy is a farce as long as there is a ruling class, or a single party, or an all-powerful chief of state. Another objection, which is as old as Plato's *Republic*, is that there can be no democracy where there is excessive political apathy, and where active citizens do not possess a high degree of intelligence and education, and a consistent concern with improving the quality of life as a whole. This, as Plato saw, could only take place in relatively reduced polities, united by community bonds and yet highly civilised. In this vein Lévi-Strauss affirms that 'true democracy . . . is to be found in communal life, even in that of the very smallest community'.[3] From this standpoint, once democracy loses its community character (the subtle equilibrium between *Gemeinschaft* and *Gesellschaft* which one finds in an imperfect state in, say, ancient Athens or in some early protestant colonies in North America), it also loses one of its most genuine traits. And, to complicate things further, the notion of democracy is so attractive that many dictatorial regimes presume to define themselves as democracies. And some socialist countries, reckless of tautology define themselves as a 'people's democracy'. But these difficulties, real as they are, are not enough to prevent recognising the fact that fairly democratic polities do exist—polities in which the law is held sovereign, where it can only be changed by peaceful means and by popular pressure, and where men are free to voice their disapproval of policies, and organise to change the government they dislike, without risking their lives or wellbeing in the process.[4]

*The sociology of democratic life*

Since timeless and perfect models of democratic polities seem to be found only in the minds of philosophers or in the holy writ of ideology, sociologists have tended to study democracy as it appears, with all its imperfections, in actual social life. That is to say that they have studied certain aspects of political life whose nature is unquestionably democratic (as, for instance, popular representation in government bodies) and their relationships to other sets of variables in each society. In so doing they have taken as much interest in factors that foster democratic life as in those which hinder it. Without attempting to exhaust the themes of the sociology of democratic life, a list of its chief problem areas can be drawn up. (Some other problem areas, not included in the present indicative list—such as 'militarism and democracy', 'technocracy and democracy'—will be treated elsewhere (VII, 5, 6; X, 3).

I   *Democracy and economic development*   That there is a very close relationship between the economic system, its degree of development, and the political system found in a society, is a platitude which begs all sorts of difficult questions (VI, 3, 4). It would be convenient if they were resolved by Seymour Martin Lipset's dictum that 'the more economically developed and literate a country is, the more likely it is to have a competitive party system'.[5] There is some truth in this assertion, which reflects to some extent some Western European and American commonsense assumptions. In the United States, for example, the two main parties share an astonishingly wide area of consensus as to both internal and external policies. Yet while Russia and most of the other Soviet states are literate and well developed economically (although their level of consumer goods is still low compared with that of some Western countries and Japan), there seems to be no indication that they are moving towards a plurality of parties. It is also true that utter poverty is nearly incompatible with a democratic order, and that one of the dilemmas of revolutionary regimes which try to bring about democracy in economically backward countries is the necessity for a disciplined regimentation of the population under the leadership of a strong party. Unless the notion of democracy is stretched to cover Chinese communism, Arab socialism of the Algerian or Egyptian type, and Cuban communism, the real chances for a fully fledged democracy will have to be reserved for societies which have reached a fairly high degree of economic development.

In the ancient city states of Greece democracy was the preserve of the affluent citizens; today, it is the privilege of affluent countries. As Lerner has shown, democracy and the several aspects of economic development—urbanisation, literacy, wealth, participation in the media of communication—are highly correlated, and, what is more, they appear in stages, the one leading to the other, with general political participation, or democracy, tending to be the crowning stage.[6] 'Economic development' is a neutral and misleading term; thus monopolistic capitalism and totalitarian socialism possess many antidemocratic features although they are both sources of economic growth. The search for the economic system of democracy presents a magnificent challenge to contemporary social scientists,[7] faced as they are with new and insidious forms of economic and political control even in the most modern and democratic countries of the world.

II *Democracy and electoral behaviour* Democracy is participation, but participation is not to be found evenly distributed over the whole of a society. In this context the study of political behaviour and that of social stratification overlap. The problems of 'middle-class conservatism', 'middle-class fascism', or 'working-class political apathy' are also those of power, status, degrees of social mobility, and life chances in each stratum of a society (VI, 3). Elections being a vital element of democracies and involving the whole of the enfranchised population, it is in the field of voting behaviour that most sociologists have concentrated their efforts. Perhaps the chief reason for this is the great ease with which data can be gathered in this field; election returns are hard, objective data, the ecology and the geography of elections can easily be drawn up, variations over time are equally easy to detect, and some correlations with class, occupation and educational background are readily obtainable. While this task is very necessary, there are other areas, harder to get at, but which need further study, such as the influence of 'political machines' over election campaigns, and the analysis of electoral motivation. However, some studies of election results have proved most fertile. Rudolf Heberle's analysis of election returns during the Weimar Republic in Germany proved that contrary to common assumptions, the Nazis did not appeal to the same electoral body as the traditional right in that country. In his study, which concentrated on the Schleswig-Holstein region, he was able to prove that it was the great landlords that were the more reluctant to vote Nazi. He also established other correlations, for instance, that purely agricultural zones show the greatest inclination towards extremist parties. (Later, Lipset was able to strengthen this hypothesis for Canada in a study on agrarian socialism in that country.[8]) The number of investigations along these lines keeps growing, and the possibilities for solid cross-national studies are now considerable, thus increasing the number of valid and complex generalisations on the subject of electoral behaviour. Studies such as Heberle's, concentrating on the phenomenon of anti-democratic parties thriving on the weaknesses of democracy, are particularly interesting for those who wish to preserve democracy.

III *Democracy and party politics* In theory one can conceive of both a partyless democracy and a single-party democracy. In practice, though, parties seem to be a necessity in order to maintain the required level of democratic public debate, non-violent opposition, and permanent countervailing check on the government which are the prerequisites of democracy. The interest of sociologists in political parties is centered around their patterns of recruitment, their rise and fall, and particularly their internal organisation. The early assumption that cleavages between parties were also cleavages in the stratification system soon had to be abandoned; religious, cultural and reference-group loyalties often play a more vital role in the whole democratic process than colour, class origins and identifications. Standards of education, occupational patterns, economic fluctuations and international events further complicate the picture, forcing sophisticated multivariate analyses in this field.[9] As for party internal organisation, the discussion still revolves round Roberto Michels' seminal work on oligarchy formation inside democratic parties. His 'iron law' of oligarchy has already been mentioned (VI, 3) in the context of stratification. In the life of parties, leaders, he thinks, possess superior knowledge, have greater political skill and keep control of internal communication lines. Eventually they become a ruling group which cannot be unseated. Even if they come from a party with a lower-class base, if it becomes successful they enter the ranks of the ruling class; in their turn they create oligarchies and are thus severed from their origins. Evidence on the soundness of Michels' thesis has been gathered by sociologists who cannot exactly be accused of conservative or right-wing leanings.[10] The point can be made, however, that experienced leaders of parties, well seasoned in democratic politics and having experienced at least several spells in opposition (and thus having tasted defeat) are not on the whole a threat to democracy itself. On the other hand, party splits, conflict between generations (IX, 6), and new revolutionary trends often have the healthy effect of shattering their hold over the party.

IV *Democracy and pressure groups* The politics of multiparty democracies do not end with the party. Other political groups are allowed to form and enter the struggle. Some pressure groups are organised *ad hoc*, by people concerned with one issue, in order to try to influence parliaments or governments to act on their behalf. Pressure groups, of course, lobby for all sorts of causes, and many of them are quite ruthless: tobacco manufacturers, for instance, will do everything in their power to prevent the passing of any anti-smoking law. In some countries in some instances pressure groups use the most undemocratic methods available, such as bribes and threats to achieve their ends. Pressure groups—or interest groups, as they are also called—concentrate on narrower and (for them) more urgent issues than those of parties; their failure or success in getting things done their way reveals many hidden elements of the real power structures of a society.[11]

V *Democracy and public opinion* The constant making of de-mands to the powers-that-be is an essential feature of a democracy. (In fact an age-old definition of democracy is that it is govern-ment by the word.) Since parliaments and other assemblies cannot exhaust the expression of opinions or ventilate all the possible issues arising in a country, public opinion forums—especially those re-presented by the press, the radio, the academic world, and the party conference—are also necessary. The flow of public opinion into the government is one of the chief 'inputs' it receives. Equally, public reaction in democratic states is used as a way of sounding out the citizenry—or concrete social groups—about future politics, with the aim of avoiding political mistakes. Public opinion must there-fore be distinguished from mere rumours, the *vox populi* and other traditional forms of popular 'opinion', which, understandably, are still very important in dictatorships and totalitarian states. This problem area of the sociology of democracy has been explored in several directions, such as the patterns of the flow of communica-tion, the influence of prominent members within groups in shaping public opinion, the role of pressure groups in controlling public opinion and distorting it to suit their own purposes, the tensions be-tween government secrecy and the press, the rise of the press as an entire new power within the polity, the insidious use of propaganda to shape public opinion, and other related questions.[12]

VI *Democracy and local power* One of the first findings the student of the sociology of democracy comes up against is that power and authority are not evenly distributed over a territory. In addition to its different distribution according to institutions, classes, parties and other social formations, power varies with local communities; thus there can be said to be an ecology of power. In fact numerous studies have shown that the structure of power varies so much that at first generalisations appeared to be almost impossible. This has naturally become a challenge to political sociologists, who have explored the structural characteristics of territorial communities (especially local communities) in order to determine their relationship to the patterns of power and the political decision-making processes. Since most studies have discovered that the upper ranks of occupational stratification occupy the key power positions in the local community, further evidence of the permanence of strong unspoken non-egalitarian trends within the framework of overtly democratic societies has been gathered. In addition to this, studies on the 'political machine' or the 'mafia' and its interference with the democratic process have served to enrich our understanding of democratic polities and their limitations.[13] It is important, however, that future students of community power structures should also look at this problem from the opposite angle, exploring the process whereby either legitimate central powers or local democratic forces undermine, and later dissolve, local patterns of political oppression and parasitism. Both phenomena occur in the democratic polity, but it is the study of the second that will finally prove most rewarding.

## NOTES on Chapter VII, Section 5

1. J. S. Mill *On Liberty* (Garden City: Doubleday, 1961 ed.) p. 532. Cf. also L. T. Hobhouse *Liberalism* (London: Williams and Norgate, 1911).
2. G. Simmel 'Das Geheimnis und die Geheime Gessellschaft' in *Soziologie* (Leipzig: Duncker & Humboldt, 1908) pp. 257–304; E. A. Shils *The Torment of Secrecy* (Glencoe: Free Press, 1956).
3. V. Mora 'Una hora amb Lévi-Strauss' *Serra d'Or*, August 1967, Vol. IX, no. 8.
4. For some of the above problems cf. C. Friedrich's chapter on 'The Dimensions of Equality and Freedom' in his *Man and his Government* (New York: McGraw Hill, 1963) pp. 288–387; and T. Geiger, 'Die Nüchterne Gesellschaft' in *Demokratie ohne Dogma* (Munich: Szczesny, 1964) pp. 211–361.
5. S. M. Lipset 'Political Sociology' in N. J. Smelser, *Sociology: an Introduction* (New York: Wiley, 1967) p. 449, basing his statement on a number of studies.

6. D. Lerner *The Passing of Traditional Society* (Glencoe: Free Press, 1958) p. 63. Relevant passages also quoted by Lipset *op. cit.* pp. 455–56.
7. On the problems of democracy and its relationship with the economy, cf. J. Schumpeter *Capitalism, Socialism, and Democracy* (London: Allen and Unwin, 1943; R. Dumont *Cuba, est-il socialiste?* (Paris: Seuil, 1970); O. Sik *Plan and Market under Socialism* (White Plains: International Arts and Sciences Press, 1967); J. Child *Sociologists, Economists and Democracy* (London: Collier-Macmillan, 1970).
8. R. Heberle *From Democracy to Nazism* (University of Louisiana, 1945); S. M. Lipset *Agrarian Socialism* (University of California, 1950).
9. Cf. R. Alford *Party and Society* (Chicago: Rand McNally, 1963).
10. R. Michels *op. cit.*; A. Gouldner ed. *Studies in Leadership* (New York: Harper, 1950).
11. H. W. Ehrmann *Interest Groups on Four Continents* (University of Pittsburgh, 1958). For Michels' thesis in the Communist countries see M. Duverger *La démocratie sans le peuple* (Paris: Seuil, 1967).
12. B. R. Berelson and M. Janowitz eds. *Reader in Public Opinion and Communication* (New York: Free Press, 1966, 2nd ed.); G. Vedel ed. *La dépolitisation, mythe ou realité?* (Paris: Armand Colin, 1962).
13. Chapters by, respectively, P. Rossi, N. E. Long and R. O. Schulze in L. A. Coser ed. *Political Sociology* (New York: Harper, 1966) pp. 132–180; P. A. Allum *Politics and Society in Post-War Naples* (Cambridge University, 1972); F. Hunter *Community Power Structure* (Garden City: Doubleday, 1963).

# 6 THE MILITARY

The systematic exercise of violence by organised groups is the origin of permanent military institutions in societies. Whether the military monopolises power or share it, or appear only as the armed branch of the state, their institutions form a subsystem of the general political system. In some societies, where a fusion of powers is prevalent, such as feudal societies, the military are identified with a particular stratum—the nobility—and therefore the same persons hold civil, military and economic authority. At the opposite end of the spectrum we find modern countries such as Sweden or Switzerland where in times of peace the phrase 'the military are very powerful' only means that they are just another professional pressure group to be reckoned with.

In the contemporary world intermediate instances between these two possibilities are common; there are cases when the military establishment, more than just another pressure group, functions as one key element in the power structure of the state—as with the

Pentagon in the United States and the Red Army in the Soviet Union—although ultimate vital decisions continue to be taken by other institutions—Congress and the President in the United States, the Communist Party Central Committee and the Secretary General in the Soviet Union. Further militarisation of the polity occurs when the army is in command of the central organs of the state. In every one of these cases the military organisation of a society consists of a set of institutions that are in direct relationship to the central authority of the state. Private armies and a fully fledged state are incompatible; thus even mercenary armies act under the authority of a state. For these reasons, although military sociology has grown into a special field of enquiry, it must be considered as a legitimate aspect of political sociology.

The study of these matters may well start with an investigation into the degree of militarisation of the society concerned. Militarisation, however, means two different things: on the one hand it refers to the degree of militancy and militaristic regimentation a society is subjected to, and on the other it refers to what Stanislav Andreski has called the 'military participation ratio'. This can be defined as the 'proportion of militarily utilised individuals in the total population'. The military participation ratio may be actual (the one that really obtains in a society) or optimum (the ratio which, within the given technico-tactical conditions, would enable a state to attain the maximum military strength).[1] Obviously the need in this context is to find out what determines the degree of militarisation of a society and its polity at a given moment in history, and what determines its effectiveness, both internally and externally. As one might expect, the variables are many and not always easy to classify. Internal strife, weakening other groups and leaving the army as 'arbiter of the situation', may be a factor in its favour; intense industrialisation combined with a cultural tradition of secular government may be a factor against it. Finer, by assuming that the great frequency of *coups d'état* in the contemporary world—especially in places such as Africa and South and Central America—cannot be a sporadic phenomenon, has been able to arrive at some generalisations in this area. He puts forward the hypothesis that military coups are the effect of several principal forces, such as the capacity and propensity of the armed forces to intervene in a coup, the level of economic development, and the age of the affected state. His two following tables[2] show remarkable regularities:

*States experiencing military coups (successful or unsuccessful)*
*in relation to per capita incomes*
(1 January 1958 to 31 December 1967)

| Class | Gross national product per capital in $ | Number of states in class | number of states experiencing coups (square brackets denote unsuccessful attempts) | Percentage of states affected |
|-------|------------------------------------------|----------------------------|-----------------------------------------------------------------------------------|-------------------------------|
| I | 45–105 | 35 | 21 [5] | 60 |
| II | 106–261 | 32 | 16 [5] | 50 |
| III | 262–835 | 29 | 6 [2] | 20 |
| IV | 836 upwards | 19 | 2 [1] | 10 |
| not available | | 8 | 1 | |
| Totals | | 123 | 46 [13] | |

*States experiencing military coups (successful or unsuccessful)*
*in relation to age of state since independence*
(1 January 1958 to 31 December 1967)

| Period since independence (to 31 December 1967) | Number of states in class | Number of states affected by coups | Percentage of states affected by coups |
|--------------------------------------------------|----------------------------|-------------------------------------|------------------------------------------|
| Over 150 years | 25 | 7 | 28 |
| 149–15 years | 55 | 19 | 34 |
| Less than 15 years | 43 | 20 | 47 |

Similar correlations could perhaps be established between coups and the relative weight of social classes (for instance with either the weakness or strength of the industrial bourgeoisie in each country); and further precision can be achieved by reference to particular cultural areas. Thus in South America 'praetorianism' has been a specific pattern of army domination and intervention, even when the army has not actually been in power.[3] (During a period of Roman history, certain legions used to select the emperor and the *praetor* was the consul who was the leader of the army.) By contrast, in the communist countries the same characteristics of the army that make it so powerful elsewhere—unified command, discipline, even the use of weapons—are assumed by the party. Under such circumstances, the army is no match for an equally disciplined and hierarchical party, with a secret police and a complete control of the means of communication. In addition to this, of course, the party itself infiltrates the army, thus controlling it from within.

All these phenomena are related to concomitant cultural patterns or ideologies. One of the most important is militarism, a cultural complex which includes militancy and the predominance of army and paramilitary organisations in a society. Militarism is not confined to whole societies and their armies but can exist in all sorts of organisations within societies. Fascist parties everywhere have adopted militarism and have organised themselves along army lines with uniforms, unified leadership, and blindly followed orders, and have made strategic use of violence. But, in curious contrast to this extreme case of non-army military organisation, we find religious and civic institutions where a high degree of militarism is equally part and parcel of their ideology and organisation (the Jesuits, the Boy Scouts, the Salvation Army, for example) although their pacific behaviour is a basic part of their existence.

Finally, military sociology focuses on the army itself—its patterns of recruitment, promotion, ideology and internal conflicts. Modern armies, especially under the increasing pressure of technological efficiency and innovation, must strike a balance between the heroic 'fighter spirit' and the organisational, technological and bureaucratic exigencies of today. This frequently results in new types of tension in the careers and expectations of the officers. The United States epitomises several of these contradictory trends, and Morris Janowitz's study of the military profession in that country has made an important contribution in this area. In the first place, and in spite of his country's military might, the American officer does not command the high status in civil society accorded to the military in other places; in the second place the contemporary world role of the United States results in constant change in its army. Janowitz has revealed the internal transformations of its authority structure, the 'narrowing skill differential between military and civilian elites', the shifts in career patterns, and the new role of ideological indoctrination. In addition to this type of investigation[5] cross-national studies of armies and their relationship to society are now creating a sound basis for future generalisations,[6] even though in some countries, because of the nature of their regime, access to reliable and interesting data is still understandably difficult.

*NOTES on Chapter VII, Section 6*

1. S. L. Andreski *Military Organisation and Society* (London: Routledge, 1968, 1st ed. 1954) p. 33.
2. S. E. Finer 'Armed Forces and the Political Process' in J. Gould ed.

*Penguin Social Sciences Survey 1968* (Harmondsworth: Penguin, 1968) pp. 16–33, tables on p. 28.
3. V. Alba *El militarismo, ensayo sobre un fenómeno político-social ibero-americano* (Universidad Autónoma de Méjico, 1959) pp. 22–23.
4. M. Janowitz *The Professional Soldier* (Glencoe: Free Press, 1960).
5. For Great Britain cf. C. B. Otley 'The Social Origin of British Army Officers', *Sociol. Rev.*, July 1970, pp. 213–39 and 'The Educational Background of British Army Officers', *Sociology* Vol. 7, May 1973, pp. 191–209.
6. M. Howard *Soldiers and Governments* (London: Eyre and Spottiswoode, 1957).

# 7 THE BUREAUCRACY

The government of groups and individuals entails, in every developed society, an administration. Administration is the routine management by the authorities of foreseeable cases that require its intervention; normally these cases are solved by the delegation of power by the authorities to specific institutions and persons. The study of administration, therefore, is also part of the study of the polity but, unlike the case of military sociology, administrative social action goes far beyond the sphere of the political. Especially in modern pluralistic societies numerous administrative bodies fall outside the political realm. This is particularly true of *bureaucratic* administration, which is the most formal and impersonal type of administrative behaviour. Bureaucracy is embodied in *formal organisations* which are, in Martin Albrow's definition, 'social units where individuals are conscious of their membership and legitimise their cooperative activities primarily by reference to the attainment of impersonal goals rather than to moral standards.'[1] The full meaning of this abstract definition will become apparent as we look into the nature of bureaucratic behaviour, which is the procedure followed by every formal organisation. Bureaucracies are only found in complex societies, for in the preliterate world lineages, oral tradition, military and religious leadership and economic activity are too circumscribed to allow for the development of these organisations. They began to appear with the rise of civilisations, first in Mesopotamia and Egypt, and reached a high degree of sophistication in some higher pre-industrial empires such as Byzantium, China, and the Spanish Empire.[2] Yet it is after the industrial revolution in England and the French Revolution that formal structures based on the bureaucratic treatment of affairs begin to attain the substantial degree of refinement we know today in armies, private enterprises, international organisations, political parties, scientific institutions, banking and large corporations.

According to Weber's classical definition, ideally bureaucracy may be characterised by the rationality of its decisions, the impersonality of social relationships, the routine of tasks and the centralisation of authority. It is obvious that this authority must belong to Weber's 'rational legal' type that we saw above, and that bureaucracy must therefore be subject to a legal code claiming obedience 'at least on the part of the members of the organisation'. Thus in bureaucracies the person who obeys and carries out an order obeys 'the law' and not the personal orders of his superior; in fact his superior, 'holds an office' in the name of that law or system of statutes, and if removed another person with the same authority will occupy his place.[3] All business is transacted in an office, which is the central focus of bureaucracy. There is in addition another series of structural traits which provide for:

1. fixed spheres of jurisdiction for each member of the bureaucratic institutions;
2. a clearly ranked or gradual hierarchical system of authority, which is centralised;
3. a central system of registers;
4. a system of administrative spheres of competence;
5. an official activity of the employee which is completely separated from his 'private life';
6. systematic and specific rules which rigorously define the procedure to be followed in each case;
7. recruitment based on technical qualification, and promotion based on seniority, with remuneration on the basis of fixed amounts of money; and
8. the official entirely separated from the ownership of the means of administration and without appropriation of his position.[4]

Looking at these traits it becomes at once apparent that bureaucracy is a very special case of division of labour, and that its consequences for the society which uses it must be far-reaching. Bureaucracy heightens the efficiency of the state to an unprecedented degree; censuses and civil registries allow a thorough military mobilisation of the population, an effective health and welfare service, long-range economic planning, and every other form of large or small operation which needs administration. In fact, the modern state is a bureaucratic state, and so are most of the different institutions of any size that exist under it, such as ministries, communication networks, universities, armies and public and private business enterprises.

As bureaucracy began to evolve and its enormous advantages began to be realised, men began to complain about it. As a matter of fact sociologists have been at pains to use the word bureaucracy in a completely neutral sense, for in common speech bureaucracy tends to be synonymous with red tape, lazy officials, unnecessary steps, and even with modern society itself, which is seen as thoroughly bureaucratised. These features are, in varying degrees, true characteristics of bureaucracy; they are its dysfunctions. Bureaucracy is the perfect example of the easy divorce between reason and rationalisation (III, 3); the Nazi extermination camps were bureaucratised. The Soviet secret police and the American Central Intelligence Agency are both formal organisations, yet it must be remembered that genocide, espionage, and counter-insurgency policies are as old as mankind, and were practised well before a rudimentary stage of bureaucracy had been reached. The less extreme and dramatic dysfunctions of bureaucracy—senseless and unnecessary delays, excessive paperwork, excess personnel, gross mistakes—certainly exist. As always, these features of bureaucracy are not capricious. Since its inception the sociology of bureaucracy has tried to relate them to concrete historical situations within the societies concerned. Tocqueville related the Napoleonic administration to the Republican state, which in turn, as he showed, was not a new construct but the direct heir to the centralising and rationalising tendencies of the absolutist Ancient Regime of the Bourbons.[4] In his view it appears as a manifestation of deeper secular trends towards rationalisation of work and egalitarianism in western cultures, for in principle bureaucracy treats its affairs as 'cases' of similar weight. (Weber himself developed his ideal type of bureaucracy on these assumptions.) Later a host of social scientists studied the problems of bureaucracy and were able to refine considerably our knowledge of the complex universe covered by the notion; Merton looked into the 'bureaucratic personalities' that are bred by bureaucracy and the negative aspects they develop; Gouldner made the much-needed distinction between 'representative' and 'punishment-centred' bureaucracy; Blau, investigating a federal law-enforcement agency in the United States, showed how infringement of certain rules improves the chances of achieving the goals of the agency; and Albrow's effort in the direction of conceptual clarification in this area has brought critically together its many strands and tendencies.[6]

The debate over bureaucracy has received a fresh impetus with the rise of 'technocracy', that is, the emergence of a new technical elite dominating the entire society. In people's minds the technocrat has supplanted the bureaucrat as the arch villain of the modern democracy, and as the new elitist in the perennial struggle against equality. Computerised bureaucracy, organisation theory and technical competence have invested experts in every field with important controls of decision hitherto reserved to the great industrialist, the high civil servant and, of course, the holder of political office. Much ideological discussion has obscured the issues at hand,[7] but in the end it has triggered off a serious concern for the true relationships between technocracy and democracy (X, 3), which might heighten our active concern for the latter[8] in this new and unexpected phase in the historical development of the logic of bureaucracy. However, with the rise of 'technocracy'—in the sense that technocrats share, not monopolise, power (and its effects) the entire concept of bureaucracy must now be questioned. In the most advanced formal organisations the old-type bureaucrat has disappeared, and new procedures—and new social structures—are being erected to replace him. The intensive use of electronic and computerised machinery is making this change possible. Accordingly a new range of important problems is emerging for the citizen from this latest stage in the history of what has until now been grouped under the general name of bureaucracy.

## NOTES on Chapter VII, Section 7

1. M. Albrow 'The Study of Organisations—Objectivity or Bias?' in J. Gould *Penguin Social Sciences Survey 1968, op. cit.* p. 162.
2. S. N. Eisenstadt *The Political Systems of Empires* (Glencoe: Free Press, 1963).
3. M. Weber *Wirtschaft . . . op. cit.* pp. 124–28; Eng. trans. *Theory of Social . . . op cit.*, pp. 329–30.
4. M. Weber *Wirtschaft . . . op. cit.*, pp. 124–28; *Theory of Social . . . op. cit.* pp. 333–34. These and the above statements about bureaucracy are set out here in a simplified form.
5. A. de Tocqueville *L'ancien regime . . . op. cit.*
6. R. Merton ed. *Reader in Bureaucracy* (Glencoe: Free Press, 1952) pp. 361–71; A. Gouldner *Patterns of Industrial Bureaucracy* (Glencoe: Free Press, 1954); P. Blau *The Dynamics of Bureaucracy* (The University of Chicago, 1955); M. Albrow *Bureaucracy* (London: Pall Mall, 1970). Cf. also N. Mouzelis *Organization and Bureaucracy* (London: Routledge, 1967); A. Sauvy *La bureaucratie* (Paris: PUF, 1961); M. Crozier *Le phénomène bureaucratique* (Paris: Seuil, 1963).
7. J. Burnham *The Managerial Revolution* (Harmondsworth: Penguin, 1962 ed.); M. Djilas *The New Class* (London: Thames and Hudson, 1957).
8. K. Renner *Demokratie und Bureaukratie* (Vienna: Europa Verlag, 1947); R. Boisdé, *Technocratie et démocratie* (Paris: Plon, 1964).

# VIII The Social Knowledge of Reality

## 1  THE SOCIOLOGY OF KNOWLEDGE

It is a postulate of the sociological concept of culture that man acquaints himself with his world through the contents of the culture in which he lives; it is also a postulate—illustrated by the nature of language and the complexities of social action—that he does not simply mirror culture and reproduce it in his life: he enters into an active relationship with it, in which innovation, environmental modifications, and dissent are as important as compliance, consensus, and identification (IV, 1, 2). Through this relationship man helps to maintain and transform his social world. To a great extent culture is the awareness of the reality which includes beliefs, accumulated experiences, transmitted information about 'objective' events or phenomena, bodies of doctrine, techniques. We can call all this a 'knowledge' of reality, well aware that we are not referring to the knowledge of ultimate truths, but to the ways a given society —or rather the groups and individual members of each of its parts— 'know' the world, or think they know it. Our axiom in this respect is that human knowledge is socially determined, though, in agreement with the above postulates about the nature of culture, it would be wrong to assume that all knowledge is social knowledge. What is meant, rather, is that the social factor in the determination of knowledge is always present; society always colours, orients and shapes the perception men have of their world, whether they are scientists, philosophers, nomadic shepherds, nuns, seamen or soldiers. It is for this reason that a sociology of knowledge is possible. It can be best defined, in the words of Peter Berger and Thomas Luckman, as that branch of sociology which concerns itself with 'everything that passes for "knowledge" in a society'.[1]

Ever since it began to be used intensively and systematically by historians of ideas and sociologists alike, the sociological contribution to the understanding of knowledge has proved most fruitful, and, thanks to it, thought has ceased to be either hypostasised or conceived as some mysterious, independent force which could not be accounted for in human terms. But one of the dangers brought about by the very success of this approach is the carelessness with which many critics and authors now presume to offer a sociological 'explanation' of a particular doctrine, work of art, belief or idea. To say, for instance, that Immanuel Kant's theory of matter reflects the secluded life of a Prussian professor during the late stages of the Enlightenment is acceptable, but it tells us absolutely nothing about the truth or falsity of Kantian metaphysics. Such metaphysics must be criticised in its own terms, according to the rules of logic and philosophical argument. There is a philosophical epistemology which is found side by side with a sociological epistemology; the realisation that far from cancelling they often illuminate each other is rewarding. Sociological reductionism in science, philosophy, and even in art and religion (ie explaining everything in sociological terms) suspiciously echoes ideological notions such as 'Jewish science' (used by the Nazis) and 'bourgeois physics' (used by the Stalinists), even though the sociological reductionists themselves generally use similar terms in ignorance rather than with malice (1, 2, 4).

Our definition of the sociology of knowledge as that branch of sociology which studies the social processes and conditions that influence peoples' perception and understanding of their world implies that its range and scope is anything but narrow. Even if, for the sake of argument, we identify the sociology of knowledge with the study of the social conditions that are necessary for the discovery of truth, we shall not be able to limit it to science and philosophy. The world is perceived in many ways; poetry and mysticism are also ways to truth. Clearly only the most insensitive of men would assert that a seascape painting by Turner has nothing to communicate about a storm that a competent meteorologist could not express better. But the actual social process of the determination of knowledge is very different in each of these instances. Confronted with its varieties, the discipline has tended to develop in several overlapping branches, of which the following is a brief list.

I *The Sociology of science and philosophy*   This is concerned with the study of economic, political and cultural factors which influence knowledge. Merton, for instance, has pointed out the role of Puritanism and religious fervour in fostering the growth of the natural sciences within the framework of the Royal Society, in Newton's England.[2] (The social sciences themselves have been the object of this type of enquiry, and the study of the 'sociology of sociology' has thus become a legitimate exercise.[3]) Though not always under the specific name of 'the sociology of science' or 'the sociology of philosophy' this tendency has a long history. Auguste Comte's theory of positivist thought in the modern age as superseding older and (as he saw it) less rational patterns of knowledge, established this interest at the very inception of sociology. Weber's studies of the growth and spread of rationality in the West under the bourgeois mentality as well as those of Georg Simmel on the effects of a money economy upon quantitative habits of thought are important stages in this trend.[4] Philosophers and historians of science have also made very valuable contributions to this branch of the sociology of knowledge. Michael Polanyi's investigation of the role of personal knowledge processes in scientific discovery, and Thomas Kuhn's theory about the internal structure of scientific revolutions, have helped to shake up the more complacent attitudes and established theories about social causation of rational, scientific and philosophical ideas.[5] Finally some sociologists, such as Pitirim Sorokin and Georges Gurvitch, undeterred by the vast complexity of the area, have boldly related the main types of social system found in the history of mankind to their cognitive systems, thus keeping alive in our day the ambitious tradition of Comte and Spencer.[6]

II *The sociology of literature*  The sociologist does not approach literature as an artistic expression but rather as a document through which the inner structures of a society can be investigated. No matter how fanciful or farfetched the literary act of creation may be, Lucien Goldman claimed, it is still a document which, if properly decoded, is bound to reveal the latent relationships, values and beliefs of the writer's world.[7] The sociology of literature is very closely connected with the study of readerships, audiences, and popular and mass culture.

III *The sociology of popular and mass culture*  The research into myths, sagas, legends and folklore has its roots in the historian's work in these fields. The sociological approach, however, has shed new light on this area, as may be exemplified by Peter and Iona Opie in their study of the language and lore of English children,[8] not to mention the considerable amount of anthropological work which has explored these traditions among the primitive. The specific problem of how the primitive know the world is, in fact, one of the overriding preoccupations of all sociologists of pre-industrial societies.[9] The spread of the mass media—popular newspaper, television, the radio—and the new patterns of communication thus established, as well as the changes in perception and their consequences, have promoted the growth of an entire new problem area and field of research[10] (X, 3).

IV *The sociology of religion* (VIII, 3)

V *The sociology of ideology* (VIII, 4)

VI *The sociology of education*   The more learning and socialisation processes have been put into the hands of secondary institutions such as schools, universities, special training courses, in the place of traditional primary group education and on-the-job learning, the more important has the sociology of education become. This branch of sociology is obviously concerned with the whole system of formal education of pupils and their teachers. However, as a branch of the sociology of knowledge the sociology of education examines the cultural contents of the knowledge transmitted, and analyses the relationship between power and knowledge and between educational and scientific policy and higher learning, as well as the role played by the knowledge gained by research into the polity and the economy.[11] (IX, 6)

VII *The sociology of intellectuals*   Every complex society has had men devoted to using, interpreting, and criticising the world of man. Since the beginning of the modern era, however, a new type of man has arisen—the intellectual, whose importance in the cultural scene can hardly be exaggerated. (Historical precedents for the modern intellectual can, of course, easily be found, especially in classical Western culture.) Intellectuals have a direct relationship with knowledge—in fact, they claim to be producing it. And 'new' knowledge—not just the pious preservation of tradition (although this is also a function of intellectuals)—has become vital to the modern world. Their marginality to power, their influence on it (or direct access to it), their role in the fabrication of ideology or in its denunciation—these are only some of the fields investigated by this branch of the sociology of knowledge.[12] (VIII, 4)

VIII *The sociology of everyday life*—Everyday life has a cognitive dimension that has long been overlooked by students of the sociology of knowledge, with the conspicuous exception of Georg Simmel; now, however, several sociologists claim that it is by a basic study of everyday situations that sociologists will come to know how people build their knowledge of others, of themselves, and of society generally. These students of society, by investigating the way people actually understand each other, how they create a language and why they accept particular assertions about reality as true (or false), have caused us to analyse important assumptions which—enthralled, as it were, by the more spectacular issues of cultural life, such as ideological strife and scientific revolutions[18]—we had previously accepted without question.

These eight fields do not cover the whole domain of the sociology of knowledge; other fields, such as the sociology of art and the sociology of language, also fall partially within its interests. Since it is impossible to examine each of them in detail, only two problem areas—religion and ideology—have been chosen as examples. Before introducing them, however, some observations will be made on the nature of belief.

## *NOTES on Chapter VIII, Section 1*

1. P. L. Berger and T. Luckmann *The Social Construction of Reality* (London: Allen Lane–Penguin, 1967) p. 26.
2. R. K. Merton *Social Theory, op. cit.* pp. 531–628.
3. R. W. Friedrichs *A Sociology of Sociology* (New York: Free Press; London: Collier Macmillan, 1970); E. A. Shils 'Tradition, Ecology and Institution in the History of Sociology' in *Daedalus* Vol. 99, no. 4, Fall 1970, pp. 760–825.
4. For Weber see above VII, 7 and below, VIII, 3; G. Simmel *Philosophie des Geldes* (Leipzig: Duncker & Humboldt, 1904) and 'Die Grossstädte und das Geistesleben' in K. Bucher *et alii die Grossstadt* (Dresden: Gehe Stiftung, 1902–1903).
5. M. Polanyi *Personal Knowledge* (London: Routledge, 1958); T. Kuhn *The Structure of Scientific Revolutions* (University of Chicago, 1962).
6. P. Sorokin see IV, 2; G. Gurvitch *Les cadres sociaux de la connaissance* (Paris: PUF, 1966).
7. L. Goldmann *Le dieu caché* (Paris: Gallimard, 1955); Eng. trans. (London: Routledge, 1946); L. Goldmann ed. special issue on sociology of the novel *Revue de l'Institut de Sociologie* (Brussels, 1969) no. 3; R. Escarpit *et alii La litterature et le social* (Paris: Flammarion, 1970); J. Rockwell 'Normative Attitudes of Spies in Fiction' in R. Rosenberg and D. M. White eds. *Mass Culture Revisited* (New York: Van Nostrand, 1971) pp. 325–340.
8. Peter and Iona Opie *The Lore and Language of Schoolchildren* (Oxford: Clarendon, 1960).

9. C. Lévi-Strauss *La pensée sauvage* (Paris: Plon, 1962).
10. R. Rosenberg and D. M. White eds. *Mass Culture* (London: Collier Free Press, 1960) and *Mass Culture Revisited, op. cit.*; G. de Torre *Minorías y masas en la cultura y en el arte contemporáneos* (Barcelona: EDHASA, 1963); J. D. Halloran *The Effects of Mass Communication* (Leicester University Press, 1964); R. Escarpit *Sociologie de la litterature* (Paris: PUF, 1968); R. Escarpit *The Book Revolution* (Paris: UNESCO, 1966).
11. A. H. Halsey, J. Floud, C. A. Anderson *Education, Economy and Society* (New York: Free Press, 1961).
12. L. A. Coser *Men of Ideas* (New York: Free Press, 1965); J. Benda *La trahison des clercs* (Paris: Pauvert, 1965); R. Aron *L'opium des intellectuels* (Paris: Calmann-Levy, 1955); Eng. trans. (London: Secker, 1957); F. Ayala *Razón del mundo* (Buenos Aires: Losada, 1944).
13. A. Schütz *Collected Papers* (The Hague: Nijhoff, 1962); P. L. Berger, J. Habermas in H. P. Dreitzel *Patterns of Communicative Behavior* (New York: Macmillan, 1970).

# 2 BELIEFS

Beliefs are firm convictions about reality, both about its ultimate nature and about its particular aspects and issues; their truth of falsity cannot always be tested empirically. The constellation of beliefs prevalent in a society, or in one of the parts of a society, can be considered as a subsystem of the general cultural system, since beliefs do not appear in isolation but in conjunction with attitudes, norms and values. The distinction between these latter and beliefs is rather fine: values are about desirability, goodness and beauty (and their opposite qualities) while beliefs are about truth or falsity. (IV, 2.) Sociology is interested in beliefs for two reasons: first, they are usually collective representations, shared by numbers of people, and thus generalisations about them become possible; second, they orient social action, and account for social cohesion.

Beliefs can be said to be oriented towards three different dimensions. First, some are about the past. They represent the historical consciousness of each group, collectivity or society. 'National consciousness', 'tribal pride', 'revolutionary tradition' are examples of such beliefs. Second, there are beliefs about the present. These shape social action and determine the future of a group. In a sense beliefs about the present and the future are one, since often the former is seen in terms of the latter. Beliefs about the present largely determine the way the situation is defined by the people concerned. (The definition of a situation is the way people evaluate their social and physical environment before making decisions about it.[1])

Third, there are beliefs about causation. Sicilian villagers take the images of their patron saints up to the streams of burning lava flowing from Mount Etna in the belief that they will stop it from advancing upon their houses and orchards. Many British, Danish and American middle-class men and women consult horoscopes in the belief that the stars guide their lives. Doctors engage in cancer research in the belief that the scientific method is the only one that will one day discover its cure. Thus, in spite of diffidence, scepticism and other related psychological processes, men must hold some cause-and-effect notions in order to function properly.[2]

A prerequisite of beliefs is that they appear as final and conclusive knowledge about reality, irrespective (as has been emphasised) of their objective truth or falsity. Often these two elements appear inextricably intertwined in beliefs, and it is a fruitless exercise for sociologists to attempt to separate them. Obviously this is not the opinion of people who quarrel endlessly about beliefs, and go to great lengths to distinguish true from false; the several splits in the Communist movement, in the Buddhist religion, and in the Christian churches testify to this. We shall simply accept that beliefs exist as psychologically internalised (deeply felt) notions, and that they frequently entail profound truths. The sociologist is not a cynic. He does not have to 'believe' in Islam to see its beautiful, noble and profound features; he does not have to belong to the Trotskyist International to see the point of it.

One of the chief areas for the sociological study of beliefs is the investigation of their effects. During the Renaissance, Montaigne warmly embraced the ancient Greek and Latin idea that one could not disregard people's opinions simply because they seemed false, for they still motivated them and had tangible consequences. This was expressed by William Isaac Thomas in a postulate, when he said that when people define something as real it is true in its effects. During the sixteenth and seventeenth centuries Europeans believed in witches and witchcraft, and also thought that pacts with the devil had to be most severely punished. In consequence thousands of unfortunate women were burnt in public for their so-called sins. Historians and sociologists are not concerned about the possibility or otherwise of devilish powers possessing into individuals, but rather they want to discover which social conflicts, tensions and frustrations, and which cultural elements, produced belief in such phenomena at that particular moment in time. They are equally concerned with these factors as they appear in less dramatic situations than the example just given, namely in phenomena of everyday life. At all levels of human activity beliefs are crucial. Even the scientist and the philosopher, devoted to a life of active scepticism, possess some basic assumptions (beliefs) that are reflected in their activities. Beliefs allow societies to function smoothly, for men find no need to question at every step their caste, class, or social position, or the orders of authority or the pronouncements of sages and religious or political leaders. Inevitably, the man who dares to question, however superficially, all these sources of consensus, cuts himself off from the group and, unless he joins or forms a new sect, increases the degree of his own isolation. Separation from prevalent beliefs increases individualism and, as Simmel suggested, the more unique an individual is the lonelier he is also.[3] For the rest of this chapter, however, we shall look into phenomena that demand a high degree of unwavering belief and a very low level of individualistic—and even rational—deliberation.

Precisely because rational and logical analyses and deliberation are not the salient characteristics of the general belief networks (religions and ideologies) their 'systematic' character is highly questionable. In fact, most men are remarkably prone to hold simultaneously beliefs that are logically incompatible and mutually exclusive. Leon Festinger has stated that through this phenomenon, which he named 'cognitive dissonance', men experience a discomfort that prompts them to modify and readapt their belief 'systems' into less self-contradictory wholes.[4] This perhaps helps to explain religious reform movements and ideological strife and critique, as well as the passage in many historical instances from syncretic accumulation of beliefs to a more synthetic belief 'system'. With the reservation that men's beliefs are frequently contradictory, we shall now treat religions and ideologies as 'systems' of belief.

## NOTES on Chapter VIII, Section 2

1. W. I. Thomas and F. Znaniecki *The Polish Peasant . . . op. cit.* Vol. I.
2. W. Bell and J. A. Mau 'Images of the Future: Theory and Research Strategies' in J. C. McKinney and E. A. Tiryakian *Theoretical Sociology* (New York: Appleton Century, 1970) p. 220.
3. G. Simmel *Grundfragen der Soziologie; Individuum und Gesellschaft* (Berlin: Walter de Gruyter, 1917); Eng. trans. K. Wolff *The Sociology of Georg Simmel* (London: Collier Macmillan, 1950) pp. 26–84.
4. L. Festinger *A Theory of Cognitive Dissonance* (Evanston: Row, Peterson, 1957).

# 3 RELIGION

*Definition and elements*

Religion is a system of beliefs about the sacred elements and forces of the cosmos, including man's place in it, which provides meanings about ultimate notions (such as life, death, salvation) and entails a number of practices or rituals. Religion always implies some sort of social structure and a system of morality for its faithful; its beliefs may cover many or most areas of the natural order, but they must always refer in some way to the supernatural. An acquaintance with the several dimensions and components of this most complex of phenomena is prerequisite to the comprehension of the full implications of the sociological definition of religion.

*The sacred and the profane* When it is said that religious beliefs refer to the supernatural it is meant that religion presupposes the existence of forces and entities that are essentially different from, and cannot be perceived in the same way as, natural events. Angels, devils, the gods, Grace, Fate, God, to cite some of the notions familiar to Westerners, are some such forces and entities. The fact that they are 'essentially different from natural events' does not mean that they are separate from them. They enter into contact with the natural world; they transform its nature; they give it a special meaning. It is perhaps only analytically that a sharp (but very useful) distinction can be made between the world of the sacred—where these forces manifest themselves—and the universe of the profane, which is outside it. The world of the sacred immediately creates a whole area of actions and places, people and things, which are possessed of religious meaning: sacred mountains, rivers, and springs; exorcisms, sacrifices, rituals; temples and places of worship; shamans, priests, pastors, bishops, nuns; myths, prayers. There is an area of the world which possesses *mana* (a Melanesian word vaguely meaning 'religiously charged') and another which seems to be separate from it, at least for a number of complex societies. Although this is not entirely so, for religion is an all-pervading phenomenon for *homo religiosus*, the assumption of this hypothesis at one stage led to some fruitful considerations. Thus Durkheim's definition of religion is based on this dichotomy between the sacred and the profane. For him 'all religion is a socially-based system of beliefs and practices relating to sacred things, that is to say, things set apart and forbidden—beliefs and practices which unite in one simple community called a church—all those who adhere to them'.[1] This means that for the faithful there is an essential heterogeneity of the world, which appears divided into these two fields, often defined by religions as incompatible; man, then, cannot fully belong to one if he does not renounce the other.[2]

If what a religion defines as sacred is also good, it is holy; if it is evil, it is unholy. In both cases the sacred is untouchable, save ritualistically, especially in the case of the holy. And what is holy is, as Durkheim stresses, separate, distinct both from the profane and the evil. The pollution of sanctity and the holy is therefore called profanation, the unholy mixture of the profane with what must be left untouched in its purity. This is very clear in the case of tangible sacred objects which need cleaning operations to keep them from pollution or to restore them to their holy state if they have been profaned or defiled. Within the realm of the sacred, the holy is, as Rudolf Otto so convincingly showed, the area that fascinates, terrifies, and enthrals the believer, attracting and repelling him simultaneously.[3] Fear of God is as important as love of God. All mystics tell us that the vision of the divine is as terrible and full of awe as it is full of overwhelming attraction and love.

*Myth and dogma*  Religious beliefs appear in the form of myths. Sociologically a myth is a belief about supernatural developments. It is irrelevant whether these events have actually taken place or not. Thus to try to prove the historicity of Jesus Christ—which is in fact quite easy to prove—in order to support the claim that he was born of a virgin and that his death redeemed the sins of mankind may be a correct procedure in theology, but it is foreign to the logic of the social sciences, whose aims do not include the theological proof or disproof of myths. Myths, in the social sciences, are approached as cultural material whose analysis will probably yield some historical, psychological, sociological or anthropological results.

Myths envelop the central wisdom of a given religion. If transmitted orally they are told and retold; if written in sacred texts they are read out and commented upon from generation to generation. Usually the faithful gather around the priest, shaman, elder, or preacher and listen to the myth, or parts of it, according to certain established patterns. Taken all together, myths form the mythology of a given religion. If analysed, we discover that they are in part made up of dogmatic elements—tenets about the supernatural which are vital to the religion. For Christians the notion that Jesus is the Messiah and the Saviour is a dogma. Likewise, the belief in Nirvana as the possible attainment of perfect beatitude is equally a central dogma in every form of Buddhism.

*Morality, evil and salvation* There is no religion without ethics. All religions demand moral responsibility of some sort and therefore must point the right way or the correct behaviour to the faithful. In connection with this all religions admit the existence of evil, and offer guidance to those who encounter it. In religion one cannot speak of morality without speaking of evil and sin. In religious terms evil is not the same as, say, sickness, frustration and slavery, although prophets and religious leaders have often affirmed that these are consequences of sinful behaviour. The notion of 'God's punishment' or the 'revenge of the gods' is linked to the belief that there has been a violation of the cosmic order established by super-natural forces. Atonement is one of the solutions offered by religion to recreate the broken harmony. When, on other occasions, religions cannot explain away transgressions as human failings, they attribute them to the forces of evil—malignant spirits, Satan, or other more impersonal destructive forces. But sin and evil forces do not exhaust the catalogue of evil in man's life. Defilement and pollution are also present as a constant fear, and in this respect they are equally important; for, as Mary Douglas has stressed, they are essentially disorder and spell danger.[4] This is why, as a result, the immediate social consequence of profanation is scandal; the inner moral harmony has been broken. In all advanced or complex religions, sin and subsequent expiation are in turn linked to a crucial notion— the notion of salvation. The role of salvation varies from religion to religion. In some it amounts only to cure or ephemeral bliss, but in other religions are messianic or salvationist, and for them this belief becomes central to the whole system. In yet others, people who refuse salvation are not exactly punished but are simply left to toil, or are excluded from the society of the 'chosen'. In still other religions, by contrast, man simply cannot be indifferent to salvation. Christians believe that a man of their faith who is indifferent to his own salvation will expiate his sins in hell or purgatory. And most religions understand man either as a sinful being or as someone capable of committing sin. The remedy for this sin is of sociological interest, for it varies considerably, and one could classify religions according to methods of expiation. The moral behaviour thus gener-ated has many social consequences. Whether expiation takes the form of contemplative retirement, public penance, hard work or charity to the poor, the social group in which it takes place will be affected differently. Thus, while expiation cannot be separated from salvationist practices, salvation itself goes beyond the mere avoidance of sin. In complex religions, such as Jainism, Buddhism, Christianity and Judaism, immunity from evil and sin is only a first step on the road to salvation and final grace. The social consequences of this are as varied as they are important; it matters greatly to the kind of life a group will lead whether they understand the attainment of final and complete salvation in terms of sanctifying grace or as predestination, or by clinging to a minute set of religious formalities. Salvationist methods are also useful indicators to help us distinguish religions from each other objectively.

*Ritual* Religion becomes evident to the observer through several patterns of behaviour. One of the most detectable is ritual, which is the set of rites performed by religions. Basically, ritual refers to myth, and very frequently has direct connections with salvationist activities, the expiation of guilt, and the creation of purity and religious cleanliness. (Cleanliness is religiously defined; thus the performance of baptism among certain Christians, has little to do with the chemical purity of the water. For Hindus the muddy Ganges is sacredly clean; ritual baths are therefore taken in it). Rituals also help to remove the frontiers between the sacred, the profane and the secular, and establish routes whereby man can gain access to the first. A considerable part of ritual is concerned with breaking down the barriers between these fields.

The effects of ritual are not entirely restricted to the religious acts in which the community of the faithful participates. Ritual also sanctions and maintains social structures, as is the case with the maintenance of social distance in caste society: pollution and contamination between *jatis* or between caste and outcast or untouchable is an act of defilement which is explained in religious terms and is healed by an appropriate ritual. (VI, 3)

*Magic* Magic is a set of ritual operations designed to obtain certain results from either natural or supernatural forces. Magic is eminently utilitarian and practical, as it invokes supernatural means in order to attain concrete and limited results. Amulets, invocations, exorcisms, are essentially circumscribed. For this reason magic has traditionally been distinguished from religion, whose scope has always appeared much wider. This attitude seems to be corroborated by the fact that magic rituals, such as a black mass, arise in clear contradiction and opposition to a given religion. It is in this vein that Marcel Mauss, in his attempt to draw up a general theory of magic, defined it as 'any rite which is not a part of an organised cult'.[5] And yet the relationships of established religions with witchcraft show that this distinction is not that simple, and that magic should be understood as a special aspect of religion in general. Very often religions incorporate and legitimise magic rituals, while magic itself is far from undermining established religion; if anything, the black mass reinforces the faithful in their beliefs. It is only secularisation, or the spread of another religion, that can undermine them.

Belief in magic is not peculiar to primitive man. A proper theory of magic, Julio Caro Baroja has said, would have to take into account its historical evolution and relationship to nation, class, and cultural and political crises. He adds that 'the conceptions of the world that allow the development of magic thought . . . are several, even contradictory, and full of connections that break up or link up again depending on the circumstances'.[6] Magic is thus an elusive and subtle reality which cannot be restricted to the conventional definition given above. Magic is also a mentality and, as such, an aspect of the collective consciousness. It is perhaps in relation to magic that the idea of *mana* is vital: the sorcerer and his community take it for granted and live in a world of *mana*: magic objects, incantations, magic beings, mysterious personal powers—all are manifestations of this deeply felt, though never well defined, force that penetrates everything.[7]

## Religious groups

Myths, rituals, sacramental notions, occur according to action patterns and within the framework of certain religious communities. These communities are structured in institutions and groups whose exact description and definition are not always easy, since emotional expression, moral (rather than material) interests, and the pervading diffuseness of everything religious are insurmountable barriers to clear-cut distinctions. Nevertheless, religious groups can be generally classified in four ideal types: cults, denominations, sects and churches.

*Cult*  A cult may mean a ritual or religious practice, but from the standpoint of religious groups it is a very loosely organised religious community in search of mystic or ecstatic experience. Its followers are not entirely and fully committed to it. Cults are essentially charismatic, non-dogmatic and dominated by collective mystical experiences.[8] They tend to be relatively short lived when they depend on the expertise of a given medium, or on the personal leadership of one individual, though they last longer when they are based on a miraculous place or object. Their non-dogmatic and circumscribed nature is reflected in the fact that they often emerge within the framework of wider religions. They may appear as quasi-sects. Precise definition is especially difficult in the case of cults; the voodoo cult is a widely established religion in Haiti, but only a marginal ritual in other Afro-American areas. The ritual eating of peyote amongst the Navaho can be either an isolated cult or a part of an established religion. The cult of the Virgin of Guadalupe has been thoroughly legitimised by the Catholic church as a Mexican national variant of its Marian myth. One thing remains constant in all these cases—the object of the cult rather than the people themselves, for cults admit a high turnover of believers, while splits or quarrels about them (heterodoxy) are rare; those who object simply abandon them.

*Denomination*   Denominations are a type of religious group that admit religious pluralism and do not pretend to possess a monopoly of truth; they are not very strict about rules of membership, but have formal rituals and, often, a professional clergy. They are typical of politically pluralistic countries, and it is not always easy to distinguish them from sects.

*Sects*   Sects are highly cohesive religious groups, whose activities completely involve the life of their adherents. Sects are very explicit about their beliefs, ritual and morality, and demand strict obedience to them. They are repositories of an orthodoxy and, unlike denominations, think that non-believers are wrong. However, they may be tolerant of other groups, as a convenient attitude for their own survival. The members of a sect enter it by their own merit, by conviction and by explicit admission. Sects are militant, often evangelical. They see themselves as encompassing 'the chosen ones', those who have 'seen the light'. For all these reasons they tend to enter into conflict with other social institutions, and suffer high degrees of tension and internal conflict among themselves. Struggles in their midst are bitter. Charismatic leadership is very important at the inception of new sects, and in them primary group feeling and ties are strong.

*Church* This is the most complex of these four ideal types of religious group. Although churches possess a clear *Gemeinschaft* dimension they are highly organised, with a complex hierarchy, a system of law—secular as well as divine—and a bureaucracy. The member of a church tends to be born into it, although the recruitment of new members through proselytising is not excluded. Churches also possess a system of punitive law divided against heretics, since they do not tolerate (or tolerate with ill grace) alien religions—which they consider as superstitions—their followers must be either infidels or heretics. Finally, a church is a conservative religious organisation, well adjusted to the secular order, both dominating it in some respects and being dominated by it in others.

This description corresponds to the ideal type of church as outlined by Ernst Troeltsch, who first used it in contra-distinction to the equally ideal type of sect in order to understand the social doctrines of Christian communities and organisations.[6] No known church fully possesses all these traits. The very Catholic Church which at one time in history seemed to meet all of Troeltsch's requirements, would not dare today to use its alleged *ius gladii* (right to punish with the sword) against infidels. Several religions —Chinese Confucianism, Caliphate Mohammedanism, and Judaism in ancient Israel—have been, or still are, churches in the sociological sense of the word, regardless of the fact that not all the prerequisites of the ideal type are fully present in them. They all possess great complexity, a considerable span in their hierarchical authority structure, professional priests and acolites—a clergy—and some form of direct or indirect authority and domination over secular society.

## The dynamics of religious groups and religious evolution

A number of the many functions of religions are immediately obvious to the observer. Man needs a map of his world, moral as well as physical, to find his way in life, and religion supplies just that for the believer. Equally, it is through his religion that the believer allays his fears, explains his sufferings, comes to terms with death, and finds a meaning to proximate and ultimate things. Through awakening solidarity and community feelings, religion is one of the most powerful agents for social cohesion, unified collective action and group identity. These inter-dependent functions of the religious experience, however, occur within groups which have to face changing historical conditions, rearrange themselves, split, expand or disappear. Nothing is more dynamic than religion; some of its elements seem to defy the passing of centuries, but on close analysis beliefs and religious groups are both seen to be in a state of flux. In spite of the interesting permanence of some archetypal symbols and principles through the ages, myths and dogmas must be perennially reinterpreted by each generation.

Inevitably an extremely brief reference to the dynamics of religious groups and institutions is bound to be quite crude and inexact. Religion is always also 'something else', and the danger of over-simplification is therefore even greater here than in other areas of the sociological task. With these reservations in mind it is possible to state that in complex societies a new religion always appears in the form of a sect. If it succeeds it often begins to develop in the direction of a church. Its initial criticism or rejection of the established order is weakened, and a reconciliation of the secular powers with the moral and supernatural claims of the religion ensues. In the process charisma becomes routinised (VII, 1) and the initial impetus of the revolutionary creative religious movement may be lost. The stage may then be ripe again for revisionist, revivalist or reformist movements inside or outside the church, and these are soon branded as heretical by its authorities. Great churches such as the Catholic church have been able at times to turn reformist movements into internal quasi-sects—as the early Franciscans—or to adapt themselves fully to them. Thus the Jesuit counter-reformers did not appear as a mere new order but took over the transformation that culminated in the Council of Trent. At a given moment after the Renaissance the Catholic church was unable, in spite of long wars of religion, to control secessionist movements by extermination and repression (as it had the Albigensian heretics by means of the Inquisition) and had to take on a new pattern of accommodation with the new secular forces. As for the Protestants, they failed to create any church that retained a universality comparable to that of the Catholic church, and split themselves into sects and denominations, though in some countries they managed to create churches such as the Swedish Lutheran Church. All these tensions, these constant movements towards the formation of sects and churches, can be largely explained by the contradictory forces at work in the religions of any complex society—the forces of worldly compromise and religious authenticity. On the one hand religious groups, when well established, must come to terms with the world, which means that they must rationalise and justify vested interests of every kind—often under a cloak of casuistry. On the other the very moral precepts they preach demand a life dedicated to principles that are blatantly incompatible with such compromise. Those believers who have systematically internalised these principles soon develop an 'inner religious state' which puts them in opposition to the Church (which they see as corrupt) and the world, whose order they submit to ruthless criticism.[6] A process of religious revival, reform, or revolution can then develop.

The internal logic of these processes is probably as much a cause of historical trends in religion as is the influence upon it of other factors—economic, political, or otherwise. The precise weight of religious influence is, of course, very difficult to assess, but it is important that the hypothesis of an internal and relatively independent life of religions be entertained. When seen in broad historical perspective, the religious evolution of mankind itself presents interesting general patterns and continuities, which accumulated research and gathered information has strengthened rather than weakened. Robert Bellah has been able to elaborate a theory of five stages —primitive, archaic, historic, early modern and modern (to use his conventional names)—which does relatively little harm to known facts, which takes account of the contradictory phenomena of world rejection and world acceptance just alluded to, and which is based on the proposition that 'at each stage the freedom of personality and society has increased relative to the environing conditions'. It appears that during the earliest stages of religion, mankind accepted the world as it was (though interpreting it mythically), as this was the only possible answer to a reality which completely pervaded the self of primitive man. By protecting man from the direct impact of the natural forces, early forms of civilised life allowed a differentiation in man's mind between his own self and the world, which was seen in a new light; as a consequence 'historic' religions (such as Buddhism, Judaism, Christianity, Islam) were all dualistic, believing in a supernatural realm and an earthly realm, the former being 'above' and beyond the latter. A parallel dichotomy between earthly life and life after death (which becomes 'true' life) also appears. All this already implies intense world rejection, though perhaps not criticism of the world in the strict sense of the word. Yet in the 'early modern' phases a considerable increase in the knowledge of human psychology and the physical structure of the universe transformed rejection into criticism. New religious impulses (especially those connected with Protestantism) opened the way to social criticism, and undermined the fatalistic and 'valley of tears' conceptions whose rejection of the world amounted, in fact, to a resigned acceptance of its painful features. Late modern religion is a continuation of these world-changing trends, but with a weakening of efforts to maintain standards of doctrinal orthodoxy and morality by coercive means.[10]

## Religion and society

The true believer lives his religion as a total phenomenon, which affects the ultimate purpose of his life. It is for this reason that it is difficult to isolate religious experience from other levels of human reality. Religions sanction family life, economic transactions, political structures, work, warfare. They all explain death, and orient man's conduct towards this supreme moment, whether it is happening to himself or to his fellows. In spite of this, sociologists have attempted to show how non-religious phenomena affect the religious and, *vice versa*, how religion, taken by itself (that is, considered as a religious factor),[11] impinges upon the other levels of social reality.

Contrary to common ideological vulgarisations, no conclusive proofs can be produced to show that religion is a mere sublimation of earthly frustrations, a great illusion, or the greatest lie in the history of mankind. But this is not to say that religion is not the field in which such frustrations are often worked out and where they find an easy, sometimes terrible, expression. Angus Mackay's study of Castilian society in the late Middle Ages shows how massacres of Jews over almost a century (1391 to 1476) closely followed sharp rises in prices of barley and other staples.[12] Violence from members of one caste against those of a lower caste who dare to break the norms in contemporary India can all too easily be traced to the desire of the aggressors to maintain their position of privilege rather than to their piety. Apart from common cases of persecution or victimisation such as these, we also encounter religion in its subtle role as a cultural enforcer of systems of social inequality. The following table, drawn up by Katherine and Charles George, eloquently illustrates the relationship between the Catholic hierarchy and the patterns of class domination through the centuries.

An even more revealing table could be formed by taking the dates of canonisation rather than those to which the saints belong, for it is the papal decree that is subject to a historical set of pressures rather than the canonised themselves. The authors compiled this list with data up to 1949, but since then, and especially after the Second Vatican Council, canonisations have taken a less aristo-

*Variations by Century in Number and Percentage of Saints in*
*Three Class Categories*[13]

| | Upper class | | Middle class | | Lower class | |
|---|---|---|---|---|---|---|
| | No. | % | No. | % | No. | % |
| First | 39 | 47 | 34 | 41 | 10 | 12 |
| Second | 56 | 74 | 11 | 14 | 9 | 12 |
| Third | 127 | 60 | 70 | 33 | 15 | 7 |
| Fourth | 211 | 66 | 89 | 28 | 18 | 6 |
| Fifth | 141 | 84 | 21 | 13 | 5 | 3 |
| Sixth | 207 | 94 | 11 | 5 | 2 | 1 |
| Seventh | 242 | 96 | 8 | 3 | 3 | 1 |
| Eighth | 125 | 97 | 4 | 3 | 0 | 0 |
| Ninth | 94 | 94 | 5 | 5 | 1 | 1 |
| Tenth | 56 | 97 | 2 | 3 | 0 | 0 |
| Eleventh | 93 | 94 | 4 | 4 | 2 | 2 |
| Twelfth | 120 | 90 | 12 | 8 | 2 | 2 |
| Thirteenth | 118 | 80 | 25 | 17 | 5 | 3 |
| Fourteenth | 85 | 72 | 20 | 17 | 12 | 11 |
| Fifteenth | 72 | 81 | 15 | 17 | 3 | 2 |
| Sixteenth | 59 | 63 | 23 | 25 | 11 | 12 |
| Seventeenth | 69 | 68 | 26 | 25 | 7 | 7 |
| Eighteenth | 13 | 39 | 16 | 48 | 4 | 13 |
| Nineteenth | 17 | 29 | 31 | 53 | 11 | 18 |
| Twentieth | 0 | 0 | 3 | 75 | 1 | 25 |
| Totals | 1,938 | 78 | 430 | 17 | 121 | 5 |

cratic turn—a trend that, as can be seen, began with the rise of the middle classes from the eighteenth century onwards.

The reverse phenomenon, the influence of the religious factor upon other aspects of social life, can now be examined. The classical example is still Max Weber's hypothesis of the far-reaching consequences of the Protestant religion upon the modern world. This hypothesis has given rise to a considerable flow of controversy, research, and further refinement of the issues involved, especially as it has been taken out of its original European and American context and has been applied to other countries. Basically, Weber's hypothesis is that Protestantism (especially in its Calvinist and Puritan branches) is *one* of the chief causes of modern capitalism. Capitalism was to be found in embryo in Rome, in Babylon and in India, but it was in modern Europe that it finally grew and, with it, a whole class system, together with a specific cultural and political world. This, Weber thinks, was largely due to the kind of ethics developed by certain Protestant communities. Thrift, hard work, constant capital formation, investment and reinvestment were all explicitly fostered by them, regardless of their dogmatic differences and disagreements. Moreover with Calvinism, with its belief in pre-destination, man could learn that he belonged to the category of the elect only by some sign of earthly success, which was regarded as a prognostication of his future bliss. As a background to all this, asceticism on the part of the powerful insured that wealth was not wasted in useless pomp but was profitably reinvested. It was thus, to put it in an oversimplified form, that the modern capitalist world found its initial impulse. Later developments, as Weber was keen on insisting, stressed the competitive and hard-working features of the spirit of capitalism, while the ethical principles of Puritan Protestantism, not to speak of its supernatural beliefs, receded into the background or even disappeared.[14] Thus the obvious realisation that a man's religious beliefs are bound to influence his economic, political or educational behaviour found in Weber a more scientific formulation, a seminal statement beyond which we can now begin to look into the effects of the religious factor upon human society in general.[15]

## NOTES on Chapter VIII, Section 3

1. E. Durkheim *Les formes élémentaires de la vie religieuse* (Paris: PUF, 1960 ed.) p. 65.
2. *Ibid.* pp. 50–51, 53.
3. R. Otto Das *Heilige* (Gotha: Leopold Klotz, 1926; Eng. trans. *The Idea of the Holy* (Oxford University Press, 1923).
4. M. Douglas *Purity and Danger* (London: Routledge, 1966) p. 2.
5. M. Mauss 'Esquisse d'une théorie générale de la magie' in *Sociologie et anthropologie, op. cit.* p. 16; cf. also L. Lévy-Bruhl, *La mentalité primitive* (Oxford University: Herbert Spencer Lectures, 1931).
6. J. Caro Baroja *Vidas mágicas . . . op. cit.* Vol. I, p. 24.
7. M. Mauss *op. cit.* pp. 101–15.
8. M. Yinger *Religion, Society and the Individual* (New York: Macmillan, 1957) p. 154.
9. M. Weber *Religionsoziologie* (Stuttgart: Mohr, 1922, 4th ed.); Eng. trans. *The Sociology of Religion* (London: Methuen, 1965) pp. 207–22.
10. R. N. Bellah 'Religious Evolution' *Am. Sociol. Rev.*, Vol. 29 (1964) pp. 858–864.
11. G. Lenski *The Religious Factor* (Garden City: Doubleday, 1961).
12. A. I. Mackay *Castile in the XVth Century* (University of Edinburgh, Unpublished Ph.D. dissertation, 1970) pp. 554–557. Rises in prices refer to 'perceived reality' and not always to 'real' prices.
13. K. George and C. H. George 'Roman Catholic Sainthood and Social Status' in *Journal of Religion* (1953) p. 155; reprinted in R. Bendix and S. M. Lipset *Class, Status and Power, op. cit.* p. 395.
14. M. Weber *Die protestantische Ethik und der Geist des Kapitalismus,* (1901–1902); Eng. trans. *The Protestant Ethic and the Spirit of Capitalism* (London: Allen & Unwin, 1930). For a discussion of the 'Protest-

ant Ethic' debate cf. S. N. Eisenstadt 'The Protestant Ethic Thesis in Analytical and Comparative Context' in *Diogenes*, no. 59 (1967) pp. 22–46.

15. Weber's study is seminal in the sense that it is dynamic and attempts to explain long-range change. Otherwise, other authors, above all Fustel de Coulanges (*La cité antique*, 1864) and his disciple Emile Durkheim (*Les formes . . . op. cit.*), are equally important in their efforts to show the integrative functions of religion. Readers interested in the effects of religion upon scientific knowledge may turn to R. K. Merton's study of Puritanism and the Royal Society (*op. cit.*) and J. Needham's massive works on Chinese science and technology; cf. especially his chapter on 'Buddhism and Chinese Science' in *Science and Civilization in China* (Cambridge University Press, 1956) Vol. II, pp. 417–31. For a brief, general introduction to the sociology of religion, B. R. Scharf *The Sociological Study of Religion* (London: Hutchinson, 1970).

# 4  IDEOLOGY

## *Definition and conceptual problems*

In complex societies, religion is not the only comprehensive belief system purporting to explain the ultimate sense of the human cosmos; ideologies, too, serve that purpose, while their integrative functions in group life are almost identical to those of religion. In fact the only truly differentiating element is the overtly secular element of ideologies. (Whether ideologies are really secular in the last resort is a moot point, but as a first methodological step in their study it seems advisable to accept the fact that ideologies do not resort to spiritual and supernatural forces.) In every other area religion and ideology overlap or possess many common elements. And yet, as will be seen, initial separate treatment appears justified.

A common approach to ideology in much contemporary sociology starts with the assumption that it is a set of received beliefs and notions about the social world and its approved values and goals.[1] In spite of its vagueness this assumption is not altogether wrong; it even has some advantages. It allows us to distinguish ideology from other belief systems such as science or religion, where other elements, either actively critical or supernatural, enter the picture. This definition shows also that ideology is a dimension of culture which is not always incompatible with other cultural levels. Thus the expressions 'the ideology of Vietnamese Buddhist monks' and 'the ideology of the Vatican' are perfectly legitimate; they mean the secular world picture and action orientation of the Buddhist monks in Vietnam, or of the Vatican, abstracted from the religious universes they represent. This definition, however, infers that each human group must possess an ideology. Once again, this is true; each group, if it is to exist at all, must possess a map of its world and a set of norms for action. One could then speak of the 'ideology of the Brown family', 'the ideology of the first-year students at the University of Uppsala', 'the Ghanaian working-class ideology', and so on. Such expressions are often used colloquially. Sociologically, though, this presents serious snags: it is a diffuse and imprecise term that applies to any group in society and which can hardly be distinguished from the notion of subculture. Moreover, there are other concepts, such as mentality, outlook, and creed, which also fit this definition and which, very often, reflect it more accurately.[2]

It seems sensible to restrict the notion of ideology to group conceptions that refer to certain precise areas; a study of the sociological literature on the subject strongly suggests that the notion be restricted to social conceptions of power and authority, to the sources of what is deemed sacred (in the secular sense of the word) *and* to a description of the social secular world. Even this may look too wide, but it seems adequate for a workable definition: an ideology is a conception of the social world explicitly and coercively maintained by a collectivity, which explains its existence through it, which derives from it a general plan of action and an identification of the sources of legitimate authority, and attempts the control of its social environment in a way consistent with this conception. Some observations on each aspect of this definition are in order.

1. No further explanation need be given of the fact that ideologies are conceptions of the social universe; they are primarily world outlooks, even if they appear within the framework of wider belief systems. In this they partake of other related phenomena, such as mentalities and creeds.

2. Ideologies, often in contrast with these latter cultural phenomena, are always partly explicit. The degree of explicitness may vary; it is highest when written down in undisputed texts (The Thoughts of Chairman Mao, Hitler's *Mein Kampf*), and lowest when the written or uttered statements are mere guide lines and are subject to relatively open discussion (as with the resolutions of the yearly Conservative Party Conference in the United Kingdom). Yet ideology is not in every case entirely implicit, diffuse and unspoken, as the subculture of the middle classes of a region in a given country may be.

3. All ideologies imply coercion in the form of sanctions for its dissenters and at least unequal treatment for its non-adherents. All ideologies possess a membership. In fact they define the boundaries of a group and have strong in-group, out-group and reference-group orientations. A person is or is not a member of the Social Democratic Party of Federal Germany; if one is, one cannot vote and campaign for the Christian Democratic Party without rendering oneself liable to expulsion. A person who is a member of the Mafia must abide by its rules; if he breaks secrecy he pays for it with his life. The member of an informal factory group of workers who 'flirts' with management or refuses to go along with a wildcat strike will soon be in trouble with his workmates. (Incidentally, unwritten and 'unofficial' conceptions such as those exhibited by an occupational group in industry may also be ideologies; not only are they very explicit and clearcut for their members but they possess all the other requirements.)

4. In spite of frequent ideological statements to the contrary, ideologies do not refer to vague collectivities but to concrete groups, such as the Yugoslav Communist League, the Mexican Institutional Revolutionary Party and the National Union of French Students. During periods of ideological ferment and change, of course, not all members of an ideology can be readily identified under the correct label. Thus it is legitimate to speak of the ideology of left-wing students in Western Europe in the years after 1968 even if complete formal membership is non-existent. What matters is that they exist as an active, expressive, and detectable collectivity.

5. All ideologies include a plan of action, usually made up of some general principles (the ideological creed) and the day-to-day policy issued by the elite (e.g. the party line). Perhaps there are eliteless ideologies but, if so, they are ephemeral, since policy formulation cannot take place without the help of small groups placed at the centres of ideological authority.

6. Ideologies are about authority and power. Even the anarchist ideology is deeply concerned about them. It is for this reason that the study of ideology is as much a branch of the sociology of knowledge as it is an aspect of political sociology (VII). Ideologies legitimise power or declare it illegitimate. This may appear in a zero-sum situation, when two contending ideologies want to annihilate each other. In pluralist polities, though, contending ideologies may agree about the power vested in certain neutral institutions or may agree to tolerate each other, according to the rules of more or less democratic competition.

7. Ideologies are agents of social control, sources of social order. In varying degrees they all fail to order the world exactly to their writ, but as long as they exist they are an active factor shaping social arrangements.

## The theoretical background of ideology

The notion of ideology forms one of the battlegrounds of sociologists. The words 'ideologist' and 'ideology' appeared during the last stages of the French Revolution and soon acquired a pejorative sense,[3] in spite of the efforts of those who coined them, for whom ideology was the name for a future 'science of ideas'. The pejorative sense of the notion was inherited by Marx and Engels, to whom ideologies were cultural distortions of social reality imposed by the ruling class, and therefore (and especially for the exploited classes) forms of false consciousness (VI, 2). For Marx ideologies reflect the vested interests of the rulers, and each historical epoch has its own ideology, depending on the dominating class. In his sense ideology covers a vast section of what we call culture; thus in the Middle Ages, religion and theology were aspects of the feudal ideology, just as in modern times liberalism was the ideology of the victorious bourgeoisie. Allegedly sacrosanct political and religious dogmas are therefore only sublimations of actual social relationships:

> The production of ideas, or conceptions, of consciousness is at first directly interwoven with the material activity and the material intercourse of men, the language of real life. Conceiving, thinking, the mental intercourse of men, appear at this stage as the direct efflux of their material behaviour. The same applies to mental production as expressed in the language of politics, laws, morality, religion, metaphysics, etc, of a people. Men are the producers of their conceptions, ideas, etc,—real, active men, as they are conditioned by a definite development of their productive forces and of the intercourse corresponding to these, up to its furthest forms. Consciousness can never be anything else than conscious existence, and the existence of men is their actual life-process. If in all ideology men and their circumstances appear upside-down as in a *camera obscura*, this phenomenon arises just as much from their historical life-process as the inversion of objects on the retina does from their physical life-process.
> . . . The phantoms formed in the human brain are also, necessarily, sublimates of their material life-process . . .[4]

Marx's approach to this subject had notable consequences for the future sociology of knowledge. In the first place it appeared that economic and political relationships were decisive factors in shaping people's conceptions about the world; in the second, ideologies were serious barriers to the discovery of truth, since they were both mere sublimations of men's frustrations and thorough distortions of reality, whereby men perceived the world 'upside-down'. Lastly, ideologies were inevitable in a class society, whose cultural 'superstructure', or system of law, morality, religion and political doctrine sustained the prevailing system of privilege. Karl Mannheim picked up the threads of Marx's theory, agreeing with him in several respects. However, he reserved the name 'ideology' for essentially conservative doctrines only, doctrines which attempt to maintain a situation or to return to the past. These he distinguished from 'utopias' or revolutionary ideologies, which are grounded on an apocalyptic or messianic vision of the future, and which are, for this reason, inevitably unscientific. (By the same token they are also partially self-fulfilling prophecies, bringing about chaos and upheaval.[5]) This led Mannheim to a study of the relationships of classes and social groups to truth and rationality. He came to the conclusion that it was the relatively classless 'unattached' intellectuals who, because of their lack of vested interests, had the greatest chance to get closest to a true knowledge of reality. Mannheim never claimed that intellectuals were entirely free of commitments, or above parties, passions and special interests, and therefore immune to ideological bias, and he distinguished several types of intellectual in the history of the intellectuals[6]—a fact which, surprisingly, tends to be overlooked by Mannheim's critics. Yet it is true that he showed a remarkable confidence in the continued critical powers of intellectuals generally (VIII, I).

The sociology of ideology was later enriched by studies of the content of its mythology. Like religion, ideology is made up of dogmatic tenets (or at least tenets which are taken-for-granted or undisputed) and these in turn often revolve around central deep-seated images. Ernst Cassirer has been able to relate the structure of mythical thought in society (whether religious or ideological) to the political institutions. His conclusions about myth are definitely pessimistic: 'Language is not only a school of wisdom but also a school of folly. Myth reveals the latter aspect to us; it is nothing but the dark shadow cast by language on the world of human thought'.[7] This position seems too extreme for there are reasons to suppose that a number of political myths and symbols have important consequences for the creation of social order and respond to deep meanings in the collective conscience, having lasted through the ages with unabated vigour. If we equate political myths to extreme, messianic, ideological notions, it would be sensible to agree with Cassirer. But political and ideological myths may be abstractions of a different nature, fundamental for the efflorescence of a civilised society. Thus Manuel García Pelayo has demonstrated the role of medieval myths and political symbols in the birth of modern political theory; he has also shown the beneficial functions of the notion of law in medieval social order, and the causes for another political myth, basic for politics after the Renaissance: the 'reason of state'.[8] For García Pelayo myths are important components of the ideologies around which these are organised. The acceptance of this position, which seems reasonable, has an important effect on our concept of ideology; as with religion, ideology cannot be defined only as a thorough distortion of reality. To be sure, ideologies are oversimplifications—frequently quite dogmatic—of a complex and changing reality which refuses to fit their Procrustean bed. But they are answers to very real crises, alienations, conflicts and deeply felt needs, and cannot be dismissed wholesale. Some, like liberalism and Marxism, incorporate very noble ideals and aspirations, such as the 'myth of progress' and the 'myth of modernity'. These may be ideological myths,[9] but it would be a tragic mistake to cast them away either for that reason, because they appear in conjunction with less appealing notions, or because the powers that be have used them to justify oppression and terror. Other myths, thoroughly repugnant from a moral point of view (such as the Nazis' belief in their own racial superiority), are much closer to outright distortion, but the social scientist must equally investigate in which sense they respond to authentic needs and conflicts. If this is taken into account it will be possible to agree with Nigel Harris's assertion that ideologies 'are not disguised descriptions of the world, but rather real descriptions of the world from a specific viewpoint, just as all descriptions of the world are from a particular viewpoint.'[10] All ideologies are the effect of very real situations, even when the element of sublimation is by far the most salient to the relatively uncommitted observer.

### Types of ideology

It is obvious that ideologies are not all the same sort, and that some kind of classification ought to be possible. In fact, a taxonomy of ideologies (or ideological groups) has proved perhaps more difficult than a taxonomy of religions. Since ideologies are about power, the polarity right wing/left wing is quite useful in common conversation or in journalism. (VII, 2) One can also think of criteria of classification such as the continuum between millennarian ideologies (highly activistic, inspiring a mass movement, and messianic) on the one hand, and pragmatic (based on *realpolitik*, and vested interests) on the other. But these, useful though they are, seem most inadequate for the nature of ideology also depends on an important question which is ignored by these distinctions—the question of whether ideology purports to encompass the entire society (such as the ideology of the Communist Party of the Soviet Union) or only a part of it, restricting itself explicitly to one area of society. In this context the word 'total' does not necessarily mean 'totalitarian' (though it is not incompatible with totalitarianism). Thus the ideology of the Christian Democratic Party in Italy is 'total' in the sense that it seeks state and government power and pretends to influence the whole pattern of Italian society but the party itself is not totalitarian. Another variable is the relative openness or closeness of the ideological group. Secrecy, strict recruitment patterns, a high degree of internal discipline, complete personal commitment to the party organisation and the like, are the hallmark of the 'closed' ideology; the opposite characteristics denote an 'open' ideology. With these observations in mind it is possible to draw up a simplified scheme of ideologies, as follows:

|  |  | SOCIAL CONTROL | |
|  |  | Goals | |
|  |  | Partial | Total |
| IDEOLOGIES | Traditionalistic closed | Mafia Ku-Klux-Klan | Legitimist movement; Irish Orangemen; Spanish Carlists; John Birch Society (USA) |
|  | Traditionalistic open | Trades Union Congress (UK); National Union of Students | British Liberal Party; German Social Democrats |
|  | Revolutionary closed | Sectlike organisations; Scientology; Opus Dei | Fascism; Stalinism; |
|  | Revolutionary open | Beatniks; Hippies | Anarchists |

Like so many classifications of wide sociocultural phenomena, the present one presents difficulties. For instance in the first place the notion of 'revolutionary' ideology must refer in the present context to any sort of ideology that pretends to break up, subvert, or undermine large sections of the established order. In the second place, social change is rapid; in many a sense Stalinism became a profoundly conservative, indeed a reactionary, ideology, for the Comintern soon became a tool for the international domestication of revolutionary fervour in favour of Soviet imperial power. Thus a diachronic conception of ideology is essential for the correct understanding of this phenomenon. Another serious difficulty stems from the syncretic character of many ideologies. Thus Fascism is a 'total' and 'closed' revolutionary ideology in the sense that it very seriously subverts the social order; but its traditionalistic elements are also evident. Thus, while the Nazi party systematically eroded the Prussian military establishment and destroyed an entire political order (with revolutionary activities) it also maintained the power of certain great capitalism industries, such as Krupp and Siemens, though, even before the war broke out, their fate as 'independent' capitalist enterprises began to look quite problematic.[11] Ideologies bring together in simplified formulas many strands of social life and therefore a perfectly satisfying classification is nearly impossible.

Ideologies must always be related to the systems of inequality prevailing in a society—something that is not referred to in the above diagram, but that has been present throughout our discussion of the problem areas of political sociology. An ideology recruits its adherents from certain layers of a given social class; it is found more frequently among certain occupational groups than among others, and arises at given stages of their development (VII). The Marxian tradition in the study of ideology, later developed by Mannheim was built precisely around this set of problems. Contemporary concern with content analysis, linguistics and the study of meaning, far from diverting attention from this tradition, has enriched its possibilities.[12] In spite of these recent developments, however, it is perhaps still too early for the elaboration of a general theory of the evolution of ideology, since this phenomenon, though in many respects as old as mankind,[13] has in recent times acquired a new slant and vigour in the framework of modernity. In its extreme closed and total forms—such as fascism—it has shown that it is one of the most destructive social processes known to us.

## NOTES on Chapter VIII, Section 4

1. Cf. for instance H. Johnson *Sociology, a Systematic Introduction* pp. 587–593.
2. E. A. Shils' article, 'Ideology' in *Int. Encyclopedia of the Soc. Sc.* (1968) Vol. 7 p. 66; G. Bouthoul *Les mentalités* (Paris: PUF, 1966).
3. For a critical description of its origin, H. Barth *Wahrheit und Ideologie* (Zurich: Manesse, 1945); G. Lichtheim *The Concept of Ideology* (New York: Random House, 1967) pp. 4–11; J. Plamenatz *Ideology* (London: Pall Mall, 1970).
4. K. Marx *The German Ideology*; Eng. trans. (Moscow: Progress Publishers, 1964) p. 37.
5. K. Mannheim *Ideology and Utopia* (London: Kegan Paul, 1936).
6. K. Mannheim *Essays on the Sociology of Culture* (London: Routledge, (1956) pp. 91–170.
7. E. Cassirer *The Myth of the State* (Oxford University Press, 1946) p. 19.
8. M. García Pelayo *Del mito y de la razón en la historia del pensamiento político* (Madrid: Occidente, 1968).
9. C. Baudouin *Le mythe de la modernité*; B. Dunham *Man against Myth* (London: Muller, 1948).
10. N. Harris *The Problem of Ideology* (London: Watts, 1968) p. 10; cf. also E. Trías *Teoría de la ideologías* (Barcelona: Península, 1970).
11. T. W. Mason 'The Primacy of Politics—Politics and economics in National Socialist Germany' in S. J. Woolf ed. *The Nature of Fascism* (London: Weidenfeld, 1968) pp. 165–95.
12. F. Mellizo *El lenguaje de los políticos* (Barcelona: Fontanella, 1968).
13. M. H. Levine 'Prehistoric Art and Ideology' *American Anthropologist* Vol. 59 (1957) pp. 949–62.

# 5  A NOTE ON SECULARISATION

The student of belief systems, religious and ideological, must sooner or later come to grips with the problem of secularisation. This is the process whereby a group evolves a system of values and attitudes which are increasingly unrelated to the group's religious orientations. A widespread assumption among the practitioners of sociology has been that modern societies have themselves undergone a vast process of secularisation. This implies the often latent dichotomy between traditional, religious societies and modern, secular societies; the first are essentially conservative and the latter essentially geared towards change. Howard Becker, without expressly restricting it to the profane or faithless, emphasises that 'secular' ought to mean something wider, namely, the opposite to the sacred.

Because veneration and inviolability play little or no part in the considerations of the secular mentality, the secular society directs itself towards what is new and only under utilitarian criteria for action.

> A secular society may be viewed as one that engenders in, or elicits from, its members, by any or all appropriate means, readiness to change customary orientation towards values regarded as essential in that society and to redefine those values. More succinctly, a secular society is one bringing its members to be willing and able to accept or pursue, in whatever measure, the new *as the new is defined in that society*.[1]

This approach appears somewhat misleading. It is true that the readiness and purposeful search for novelty, so typical of the Western mind in the past, have become ingrained attitudes in every modern society. (A whole set of myths have developed in European culture around variations of this theme: Prometheus, Faust, Don Quixote.) Modernising elites and groups in every country in the world have now joined in this attitude. It is also true that this has meant a great deal of secularisation, and often a frontal attack on religion. Voltaire's slogan for progress, '*écrassez l'infame!*' (smash the infamous one [religion]!) did not fall on deaf ears. And the Voltairean attitude has lingered until today among 'enlightened' and agnostic intellectuals everywhere.

The rise of extreme totalitarian ideologies and the widespread development of modern forms of fanaticism have tempered the revolutionary impetus of many of these modern intellectuals, and have led them to believe that an explanation could be found for the fact that secularisation was not bringing about the peaceful progress and the new civilisation they thought it would. The infamous one was only apparently dead, for ideology was religion in disguise; and it had equally undesirable, if not worse, consequences upon men's minds. These are, however, naive conceptions, for they are only half truths. In the first place, to go back to Becker's notions, it is true that the utilitarian mind (of all ages, incidentally) finds nothing that is sacred. It attempts to manipulate the world (objects, beliefs, people, symbols) for its own selfish goals. But a society, no matter how modern, cannot live without a sense of order which is in itself sacred and awe-inspiring. That is why it has been asserted that ideologies, too, refer to the realm of the sacred. In the second place, it would be amazingly simple if it were true that a decline in religion has been followed by a parallel rise in ideology. Instead, a complex set of cultural sequences has been unleashed.

Secularisation has not meant the demise of religion. The growth of rationalism, utilitarianism and science, and of a generalised non-religious approach to life, has elicited a series of specifically religious responses. Old religions have adapted themselves to the new situation by an effort to assimilate science, rationality, and 'modernity'. An indication of Christianity's response is provided by Christian Science, with its claim to be scientific and its entry into the arena of public opinion through its international newspaper, *The Christian Science Monitor*. Universalistic religions, from Theosophy to the Baha'i, have developed from the combination of two forces: the confrontation and mixture of Eastern and Western religions in the modern setting, and the widespread signs of a 'world government' and internationalist movement. Millennarian religions, such as the Jehovah's Witnesses in the Western world and nationalist religious reinterpretations of the past (such as the Asoka cult in India) also flourish. Finally, religions verging on the virtually ideological—actually borderline cases between ideology and religion—like the Japanese Soka Gakkai movement, have made their appearance, and are well established. All this, of course, has been happening while the old established religions give no sign of early collapse. Some, like Islam, seem to receive new impetus from the forces of nationalism, ethnic reassertion, or antiEuropean feeling: for example, its expansion in certain African areas, and the Black Muslim movement in America. In connection with this last phenomenon it is of interest to note the great number of new religions which have appeared in the non-Western tribal or formerly tribal areas of the world, as a consequence of deep crises unleashed by the impact of Western technology or even simply the Western presence in their midst.[2]

Because of these, and other more subtle phenomena, some sociologists have become uneasy about the notion of secularisation. Michalina Vaughan and Margaret Archer have shown that even when it exists it is not a linear process; phases of desecularisation have occurred in several countries, such as Israel or Spain, over periods of their contemporary history.[3] This uneasiness has led others, like David Martin, to question the whole idea of secularisation, and to dismiss it altogether. His argument against it is certainly interesting, for he aptly shows that the very notion of secularisation is essentially ideological—one of the leading myths, one could add, of Western intellectuals for a very long time. (Myth, that is, in the strictly sociological sense of the word!) Martin also shows the weakness of the concept in dealing with religion, which, of course, cannot just be defined in terms of 'churches and chapels', or church attendance.[4] Other criticisms can be levelled against the belief that secularisation is a general and overriding fact, especially those implicit in our earlier comment about the inner core of ideological thought and its definition as being that which is held sacred and cherished above all by an ideological community. And yet the sociologist will be hard put to it to give up the concept entirely. Secularisation *has* taken place in large spheres of the modern world; it is a detectable, clear, cultural process in many instances, and one simply cannot explain modern society without it—at least until a new, more precise, notion is found. What we must shed is any pretence that we know for sure that mankind can live in a thoroughly secularised universe.

## NOTES on Chapter VIII, Section 5

1. H. Becker 'Secular Society' in J. Gould ed. *Dictionary, op. cit.* p. 626.
2. V. Lanternari *Movimenti religiosi di libertà e di salvezza dei popoli oppresi* (Milan: Feltrinelli, 1950).
3. M. S. Archer and M. Vaughan 'Education, Secularization, Desecularization and Resecularization' in D. Martin ed. *Yearbook of Religion in Britain* (London: SCM Press, 1970).
4. D. Martin, 'Towards Eliminating the Concept of Secularization' in J. Gould ed. *Penguin Survey of the Social Sciences 1965* (Harmondsworth: Penguin, 1965) pp. 169–82. See also R. Thomas *Religion and the Decline of Magic* (London: Weidenfeld, 1971).

# IX Social Conflict

## 1 TOWARDS A THEORY OF SOCIAL CONFLICT

When a definition of social conflict was attempted earlier on (III, 6) the difficulty of constructing a unitary theory about such an all-pervading phenomenon was stressed. Nevertheless, contemporary sociology has inherited a considerable tradition in the study of conflict out of which efforts aimed at integrating the several contributions of the several schools which study social conflict are now being made. Yet, since we are still very far from an adequate sociological theory of conflict,[1] the best method of approaching the field is perhaps to show which are the chief lines of research being pursued.

1   *The biological basis of social conflict*   For quite a long period of time sociology was largely dominated by the doctrine of the Social Darwinist school. In the latter part of the nineteenth century sociologists on both sides of the Atlantic were enthralled by the apparent scientific character of such notions as 'natural selection', the 'survival of the fittest', and 'the struggle for life', which they derived from the theories of Herbert Spencer and Charles Darwin (neither of whom was a Social Darwinist). They forgot that social conflict was, among humans, intra-specific and that other species were immune to this latter form of conflict—their selection, survival and struggle being related to their environment, and their aggression never being directed against their own kind, except in the form of competitive quarrels. However, the efforts of the Social Darwinists were not altogether in vain; they gathered and ordered considerable comparative information about social conflict, they developed several plausible partial theories (eg the 'conquest theory of the origin of the state' VII, 3), and showed that a theory of human pugnacity[2] was necessary for the development of a fully-fledged sociology of conflict.

After a decline in interest in these issues—surprisingly (as

Bottomore points out) in this century of war, ideological strife, revolution and dictatorship[3]—there has recently been a marked reawakening of interest in some of the areas first explored by the Social Darwinists. In the meantime Freud and the psychoanalytical school had kept alive the notion of the innate existence in man of an aggressive and destructive element that only culture and proper socialisation could keep in check and help sublimate into peaceful and creative expression.[4] Modern biologists and zoologists have begun to explore aggression among animals and to apply their approach to man. The zoologist Konrad Lorenz has shown that intra-specific warfare in animals is produced only when certain serious environmental strains are introduced, mainly overcrowding.[5] For him, and for many of his colleagues, the 'fighting spirit' which is necessary for a species in its struggle for survival—defence, hunting—is directed by man against his own species also because of environmental strains. Man first removed all other species he regarded as threats to his wellbeing and then expanded all over the face of the earth. At a given moment in history free and adequate territory became rare, and men began to encroach upon territories and food supplies of other men. Warfare between bands and tribes began, and has continued ever since. Excessive population exhausts food supplies, imposes oppressive forms of distribution of wealth, inclines some people to be parasitical on others, imposes levels of density which are psychologically harmful, and heightens people's aggressive and destructive tendencies. This is a general hypothesis which is potentially a fertile area of study. It has nevertheless already led to crude oversimplifications and popularisations. A journalistic 'sociology' has sprung up which pretends to explain every form of war, exploitation and conflict in terms of population pressure or closely related phenomena, such as the ensuing territorial scarcity.[6] Excessive population is a serious problem—it may even prove disastrous for mankind's future—but not all social conflict can be explained in its terms. We have already seen that sparsely populated areas show degrees of violence which are higher than those exhibited by thickly populated regions. Social stratification, political organisation and cultural patterns are just as important as density in determining the intensity and the direction of social conflict (IV, 1).

2 *Social conflict and class conflict*   The view, 'the history of all hitherto existing society is the history of class struggles', put forward by Marx and Engels in the *Communist Manifesto* unambiguously

reflects the basic assumption of those who believe that the only key to the explanation of social conflict is stratificational antagonism. Even though most sociologists have not subscribed to this extreme attitude, on the whole the importance of class conflict has received the central attention it deserves. While accepting the correctness of the Marxian analysis of class conflict for many aspects of societies in the early phases of capitalist industrialisation, many non-Marxist sociologists, have seriously questioned its validity for the contemporary industrialised world. In so doing they have not precisely denied the importance of class conflict but have explored its new directions as well as the new strata, occupational groups and collectivities that now enter the arena of stratificational strife. (This theme will be treated at some length in IX, 3, 4, 5 and X, 3.) Marxist thinkers, for whom the class struggle is the cornerstone of their world-view have made important efforts to bring the concept up-to-date with the known facts. Rudolf Hilferding, Rosa Luxemburg and Lenin, confronted with the imperialist expansion and subsequent prosperity of the capitalist countries which ran counter to predictions of impending collapse, developed the explanation that these phenomena, as well as international wars among imperialist nations, were the outcome of internal class struggles.[7] Thus, for Lenin, the well-being of the English working classes largely depended on the squalor of the British colonial peoples. Later, theorists of the revolutionary 'third world' conception (such as Franz Fanon) have seized upon this argument and have developed the notion of the 'proletarian nations' in revolt, not against one class but against a whole system of exploiting nations. These arguments may seem in many respects crude and simplistic, but their sociological relevance is twofold. In the first place there is an element of truth in the argument that international warfare and imperialist expansion is a byproduct of internal class strife: ruling classes have throughout history found it expedient and profitable to channel internecine conflict into external expansion, military expeditions, and the opening up of new markets. This they have done with the active cooperation of other strata, such as the poorest citizenry in classical Athens or the European middle classes during the industrial revolution. (It could even be said that these two groups took the initiative in empire building.) In the second place these communist theorists were stressing phenomena that had been either obscured or consistently forgotten by the sociologists of the Victorian era, as well as by those who, after the First World War, insisted on seeing class conflict as merely a form of internal friction amongst ranks, without further consequences. Other communist thinkers have made contributions to the theory of class conflict: Gyorgy Lukács reinterpreted the notion of the proletariat in more radical and revolutionary terms than the communist orthodoxy of the 1920s admitted.[8] In so doing he made a contribution to conceptual clarification in the sociological interpretation of the direction of modern history: if Lukács is right, the proletariat with its class consciousness (rather than the party) is the sole transformer of modern society and our system of values and knowledge. If he is wrong, the proletariat (or the working class) will have to be rejected as the chief or only subject of modern history. Thanks to Lukács' cogent argumentation, sociological theory cannot fail to be enriched by a critique of his contribution. Certainly Lukács showed that the fragmentary positivistic analysis of conflict in the process of research could only lead to meaningless interpretations. Classes and their conflict must be understood in their totality. Also in the Marxist tradition we find Antonio Gramsci's agile and illuminating theory of class domination in advanced industrial capitalist societies, which, in contrast to Mannheim's notion of the unattached intellectual, emphasised the important role of intellectuals in legitimising and maintaining the prevalent system of class inequality (X, 3).

3 *Social conflict and power* A great part of political sociology has been concerned with this theme. It covers the political expression of social conflicts as well as direct political struggles for power (VII, 3, 4, 5). In this context sociological theorists who, like Ralf Dahrendorf, have affirmed that 'stratification is about power' have tended to transfer the traditional Marxist emphasis on class as the expression of economic unequal relationships to an emphasis on class and the economy as byproducts of power groups and the distribution of power in a given society. Yet empirical evidence indicates that other variables are also at work. Conflict is often about domination or control of goods or services (e.g. higher salaries, better amenities, greater occupational opportunities, less social discrimination), and the direct enjoyment of power over people may not be desired by all the contending parties. The fact that a section of the population is always moved by the desire for sheer power does not warrant such a generalisation about society as a whole. And, as Dahrendorf himself acknowledges, the assumption that the 'structure of power and subordination in human societies is the ultimate reason for the presence of protest and resistance, . . . antagonism and unrest . . . is a question beyond the reach of empirical test'.[9]

4   *Social conflict and game theory*   The notion that power is at stake in most forms of conflict logically leads to the study of strategy. Blind, head-on clashes are rare in social life. The contenders practically always plan their moves, marshal their forces, and measure their resources. The development of the mathematical method of the 'theory of games' has come to the help of those who want to explore the possibility of studying conflictive processes from the standpoint of very formalised quantitative models. (Basically, game theory attempts to work out the ideal strategy for a player to follow when in competition with one or several competitors.) In spite of the serious drawback that game theory cannot account for irrational behaviour, it offers an interesting perspective that helps us to observe human conflict with total detachment. The student of social conflict cannot ignore its solid though incomplete contribution to the subject.[10]

5   *Social conflict and quantification*   An important datum for the study of the strategies of conflict is the size of the contenders, the volume of their resources, and other quantifiable data. Systematic studies of conflict have been careful to accumulate data such as casualties, numbers of battles, nature and size of the resources employed, police arrests, workers' strikes and the like, as well as their frequencies over time. Thanks to this approach, contemporary theories of war, revolution and crime have become somewhat more reliable than they used to be.

6   *The effects of social conflict*   Destruction and loss for the loser and gains and rewards for the winner are only some superficially obvious effects of social conflict. For a very long time historians and moralists had reflected upon other effects, such as Pyrrhic victories and unwilled and unexpected economic, political and cultural results of conflict. But it was Simmel who opened the way for the proper understanding of the effects of conflict upon the social structure of contending parties. It was not upon the dysfunctional, as had traditionally been done, that he concentrated his attention, but upon the functional. Conflict, he showed, is one of the strongest integrative forces of any group; it heightens its internal solidarity; it helps maintain discipline; under its pressure bold measures are taken by governments and great sacrifices asked from the population. Milder (but permanent) forms of discord may even maintain an entire social structure; thus, 'the Hindu social system rests not only on the hierarchy, but also directly on the mutual repulsion, of

the castes'.[11] Personal and group antagonism is also a precondition of scientific, artistic and intellectual forms of emulation and creativity. Following this line of thought Lewis Coser attempted to work out a general theory for the integrative functions of social conflict. In so doing, he approached the phenomenon from a neutral point of view: the effects of conflict can be seen as 'beneficial' for the structure of a given group, class or institution, regardless of the moral interpretations we may attach to this process.[12] Simultaneously Max Gluckman's study of social conflict and custom in African society came to conclusions similar to those of Coser: it showed that 'men quarrel in terms of their customary allegiances, but are restrained from violence through other conflicting allegiances which are also enjoined on them by custom. The result is that conflicts in one set of relationships . . . lead to the reestablishment of social cohesion'.[13] Ever since these studies appeared the integrative or reinforcing effects of conflicts could not be ignored in the sociological study of the phenomenon. However, as Coser notes, the recognition and investigation of such effects do not necessarily have to be accompanied by a corresponding neglect of the important disruptive effects of most types of social conflict upon social structures.[14]

Since it is clear from the above that a unified, plausible theory of social conflict is not extant, it is advisable to look instead at a selected number of important fields of enquiry. War and revolution have been chosen first. Two other types of conflict will then be examined: delinquency and generational antagonisms, preceded by a short exploration of anomy, which is a decisive theoretical notion for the proper explanation of these two last phenomena.

*NOTES on Chapter IX, Section 1*

1. T. B. Bottomore 'Sociological Theory and the Study of Social Conflict' in J. C. McKinney and E. A. Tiryakian *Theoretical Sociology* (New York: Appleton Century, 1970) p. 138.
2. W. McDougall *An Introduction to Social Psychology* (London: Methuen, 1915) Chapter 11; reprinted in L. Bramson and G. W. Goethals eds. *War* (New York: Basic Books, 1964) pp. 33–43, on the 'Instinct of Pugnacity'.
3. T. B. Bottomore 'Sociological Theory . . .' *op. cit.* p. 139.
4. See Freud's letter to Albert Einstein in L. Bramson and G. W. Goethals *op. cit.* pp. 71–80; also his *Das Unbehagen in der Kultur*; Eng. trans. *Culture and its Discontents* (London: Hogarth, 1930).
5. K. Lorenz *On Aggression* (New York: Harcourt, 1966).
6. Cf. literature by R. Ardrey (*The Territorial Imperative*), D. Morris

*(The Naked Ape, The Human Zoo)*, both typical examples of 'popular sociology'.

7. V. I. Lenin *Imperialism, the last Stage of Capitalism* (London: Lawrence, 1933).
8. G. Lukács *Geschichte und Klassenbewusstsein* (Berlin: Luchterhand, 1962).
9. R. Dahrendorf *Conflict after Class* (University of Essex, 1967) pp. 15–16.
10. A. Rapoport *Fights, Games and Debates* (University of Michigan Press, 1960); K. Boulding *Conflict and Defense* (New York: Harper, 1962).
11. G. Simmel *Conflict, op. cit.* p. 18.
12. L. Coser *The Functions of Social Conflict, op. cit.*; T. B. Bottomore 'Sociological . . .' *op. cit.* p. 149.
13. M. Gluckman *Custom and Conflict in Africa* (New York: Free Press, 1956) quoted by L. Coser *Continuities in the Study of Social Conflict* (New York: Free Press, 1967) p. 2.
14. L. Coser *ibid.* p. 5.

# 2 WAR

Wars and different kinds of fighting have occurred in the world since God created it. The origin of war is the desire of certain human beings to take revenge upon others. Each party is supported by the people sharing in its group feeling. When they have sufficiently excited each other for the purpose and the parties confront each other, one seeking revenge and the other trying to defend itself, there is war. It is something natural among human beings. No nation and no race is free from it.

The reason for such revenge is as a rule either jealousy and envy, or hostility, or zeal in behalf of God and His religion, or zeal in behalf of royal authority and the effort to found a kingdom.

The first kind of war usually occurs between neighbouring tribes and competing families.

The second kind—war caused by hostility—is usually found among savage nations living in the desert, such as the Arabs, the Turks, the Turkomans, the Kurds, and similar people. They earn their sustenance with their lances, and their livelihood by depriving other people of their possessions. They declare war against those who defend their property against them.

The third is the war the religious law calls 'the holy war'.

The fourth kind, finally, is dynastic war against seceders and those who refuse obedience.[1]

During the early stages of the Second World War, Robert Park complained that there was a vast literature on war, but that 'aside from what has been written about the science and art of warfare, there is little or nothing in the literature that throws light on the nature of war or its role and function in the natural history of society'.[2] This may explain why Ibn Khaldūn's typology of the causes and types of war—quoted above—is still relevant, even though it was written in the late Middle Ages. This quotation contains our basic, almost commonsense, knowledge of the chief features of war—its universality, its existence throughout human history, its root in man's aggressiveness. It also classifies wars into four kinds which, given modern names, are still entirely acceptable: (1) war among different nations, clans, or tribes, competing for territory, wealth or sovereignty rights; (2) war waged by professional warriors, that is, war as a way of life for plunderers, pirates, or mercenaries; (3) ideological and religious war; (4) civil war. Of course, Ibn Khaldūn's four types often appear mixed in actual armed conflict. For our purposes, war can be defined as the type of social conflict which occurs through the organisation of a collectivity aimed at the partial or total physical destruction and subjugation of people, always involving bloodshed. War is thus an organised, deadly quarrel.

Ibn Khaldūn started his treatment of war by assuming its basic cause to be an innate vengeful desire in men. It has just been seen how the hypothesis of innate human aggressiveness is now being explored by psychologists and biologists. Although a final answer has not yet been found, there is conclusive evidence that environmental pressures over population and scarcity of goods and territory may be among the factors that unleash violence. Social scientists have studied these problems as they appear in a wider, non-clinical setting. To do so, they chose tribal societies where complexity was reduced to a minimum and a great number of variables could properly be observed. From the evidence collected by social anthropologists it emerges that war is not a biological necessity, but a 'cultural invention' (to use Margaret Mead's expression). The varieties of primitive warfare are such that not one single pattern, common to all men, emerges. Types of armed contest range from ceremonial and ritualistic warfare, to all-out wars of extermination, through pillaging expeditions, jousts and family or lineage feuds strictly regulated by tribal or inter-tribal law.[2] Environmental factors may have played a role in the remote past of a people, but they often fail to explain its present attitudes toward war. Some tribes educate their children in the ways of ferocity and warfare, like the notorious Jibaro Indians of Ecuador for whom vendettas and professional war are the only worthy occupations for a male. Other tribes raise men in the opposite virtues, like the Pueblo Indians in North America. In every case, though, violence and war are not left to their caprice: the proper manner, place and time of conducting them and the choice of group to be attacked are regulated by intricate laws and customs. Headhunting, raids, ordeals, the taking of prisoners, all obey such rules,[3] further confirming the all-important cultural dimension of organised violence, and thus invalidating any explanation solely based on the supposedly innate urges of man.

Of all efforts made by sociologists towards a systematic explanation of war, Quincy Wright's is perhaps the most massive and thorough. He has been able to give detailed accounts of the several historical stages of war ('animal', primitive, historic or civilised, and modern), as well as to show patterns and fluctuations in the intensity of modern wars, and their functions and dysfunctions for the societies involved. Wright's monumental effort is however, only a basis or platform from which further studies will have to be carried out, for in spite of the wealth of information presented by him his theoretical conclusions are still elementary. According to Wright war depends on four factors: (1) technology, especially military technology; (2) law; (3) social structure, especially in regard to the political units within which it exists: tribes, empires, nations; (4) the network of opinions and attitudes present. Conflict may arise at each of these levels and, as Karl Deutsch explains presenting Wright's theory:

> violent conflict becomes probable whenever there is an overloading or breakdown of the mechanisms or arrangements that have controlled the interplay of actions and actors at any level and that previously have preserved some non-violent balance or equilibrium . . .
> Whenever there is a major change at any level—culture and values, political and social institutions, laws, or technology—the old adjustment and control mechanisms become strained and may break down. Any major psychological and cultural, or major social and political, or legal, or technological change in the world thus increases the risk of war, unless it is balanced by compensatory political, legal, cultural and psychological adjustments. Peace thus requires ever new efforts, new arrangements, and often new institutions to preserve the peace or to restore its partial or worldwide breakdown.[4]

The accumulation of historical data about past wars and the tabulation and quantification of those data, interesting as they are, seem to pose fewer difficulties than the direct sociological study of warfare and its effects. Nevertheless, sociologists have been able to produce valuable studies on the military (VII, 6), on armies under the strain of battle, on social cohesion and the functions of primary group solidarity in battle, on racial integration in platoons, on tacit conventions amongst enemies whereby unofficial and regular truces are established, and on several other related phenomena.[5] The study of the cultural aspects of war—especially war propaganda and aggressive ideologies—has also attracted much attention. Sumner had already stressed that the mental and physical preparation for war is a self-fulfilling prophecy that itself leads inevitably to war. 'What we prepare for—he said—is what we shall get'.[6] This phenomenon, later called 'war expectancy' by Gordon Allport, is based on the fact that people's behaviour is determined by what they expect. One of the problems then, is to determine when and how certain groups, elites or leaders, can provoke and organise the people of a nation to fight.[7]

Neither sociologists nor other groups of social and natural scientists have been very successful in contributing to mankind's efforts to stop war. However—and contrary to some popular beliefs about their supposedly neutral and aloof attitude towards this harrowing characteristic of human society—many sociologists have geared their efforts to the study of the conditions of peace and the avoidance of war. In this their research has been naturally tinged with their political attitudes and personal and moral convictions, but their overriding idea has been to work towards the abolition of warfare, especially under its contemporary forms, where thermonuclear weapons would cause irreparable damage and spell the worst moral failure in human history—the very failure of our modern civilisation which is, in several senses, the highest ever to develop on the face of the earth. The advice given by contemporary sociologists and social philosophers on these matters may be imperfect, and uncompelling in a world carried away by its own narrow ideologies and passions, but the risks of ignoring it altogether are perhaps too great. All one can do from these pages is to invite the concerned reader to turn to these sources.[8]

## NOTES on Chapter IX, Section 2

1. Ibn Khaldūn *The Muqqaddimah* (London: Routledge & Secker, abridged ed. 1967) pp. 223–24.
2. M. Mead 'Warfare is Only an Invention, not a Biological Necessity' in L. Bramson and G. Goethals *op. cit.* pp. 269–74; in the same volume B. Malinowski 'An Anthropological Analysis of War' (pp. 245–68) and J. Schneider 'Primitive Warfare' (pp. 275–83).

3. O. Sohannan ed. *Law and Warfare* (Garden City: Natural History Press, 1967).
4. K. Deutsch's Preface to the second edition of Q. Wright *A Study of War* (University of Chicago, 1964) pp. xiii–xiv.
5. In general, the *Journal of Conflict Resolution* is a good source for these matters. Cf. also A. E. Ashworth 'The Sociology of Trench Warfare' *Brit. Jnl. Soc.* (1968) Vol. XIX, no. 4, pp. 407–23.
6. W. G. Sumner 'War' in L. Bramson and G. Goethals *op. cit.* p. 227.
7. G. Allport 'The Role of Expectancy' in *ibid.*, p. 177; R. Aron *Peace and War* (London: Weidenfeld, 1962).
8. R. Aron *The Century of Total War* (Boston: Beacon, 1955); C. W. Mills *The Causes of World War III* (New York: Simon & Schuster, 1958); J. U. Nef *War and Human Progress* (Harvard University, 1950); A. Etzioni 'War and Disarmament' in R. K. Merton and R. A. Nisbet *Contemporary Social Problems* (New York: Harcourt Brace, 1966) pp. 723–823; M. Nicholson *Conflict Analysis* (London: English Universities, 1970); also Brian Crozier 'The Study of Conflict' in *Conflict Studies* special number (Oct. 1970) no. 7. The most important general statement on war and society remains Thucydides' *The Peloponnesian War*. (Clausewitz's classical study *On War*, 1873, is about strategy and its underlying philosophy).

## 3   REVOLUTION

Revolution is a form of war, specifically of civil war, whose results in many ways differ from those of other forms of social conflict. Revolution may be defined as an intense and rapid societal process of change involving an armed insurrection which results in profound and wide structural transformations. Of all social disturbances and forms of social change only those that bring about changes in the relationships of power, hierarchy, prevailing ideology, and similarly important features of the society as a whole can receive the name of revolutions. We say that the French conflagration of 1789 was a revolution because, after it, the bourgeoisie and the middle classes came to predominate in the state, the Church lost much power, new educational policies were pursued, the franchise began to spread, and the notion of citizenship was established in France. In contrast with events such as this one, military coups, palace 'revolutions', pronunciamentos, abdications and other changes of government that do not alter the fundamental nature of society are not revolutions. (Strictly speaking, even important trends such as the industrial revolution or the educational revolution are not revolutions in the sense of the definition just given, though, to complicate matters, these very trends can either help provoke a revolution or, conversely, be the result of revolutionary policies or social movements.)

Modern students of revolution have had an important tradition on which to build. The earliest classic in the field, Aristotle's work on politics, already contains unsurpassed observations on the behaviour of classes and individuals under rapid social change and on their role in bringing it about. (It is from Aristotle's use of the Greek word for this phenomenon, *stasis*, that the study of revolution has recently received the name of *stasiology*.) Machiavelli's work (both his *Prince* and his *Discourses*) and that of Hobbes' (the *Behemoth* especially) are also outstanding examples of this tradition. The modern phase in the study of revolution began with Edmund Burke's contemporary *Reflections* on the French Revolution and Tocqueville's later study. Both these authors began by discerning patterns and continuities that were later to be confirmed by sociologists. Marx's work was decisive for the analysis of class relationships in the revolutionary process, as well as for its contribution to the notion of counterrevolution. Since Marx revolutionary authors and even politicians have enriched our knowledge in many ways; Georges Sorel's *Reflections on Violence* (1908), Lenin's *The State and the Revolution* (1917) and Ernesto Guevara's (*el Che's*) writings on revolutionary guerrilla warfare are just a few examples of political literature with great indirect sociological value. These texts have been essential for the development of the contemporary theory of revolution.

Revolutions are 'total' phenomena which leave no area of society untouched. The social transformation is accompanied by transformations in values, laws, religion, power and technology, even though the new society never entirely differs from that which gave it birth. As Tocqueville showed, post-revolutionary France (and Europe) was in many a sense the continuation, even the fulfilment of the *ancien regime* world. Even Marx (who envisaged a revolution as a mutation rather than as a deep, though continued, sequence of changes) thought of the epoch before the revolution as carrying its seeds in it and embodying the logic of its own destruction. Next to being total, revolutions are characteristic of their historical period. The revolution that took place in Egypt during the reign of Amenhotep IV (1380–1362 BC) which destroyed the power of the old-temple aristocracy and implanted a universalistic monotheism, abstract thinking in law and a more popular form of art, and which gave social prominence to soldiers and upstarts, was essentially different and led Egyptian society in an entirely different direction from, say, the Athenian democratic revolution, exemplified by the appointment of Solon as a law giver (VII to VI BC). Each historical period possesses its own revolutionary patterns. It is for this reason that the generalisations that follow will be restricted only to modern revolutions—that is, those taking place since the Puritan revolution of 1640 in England. (This revolution was probably the first modern one in history and, by the same token, the last of the pre-modern ones; on the one hand it opened the way to the triumph of the bourgeoisie and parliamentarianism, on the other it was still a deeply religious affair.)

Revolutions that may be termed 'modern' occur when a specific number of circumstances concur in the same country. If only one or several of these appear it is likely that we are confronted with a quasi-revolutionary situation, or even with a great deal of upheaval and disturbance, but not with a fully-fledged revolution. For a revolution to take place the following factors—which appear here somewhat arbitrarily under nine headings—must all be present in one single society:

1 *Intense class antagonism* The popular conception of revolutionary situations always sees them largely as the outcome of a great deal of hostility between the 'haves' and the 'have-nots'. This is of course a truism but, as usual, the matter is far from simple. A great number of *jacqueries*, bread riots, proletarian or slave outbursts, urban revolts, have been directed against a privileged class deemed the culprit of the people's distress. Very frequently these disturbances have occurred when the people have been driven to despair by famine, ruthless taxation, or some form of painful oppression. Countless times, however, these outbursts have not been oriented towards the conscious revolutionary transformation of society, but only towards the restoration of 'justice'. (In the process, wanton destruction may have become an ephemeral end in itself.) Just as frequently, traditional patterns of inequality are restored, often after a successful pacification campaign, aimed at punishing the rebels and harnessing the majority. If anything, class antagonism and hatred may be greater after these phases of reaction than before. What matters for the possible revolution is that such feelings of antagonism exist, or that they can be easily created in a population whose consensual attitudes and political culture still reinforce the prevailing system. Otherwise failure awaits the would-be revolutionary leaders. Under the impact of Western revolutionary ideas,

Russian intellectuals turned to the peasantry in the early phases of the nineteenth century, only to find a deaf ear. And while the peasants remained in serfdom they never posed a threat to the Czarist system. Genuine class antagonism includes the development of acute class consciousness (IV, 3) in the lower classes *and* a loss of deference for traditional authority. When these two elements have not been present together, mankind has toiled under the most oppressive systems without engaging in revolution, save for periodic explosions of blind wrath. Other elements must intervene to turn the diffuse if deep discontent generated by certain forms of domination and inequality into a truly revolutionary force.

2  *The frustration of rising economic expectations*   As both Marx and Tocqueville clearly pointed out, it is not utter poverty that triggers off revolution but the perception of inequality as unjust and unbearable. This has the important corollary that revolution may actually break out under conditions of unprecedented 'prosperity' for the lower class; as Marx and Engels say:

> A noticeable increase in wages presupposes a rapid growth of productive capital. The rapid growth of productive capital brings about an equally rapid growth of wealth, luxury, social wants, social enjoyments. Thus, although the enjoyments of the workers have risen, the social satisfaction that they give has fallen in comparison with the increased enjoyments of the capitalist, which are inaccessible to the worker, in comparison with the state of development of society in general. Our desires and pleasures spring from society; we measure them, therefore, by society and not by the objects which serve for their satisfaction. Because they are of a social nature, they are of a relative nature.[1]

Now, when 'the enjoyments of workers' steadily rise over a prolonged period it is sensible to suppose that people's expectations of greater prosperity will also steadily rise, until people find this a 'normal' fact of life. It is then that the possibility of revolution begins to materialise. 'Nations that have endured patiently and almost unconsciously the most overwhelming oppression often burst into rebellion against the yoke the moment it begins to grow lighter' says Tocqueville.[2] Combining this idea with that contained in the previous quotation by Marx and Engels, James Davies has concluded that an explanation of revolutionary change based on the relationship between rising expectations of an important section of the lower classes and economic fluctuations can be given. As he puts it, 'revolutions are most likely to occur when a prolonged period of objective economic and social development is followed by a short period of sharp reversal'. Davies encloses the following figure to illustrate this statement:

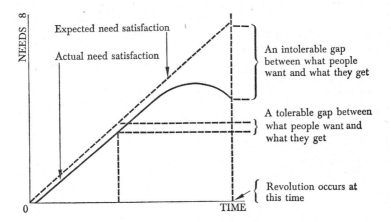

This curve is, of course, simplified, but Davies takes several concrete instances of revolutions, revolts and coups, and observes that they occur when rising expectations are frustrated (Marx), though general conditions are actually improving. By way of example, here is Davies' diagram for the Bolshevik revolution:

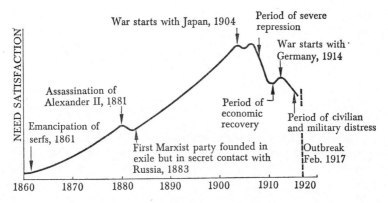

Once again, if other factors do not concur with these economic and psychological trends, revolution becomes an impossibility: a powerful government, as we shall see, can perfectly well ride this very delicate phase in the dynamics of long-run and short-run economic fluctuations. What really makes the situation explosive is the combination of two kinds of frustration—that of rising economic expectations and that of rising status and power expectations.

3 *The frustration of rising status and power expectations* The kind of social change that precedes the actual outbreak of revolution involves the development of new strata of upwardly mobile people who cannot find what they deem a proper place in the society. The rigidity of the social world in which they live becomes increasingly stifling for them, until they decide to challenge the entire system. The denial of access to higher rank to people who, by other standards, already rank fairly high, may incite them to the use of violent means to achieve this end. This means that serious status discontinuities and incongruences are at play in every pre-revolutionary period. Thus, the bourgeoisie in pre-revolutionary France ranked high in wealth as well as in importance for running public affairs (often as civil servants), banks, industry and trade, but were barred access to the state apparatus, the officer corps, and the high ranks of the Church. Since no substantial concessions were made, they became increasingly radical in their demands. Though the ennoblement of commoners, the intermarriage of the noble with the merely wealthy, and the buying of office were not uncommon in France and elsewhere on the Continent they were not common enough to forestall the final explosion. By contrast, after the Glorious Revolution in England (1688)—actually the last phase of the revolution begun in 1640—big Whig landowners and merchants were able largely to consolidate the resulting openness of the British polity, and thus to exclude the possibility of future cataclysms of the proportions of the French or Russian revolutions. 'The more a social class is capable of absorbing the best men of the oppressed class, the more solid it becomes, the more dangerous is its reign' said Marx, looking at the problem with the eyes of a true revolutionary.[4]

The strata that most strongly feel the frustration created by the rigidity of the social rank system are those nearest the class to be overthrown. Proletarian discontent may be an important factor in the overall pattern of revolution, but in some of its decisive phases the petty bourgeoisie and the intellectuals (see below) may become the spearhead of revolutionary change. The most demanding revolutionaries are those for whom the status rewards seem closest, and yet are out of reach. This generalisation can be extended to all classes. Better-paid workers tend to be more vocal, articulate and less 'reformist' than their lower-paid fellows. In contemporary situations technicians, experts and often white-collar workers press for workers' management and participation (as against mere salary rises) with greater frequency than people in lower occupational groups. Commenting on the failed revolution of 1968 in France, Alain Touraine says:

> ... The workers movement was largely inspired by men who were at the borderline of the worker condition (*condition ouvrière*), as near to artisans as they were to workers ... the strata that manifested the strongest class consciousness were not manual workers (*manoeuvres*) locked up in the proletarian condition who, for this very reason, did not transcend what has often been called 'economism', that is, the revindication of only a higher salary and better working conditions.
>
> ... It is only the skilled worker who makes the critique of the power of the boss (*pouvoir patronal*) and transcends the pure economic defence invoking production against property, progress against profit.
>
> [Today] class consciousness appears strongest not amongst those who are marginal and excluded from the system, but amongst the technicians who belong to the great modern organisations, who share in economic growth, but who can simultaneously oppose the creativity of technology and knowledge to the power of the organisation.[5]

4 *The incapacity of the ruling classes*   There are three senses in which the ruling classes must be capable in order to survive and to defuse revolution in modern times. First, they must be able to open their ranks to other people. In the second place, they must be able to cope with inevitable technical and economic transformations. In the modern world wherever they have entrenched themselves in a policy of traditionalism and rejection of industrialisation, they have quickly perished. But there are opposite examples. When the Japanese upper classes realised the futility and the dangers of their artificial prolongation of feudalism, they began a formidable 'revolution' from above aimed at transforming their country into a capitalist industrial nation. The first industrialised country in the world, England, had already seen a not altogether dissimilar process. In other countries by contrast, such as Russia, Spain, Hungary and even Germany until quite late, the nobility had by and large been very reluctant to invest the product of agricultural surplus into industrial ventures,[6] thus creating conditions for revolutionary violence.

Thirdly, it is also vital that the upper (especially the ruling) classes show a vigorous and creative political capacity in conditions of change. Revolution is unlikely where an efficient government operates with a well-defined policy. In Russia neither the last Czarist rule nor Kerenski's provisional government were efficient in any sense of the word. (The muddled and erratic Czarist police force, though more efficient than it looked, was no match in the end for the revolutionary clandestine organisations.) In Cuba, the government of dictator Batista and his army were incapable in every sense. It is understandable that revolutionaries magnify the size and power of their defeated enemy, but their success depends largely on the political ineptitude of the ruling groups, as Lenin implied in his writings. It is this ineptitude that may prompt the abandonment of the bourgeoisie by the army when matters begin to get out of hand. And, as Lenin explicitly added, it is a requirement of revolution that the army ceases to be loyal to the upper classes.[7] In modern times no uprising can face a united upper and middle class which is backed unflinchingly by a loyal army.

5 *A fraction of the upper classes joins the enemy*　Provided that the defection of the army from the government does not involve a *coup* that saves the established system, its disloyalty is accompanied in revolutions by another, perhaps more serious, kind of defection —the 'going over' to the enemy of segments (or whole strata) of the upper classes. In 1959 Fidel Castro and his guerrillas commanded the enthusiasm and the respect of the Cuban middle classes fed up with the corruption of the regime. Cromwell summoned the help of the middle and a great part of the upper bourgeoisie. In Russia the Kerenski government, which guaranteed the freedom of all parties, was a bourgeois government. Even during the later, more extremist, phases of revolutions, upper middle class and even formerly upper class individuals are prominent in the hierarchy of power.

6 *The hostility of the intellectual community*　A great segment of this part of the middle and upper classes that goes over to the enemy is formed by the intellectuals. Their role in modern revolutions can hardly be exaggerated, even though it is complex, since intellectuals themselves tend to be prominent amongst the first victims of the triumphant revolution. Intellectuals tend to perceive status deprivation perhaps more painfully, feeling doubly isolated and 'useless' under the tyrannical regime whose overthrow they plan. They move in a world of doctrines and ideas and in revolutionary periods these appear to be in great demand. They can also be very useful in fulfilling the technical gaps left by the former ruling

groups, and helping far less competent revolutionary individuals. A Jewish revolutionary such as Trotsky, who became a great general and created the Red Army, is perhaps the classic example of the rise of the intellectual to power. As the composition of the Jacobin, the Bolshevik and other governments shows, the share of intellectuals in revolutionary power is more than marginal. On a larger plane, as creators and developers of doctrines and ideas—their stock in trade—their role is even greater.

7 *The revolutionary myth* No proper revolution has ever occurred without an ideology. In the long run ideologies often harden into dogmas and are manipulated by bureaucrats and politicians who are hardly sympathetic to the most cherished values of the intellectual community—freedom of thought, and creative criticism of the world. In the process ideas become the opposite of what they were meant to be. Darwin's 'survival of the fittest' and Nietzsche's 'superman' had nothing to do with the Nazi *Herrenrasse*; there was no room in the thought of Proudhon, Marx, Engels and Kropotkin for nationalism, imperialism, and concentration camps. But the intellectual sources of what will later become a stereotyped, degraded doctrine must be there, especially during the earliest phases of a revolution. Only the creation of a pluralist polity to forestall the monolithic crystallisation of a totalitarian regime can guarantee that this process does not occur. But this is another matter: what has to be stressed is that no modern revolution begins without a doctrine which is basically a myth in the sociological sense of the word (VIII, 2, 4). Moreover, a revolutionary ideology is a central element in the whole process. Peter Calvert does not exaggerate when he says that 'the generation of revolutionary energy implies the creation of a rival centre of ideological interpretation. The actual efficiency of the revolutionary machine...is not necessarily as important as it seems'.[8] What is decisive is that some key aspects of the revolutionary ideology find a proper positive echo in large sections of the population and that they are not only fully adopted by certain small strategic action groups. Members of threatened governments are frequently paranoic and so misinterpret this phenomenon. They deny that broad sectors of the population can declare themselves for any seemingly just cause; if they are unruly, or in open rebellion, it is a handful of traitors and a sinister conspiracy of a few men behind the entire affair. Yet we know otherwise from the study of ideology: at least in its decisive early stages, the revolutionary ideology, to succeed, must express a historically correct formulation of the aspirations, longings and frustrations of many people.

8 *The duality of power*   The authoritative production of an alternative ideology to the one officially established indicates that as the
revolutionary process gathers momentum power is split in two.
Lenin stressed the importance of this. The revolutionary elites take
over at a given moment the leadership of a certain section of the
population, and challenge the legitimacy of established power; a
revolutionary civil war ensues. (In many revolutions, this process
may repeat itself by the emergence of a new centre of power
challenging the new government that overthrew the previous one in
the first place, and all in the name of 'revolutionary legality'.
The French and the Russian Revolutions are examples of several
stages of a movement towards the left. The Thermidorian Reaction
in France, which ended the rule of Robespierre, was the beginning
of an opposite set of counter reactions—this time towards the right
—culminating in the proclamation of an Emperor and the dissolution of the Republic.) The clearest instance of a duality of power is
usually found during the first stages of the revolution. Roundheads
and Cavaliers, Cromwell and Charles I are the dramatic embodiment of this duality, the representation of cleavages and opposed
forces in a society whose contradictory paths could find no solution
other than to clash on the field of battle.

9 *The appropriate international situation*   Favourable external conditions are obviously essential for successful revolution. Whether it is
to nip a revolutionary movement in the bud, or to promote it,
foreign intervention is often decisive. The same Soviet troops that
toppled a liberal, Western-type democracy in Czechoslovakia in
1948 destroyed a quiet, internal revolution towards a humane and
democratic socialism twenty years later. In Russia itself, foreign
intervention at the time of the revolution was not only unable to
hinder its development but actually reinforced it, making it even
more radical.

The study of revolution does not end with the analysis of its
conditions and the factors at play. Detailed research on the social
origin of revolutionaries, the techniques of insurrection, propaganda,
the function of crowds, and several other aspects are also pursued
by sociologists. Of particular interest is the study of the several
periods into which revolutionary movements can be divided. In all
these fields the literature is abundant, though not entirely satisfactory.[9] One of the reasons for its gaps and imperfections is a
function of the inevitable secrecy which surrounds revolutionary

events. Unfortunately the sociological study of some of the most interesting revolutions—the Chinese and the Cuban—is still very difficult. And yet this is a field of endless fascination, which seems stubbornly to conceal some basic truth about the modern predicament and about modern man's restless search for an earthly paradise,[10] for all modern revolutions are about progress, and all include some notion of Eden.

*NOTES on Chapter IX, Section 3*

1. K. Marx and F. Engels 'Wage Labour and Capital' in *Selected Works* Moscow: Foreign Languages Publishing House, 1955) Vol. I, p. 94; quoted by J. C. Davies in 'Toward a Theory of Revolution' *Am. Sociol. Rev.* (1962) Vol. 27 no. 1, p. 5.
2. A. de Tocqueville *The Old Regime and the Revolution* (Garden City: Doubleday, 1955) pp. 176–77; also quoted by J. C. Davies *ibid.* p. 6.
3. *Ibid.* p. 6; for a study of actual cases see rest of article, pp. 8–19.
4. K. Marx *Das Kapital* (Berlin: Dietz, 1949 ed.) p. 140. For a contemporary Marxist view of this problem cf. J. R. Recalde *Integración y lucha de clases en el neocapitalismo* (Madrid: Ciencia Nueva, 1968).
5. A. Touraine *Le Mouvement de mai ou le communisme utopique* (Paris: Seuil, 1968) p. 23.
6. For these questions about 'industrialisation from above' and the origins for the bourgeois revolution see B. Moore *op. cit.*
7. Quoted by G. Lenski *Power and Privilege, op. cit.* p. 71.
8. P. Calvert *A Study of Revolution* (Oxford: Clarendon, 1970) p. 175.
9. Apart from the sources quoted above (notes 1, 2, 4, 5 and 8), see C. Brinton *Anatomy of Revolution* (New York: Doubleday 1957 ed.); S. Chakhotin *The Rape of the Masses* (London: Routledge, 1940); C. Johnson *Revolution and the Social System* (Stanford University, 1964); H. D. Lasswell and D. Lerner eds. *World Revolutionary Elites* (Cambridge, Mass.: MIT, 1966); J. Monnerot *Sociologie de la revolution* (Paris: Fayard, 1969); E. Lussu *Teoria dell'insurrezione* (Paris: Giustizia e libertà, 1936); A. Decoufle *Sociologie des Revolutions* (Paris: PUF, 1968); G. Baechler *Les Phenomènes Révolutionnaires* (Paris: PUF, 1970).
10. J. Passmore, *The Perfectibility of Man* (London: Duckworth, 1970) pp. 304–327.

# 4 ANOMY

Social life is a constant struggle for order. Instead of proving the contrary, conflict illustrates this proposition all too well, for it is a source of cohesion, authority and group bonding, as well as a contest directed towards the ultimate establishment of a new equilibrium of forces. A closely related phenomenon, which also illustrates the permanent need for order found in every society, is anomy. Anomy can be broadly defined as a state of normlessness which, by leaving man without moral guidance, results in a 'lack of restraint' on his part and in a disorderly 'liberation of his desires'. This concept was introduced in the modern sociological literature by Emile Durkheim. He realised that there were situations that produced a void of norms and therefore a state of mental and moral confusion in the individual who found himself at the centre of them. Such situations were produced by a varied number of causes, such as contradictory economic forces, political chaos, certain ideological cleavages, and weak and confused moral standards. These causes arise either singly or all together, as in times of deep social crisis. They are all essentially external to the individual, which means that the source of his anomic state of mind must not be sought in his personality but rather in the social processes of anomy to which he is subjected.

Under conditions of crisis the individual loses his orientation, and does not know which values to uphold. Much crime, violence and suicide arising at times of social confusion can be traced to anomic states. The latter, it must be stressed, are the consequence of contradictory demands and goals and are therefore not to be identified with any situation of crisis, though these can also play a role in creating a void of moral norms. If the norms are clear, if the group is well integrated, and its cultural, economic and political goals are well established, a group may successfully ride a storm or face penury. Some excerpts from Durkheim will help clarify the broad implications of this important notion:

> No living being can be happy or even exist unless his needs are sufficiently proportioned to his means. In other words, if his needs require more than can be granted, or even merely something of a different sort, they will be under continual friction and can only function painfully.
>
> ... Human nature is substantially the same among all men, in its essential qualities. It is not human nature which can assign the variable limits necessary to our needs. They are thus unlimited so far as they depend on the individual alone. Irrespective of any external regulatory force, our capacity for feeling is in itself an insatiable and bottomless abyss.
>
> ... But if nothing external can restrain this capacity, it can only be a source of torment to itself. Unlimited desires are insatiable by definition and insatiability is rightly considered a sign of morbidity.
>
> ... when society is disturbed by some painful crisis or by beneficent but abrupt translations, it is momentarily incapable of exercising this [necessary and restraining] influence [on man's

unlimited desires] thence come the sudden rises in the curve of suicides...

In the case of economic disaster, indeed, something like a declassification occurs which suddenly casts certain individuals into a lower state than their previous one. Then they must reduce their requirements, restrain their needs, learn greater self-control ... their moral education has to be recommenced.

... It is the same if the source of the crisis is an abrupt growth of power and wealth... Since the relations between various parts of society are necessarily modified, the ideas expressing these relations must change. Some particular class especially favoured by the crisis is no longer resigned to its former lot, and, on the other hand, the example of its greater good fortune arouses all sorts of jealousy below and about it. Appetites, not being controlled by public opinion, become disoriented, no longer recognize the limits proper to them... With increased prosperity desires increase... The state of de-regulation or *anomy* is thus further heightened by passions being less disciplined, precisely when they need more disciplining.[1]

In spite of the very general level at which these words were written, anomy has proved to be an empirically testable notion. Thus, Robert Merton was able to show how the conflict between 'cultural goals'—culturally defined ambitions—and 'institutional norms' gave rise to concrete anomic situations in contemporary American society and, moreover, how these situations are consistently related to the different areas of the social structure. American ideological tenets often inculcate in individuals unwarranted hopes and expectations of social success, riches and power. The myth is that the world is open to fair competition amongst equals. As the individual grows and enters the fray, serious discrepancies arise between his orientations—culturally defined goals—and the harsh realities of prejudice, favouritism, scarcity of jobs at the top, and other barriers. Human ambitions, as Durkheim's above quotations tell us, can be limitless unless some sociocultural restraint is put on them; the American myth of success does precisely the opposite.

Confronted with anomy, individuals may turn to other means to obtain the goals that they continue to cherish. Italians are prominent in American gangsterism, not because they are Italians but because over a long period of time white, Catholic, Southern Europeans were discriminated against in business, politics and status circles by the white Protestant majority of 'Anglo-Saxon' America.[2] These immigrants avoided, if they could, industrial manual labour, but found white-collar, 'respectable' occupations out of their reach. For some of them, especially those who already had had some experience of organised *mafia* or *camorra* crime in Sicily or Naples, the networks of illegal 'protection' rackets or bootlegging became a source of the money they needed for the kind of success they wanted. Though this is only one sketched example, one thing immediately becomes apparent: precisely because anomy implies normlessness, it prompts men to reorganise and restore order. Organised crime is far from being the only possible solution to anomy; ideological subservience, sect formation, the creation of voluntary associations, are other examples of social reorganisation as a partial response to it. Crime and delinquency cannot be solely explained in its terms, but frequently the aimlessness and normlessness of anomic situations are the remote causes leading to criminal behaviour.

*NOTES on Chapter IX, Section 4*

1. E. Durkheim *Suicide op. cit.* Quotation in Eng. trans. L. A. Coser and B. Rosenberg eds. *Sociological Theory* (New York: Macmillan, 1969 ed.) pp. 523–29.
2. R. K. Merton *Social Theory . . . op. cit.* pp. 125–33.

# 5 FROM DEVIANCE TO DELINQUENCY

*Consensus and deviance*

We have seen how great is the effort people put into the creation of the kind of consensual behaviour that is expected to maintain the specific structures of their societies. Even physical coercion and forced indoctrination are aimed at the creation of a 'spontaneous' state of consensus (III, 4). But social life constantly involves institutions, individuals, groups, classes and collectivities of every kind, with problems which are not always foreseen and which demand an immediate response for which there is not always a readymade answer in the consensual system of norms. The formulation of new policies, doctrines, beliefs and orientations of behaviour by community leaders, politicians, local notables, opinion leaders and others, or even by the collectivity at large, may not satisfy the needs of an individual, subclass or subgroup. Under such circumstances, they begin to deviate from the accepted norms, and follow courses of action which are at variance with custom, law, or folkways. Deviance, then, is behaviour that does not follow the accepted norms of a group, and which occurs where they ought to apply. (If this behaviour occurs in areas which are outside the reach of the group, we simply say they are exotic.)

The notion of deviance poses many problems as soon as it has been defined. Deviance covers a spectrum which goes from the tolerated (and even popularly approved of) antics of the harmless eccentric to the pernicious activities of the dangerous criminal. The new fads and habits of a younger generation may be considered as deviant. The age-old traditions of an immigrant people will also be considered aberrant by the host population. The boy who abandons his lower class regional accent in favour of an upper class one will also be derided by his friends and perhaps his family for deviating from the accepted speech norms. It is not surprising then, that deviance has been called one of the 'sloppiest terms in the sociological vocabulary' which 'no longer seems adequate to embrace the varieties of dissent, conflict, rebellion, and repression which occur in all societies and which have assumed such vast dimensions in the twentieth century'.[1] And yet, until a new concept or series of concepts is found, deviance will have to be used to denote one of the basic phenomenon which is behind all these developments. Crime, especially, must be partially expressed in its terms, though (one must hasten to say) the identification of crime with deviance is one of the most serious mistakes a sociologist can make.

Crime is crime because the law defines it as such. The same can be said of deviance; if crime is an offence against the law, deviance is an offence against the mores, which also define 'right' and 'wrong' behaviour. Without denying the possibility of universal ethical principles at work in every human society, this is the only acceptable position in its study by the science of criminology. The relationships between lawfulness and illegality, morality and immorality, the honourable and the dishonourable, are so intricate that no simple and brief treatment of the question can ever be given.[2] Crime and delinquency are deviant behaviour because a group defines them so, although other groups may think exactly the opposite. The same man is a bandit for some and a heroic guerrilla for others. In gaol some prisoners are held in admiration and respect precisely for the kind of crimes they once committed. The admission of these facts does not imply that sociology ignores morality, or that it can be used as a justification of moral relativism.

It just means that it takes a very cautious attitude in the analysis of the basic moral indignation which is often at the root of the reaction of a group or the public to certain transgressions. If anything our evidence points to the existence in some vital areas of the social order of clear regularities common to very diverse societies, in spite of the also present moral discontinuities. The following table illustrates this point in one such important area.

*Number of societies punishing specific types of sexual behaviour*[3]

| Number of societies measured | Percentage punishing | Type of behaviour and person punished |
|---|---|---|
| 54 | 100 | Incest |
| 82 | 100 | Abduction of married woman |
| 84 | 99 | Rape of married woman |
| 55 | 95 | Rape of unmarried woman |
| 43 | 95 | Sexual relations during post partum period |
| 15 | 93 | Bestiality by adult |
| 73 | 92 | Sexual relations during menstruation |
| 88 | 89 | Adultery: paramour punished |
| 93 | 87 | Adultery: wife punished |
| 22 | 86 | Sexual relations during lactation period |
| 57 | 86 | Infidelity of fiancée |
| 74 | 85 | Illegitimate impregnation: woman punished |
| 62 | 84 | Illegitimate impregnation: man punished |
| 30 | 77 | Seduction of prenubile girl (man punished) |
| 44 | 68 | Male homosexuality |
| 49 | 67 | Sexual relations during pregnancy |
| 16 | 44 | Masturbation |
| 97 | 44 | Premarital relations; woman punished |
| 93 | 41 | Premarital relations: man punished |
| 12 | 33 | Female homosexuality |
| 67 | 10 | Sexual relations with own betrothed |

## Criminology

Criminology is the science and technique that studies crime, delinquency, crime prevention, and punishment. It consists of a complex set of practical methods, research techniques, broad theories, and inherited practices which are all concerned with the specifically criminal form of social deviance. Sociology has become a very important part of criminology over the years, but crime itself is too important to be left to sociologists: legislators, the police, governments, psychiatrists and social workers are professionally concerned with it. Despite these varied institutional and occupational sources with a direct interest in the problem of delinquency and crime, criminology is not just a hotchpotch of issues, doctrines and practices. To a very large extent it is the sociology of crime that has given criminology its increasing unity and internal coherence.

From its early days sociology showed a systematic and scientific interest in the discovery of the causes of crime, in crime prevention, and in the best and least inhuman methods of redress, treatment of criminals, and punishment. In this, it immediately had a positive effect upon the agencies concerned with it. Its critical appraisal of police records, the sentencing process and the administration of justice, for instance, have helped to improve them in several countries. Today, the formulation of policies for the prevention of crime or those affecting the penal system have come to rely heavily on the work of criminal sociologists. Criminal sociology now fulfils the most demanding requirements of those practically-minded utilitarians for whom social science is not justified merely by its claim that it helps us understand social reality.[4]

## Crime and the social structure

Although the contribution of sociology to the study and prevention of crime does not stop at the study of its relationships to the social structure, it is in this field that it seems most relevant. Common sense tells us that crime is not evenly distributed over a population —prostitution is less common among the middle classes than it is amongst the poor; financial crooks can obviously be found only in certain social circles; certain areas of a town obviously present higher rates of crime than others, and so on. The first task of criminal sociology has been to establish correlations between types of crime and several variables in the social structure. From this initial task it soon became evident that no single factor can account for crime. In fact when one single factor—say, poverty or illegitimacy—is taken in isolation it tends to explain nothing. Robbers and burglars are more common in relatively affluent, but disorganised and anomic, urban areas than in a poor, but culturally well integrated, countryside, where the ties of kin and local community are very strong. This is not to say that correlations cannot be found between crime and economic and political fluctuations, or between crime and other types of violence, such as war and revolution. But they must be always further qualified by other variables —class, sex, age, profession and so on.

A very interesting aspect of criminality as it relates to the social structure is its existence as a group phenomenon. The study of criminal gang organisations has led to the formulation of several theories about their criminality and about the factors accounting for their endemic institutionalisation in certain societies. In this connection the idea that a criminal gang, once established, may generate its own patterns of socialisation and its own subculture, leading into crime those individuals who happen to be within its influence soon began to take shape in the literature. Edwin Sutherland's theory of 'differential association' is based on this assumption. Simply put it assumes that criminal behaviour is, first of all, learned behaviour. This learning happens in intimate groups which also teach the motives, drives, rationalisations, and attitudes of crime, and not just the techniques of delinquent occupations and habitual crime. According to this postulate a person becomes a criminal by being immersed in criminal surroundings—though this is obviously not the only source of criminality. Greater association with criminal surroundings creates a 'differential' for the person who is in contact with them, as he is taught, socialised and persuaded to conform to the criminal culture of his milieu. This is not simply a more complicated way of stating the well-known fact that 'bad company' and the 'vicinity of criminals' breeds a contempt for the law, because for Sutherland, crime is not the product of certain criminal groups only. Every human group presents a particular index of criminality just as it presents a specific pattern of conformity and adjustment to the other groups and institutions of society. Each conceivable community, collectivity and group is 'organised both for criminal and anti-criminal behaviour and in a sense the crime rate is an expression of the group organisation'.[5] Even the most law-abiding community will teach its own members its own version of what is right and what is wrong, what is allowed and what is specifically forbidden to them, as opposed to the law of the wider society. The proof is that even the best integrated and well established groups need constant internal restraint and supervision from outside the circle of their activities for them to lead a lawful life. The elementary criticism to this theory is that the individual's criminal behaviour is not so much the consequence of his association with a criminogenic environment as it is a consequence of his own inclinations towards criminality, which lead him to frequent delinquent milieux. However, the conclusion that both trends exist and reinforce each other seems most plausible in the light of both psychological and sociological research.

There are important precedents to the contemporary trend of looking at delinquent communities as particular subcultures geared towards the transgression of the norms of established society such as Rafael Salillas' 1898 study of the underworld as a sociocultural universe in its own right.[6] Albert Cohen's study of delinquent youths in the United States is a contemporary example of this approach. For Cohen the delinquent subculture of juvenile crime is, to a large extent, non-utilitarian, malicious and negativistic. The gang does not steal to accumulate wealth and grow in status and respectability within the adult or law-abiding society, but is oriented in the opposite direction towards flouting society (in the person of teachers, for instance), terrorising 'conventional' children, practising vandalism, fighting other gangs, and showing that it is better than them at activities it regards as important. Short-run hedonism ('fun') and the glorification of their own gang, asserting, above all, its complete autonomy, are also important characteristics of this subculture. What makes Cohen's observations pertinent is that in the first place he relates youth subculture to adult delinquency. He sees non-utilitarian criteria in theft, vandalism and inter-gang warfare as a training ground for the thoroughly utilitarian criteria of the adult professional criminal. In the second place he relates juvenile delinquency to social inequality. The child's growing awareness of the class barriers that he is going to encounter as a grown-up in a world where he is officially promised equality and opportunities of all sorts makes him the victim of an intensely anomic state.[7] Of course, not all lower class boys under these pressures choose delinquency. A great number of the ambitious ones—who do not resign themselves to being law-abiding unskilled or semi-skilled workers either—desperately struggle towards 're-spectability' and assimilation into the middle classes. William Whyte showed this in an earlier study than Cohen's where he distinguished between college aspiring boys and 'street corner' boys as two types produced by lower class culture in disorganised industrial, urban areas.[8]

The close relationships between these subcultures and their physical environment has opened an important area of research for criminologists: the ecological study of delinquency. Overcrowding, deficient housing, lack of schools, and other problems of the modern metropolis have been analysed as factors in the creation of crime. The correlations between these variables and crime are by no means simple, for family patterns, religion, political attitudes and country of origin also colour the situation. It is becoming clear however that government and community power structures (VII, 2, 5) have an indirect effect upon criminality by their direct intervention in the varied matters of land speculation, slum clearance, settlement of immigrants, and the like.[9] This is a field where the sociology of politics, urban sociology, criminology and psychiatry intersect, presenting responsible people in each of these fields with a common challenge. Mental disorders, drug addiction, family disorganisation, poverty, and community disintegration are closely related to crime and are increasing sources of great suffering in our troubled times. Together they form a vast area of social problems towards whose solution sociology is now playing an increasingly important role.[10]

*NOTES on Chapter IX, Section 5*

1. T. B. Bottomore 'Sociological Theory and the Study of Social Conflict' *op. cit.* p. 153. See also S. Box *Deviance, Reality and Society* (London: Holt, Rinehart, Winston, 1971) pp. 1–25.
2. Yet, see H. Mannheim's excellent Chapter on these matters in *Comparative Criminology* (London: Routledge, 1965) pp. 22–67; cf. also M. Ossowska *Social Determinants of Moral Ideas* (London: Routledge, 1971).
3. J. S. Brown 'A Comparative Study of Deviations from Sexual Mores' in *Am. Sociol. Rev.* (April 1952) Vol. 17, p. 138, reproduced by A. K. Cohen in *Deviance and Control* (Englewood Cliffs: Prentice Hall, 1966). This book attempts to develop a general theory of deviance.
4. For a general overview see H. Mannheim *op. cit.*, or the simpler and much shorter introduction by R. Hood and R. Sparks, *Key Issues in Criminology* (London: Weidenfeld, 1970). For a study of new and 'unorthodox' forms of crime see T. C. Willett's *Criminal on the Road* (London: Tavistock, 1964).
5. E. Sutherland *Principles of Criminology* (Philadelphia: Lippincot, 4th ed., 1947) p. 7.
6. R. Salillas *Hampa, antropología picaresca* (Madrid: Victoriano Suárez, 1898).
7. A. K. Cohen *Delinquent Boys, the Culture of the Gang* (Glencoe: Free Press, 1955).
8. W. F. Whyte *Street Corner Society* (University of Chicago, 1955, 2nd ed.).
9. T. P. Morris *The Criminal Area* (London: Routledge, 1957); H. Mannheim *Juvenile Delinquency in an English Middletown* (London: Routledge, 1949).
10. R. Nisbet and R. Merton eds. *Contemporary Social Problems* (New York: Harcourt Brace, 1966, 2nd ed.); K. Scothill *The Prisoner's Release* (London: Allen & Unwin, 1974).

# 6  GENERATIONAL CONFLICT

Socialisation, as we saw, entails the transmission of the values, norms and attitudes of the older to the younger members of a society (IV, 3). Usually there is a degree of disagreement between such cultural contents and the new situations with which the young are faced, since culture is largely a product of past experiences and received traditions. Thus a latent conflict between the generations has always existed, and its manifestations have often been attributed to the natural impetuosity and idealism of the young and inexperienced. There is much truth in this age-old contention of popular wisdom, but it cannot alone account for the important open conflicts, confrontations and cleavages that have arisen in modern societies between the older and the younger generations. These have their origin in the pace of social change in modern times; the life experience and life chances of the young are so different from those of their parents when they were young that different and conflictive outlooks arise under the same roof. But the problem does not remain at home. Young men and women no longer live in extended families and in communities (like the traditional village) where people of all ages are integrated in one way of life and in one single environment. Numerous educational institutions now give shelter to very large populations of young people for a number of years, which happen to be the years of decisive phases of sexual and emotional maturation; while they learn a skill or discipline, they are faced with the decision of finding a first serious job, and undergo their first ideological, political and religious crises. In the past, the pressures of the family and local community often gained the upper hand in resolving all these conflicts, at the expense of the initial longings, ambitions and dreams of the young man or woman. Today, however, such constraints—which have by no means died out—have become secondary in many countries. Yet their removal as serious obstacles to personal fulfilment has not always meant a fuller and richer life, for other forms of disenchantment, which are no less serious, now await the young.

Generational conflict is now taking place in all sorts of societies, and plays an important part in developments which are as different as the Chinese Cultural Revolution of the late nineteen-sixties, the urban guerrillas in South America, the student revolts in Japan, France and Germany, and the hippy movement in the United States. This type of conflict is equally important in the much less publicised setting of the countries whose societies still have or recently had, predominantly tribal social structures. In them modern education, urbanisation and detribalisation processes are sources of even greater strains. As recent wars in Africa have abundantly shown these events are far from simple. Small tribal units may be eroded, but a larger 'feeling of ethnicity' amongst people of similar racial, religious and linguistic stock may arise. Changes in the political and kinship organisation of ethnic collectivities in turn change the meaning of such feeling between members of different generations, especially if they are migrants to towns. Enid Schildkrout has shown that for Mossi immigrants into Kumasi, the old Ashanti capital in Ghana, ethnicity persists through the generations, but it substantially changes its meaning for each one of them. Amongst second-generation immigrants, cultural differences are minimal, and the neighbourhood becomes a more important basis for association than the original kinship system. In Kumasi a Mossi Youth Association sprang up during the Nkrumah regime and, though allegedly apolitical, it was clear that it could cope with the problems of the Mossi people in the midst of modern Ashanti society better than their 'tribal' elders, whose background was far less adequate for the new situation.[1] In such societies the gulf between the old and the young is much greater than it can ever be in the West, although paradoxically intergenerational violence does not necessarily have to erupt in them with the same intensity. The new states often offer varied opportunities for a number of young men, for whom the mere possession of a higher degree gives them great chances of personal advancement. Paradoxically, a great potential source of generational conflict in such countries is also the lack of opportunities for science and technology graduates. Contradictory occupational trends are thus an important part of the tensions building up in such areas.

By contrast both the frustration and the opportunities that present themselves to young men in the industrialised societies are of a very different kind. In those countries educational expansion, technological growth, affluence, and new political trends have combined to create an attitude of revolt amongst certain sections of the young. By and large such revolt is against 'the system' (a vague term, perhaps meaning the way in which the entire society is organised) but it takes place against concrete institutions, usually the most vulnerable and easy targets—the universities and institutions of higher education and technology where young people are enrolled. Yet, further generalisations about them are difficult to make. Although there might be some common problems running through the entire modern world of the young rebels—a search for *Gemeinschaft*, a struggle against the impersonality of the 'technological society', and so on—national, class, political, and cultural differences are far more pronounced than the coterminous eruption of such revolts may lead one to think. An initial sociological analysis of these problems would have to start distinguishing several distinctive trends, of which the following are but four:

I *The 'institutionalised' left-wing political revolt*   In some countries the young are in a position to identify their grievances with 'conventional' left-wing socialist and communist parties struggling for political pluralism or democracy. Spanish students who have incessantly opposed the regime in their country since 1956 identify their aspirations with those of republican legitimacy, left-wing reform programmes, and the like, although other more extremist trends have also been at work since 1969.[2] The same can be said of the Czechoslovak youth of 1968 in their very active backing of the 'Prague Spring' reform movement and of the struggle of Mexican students against the monopoly of power of one party—a struggle so murderously repressed in 1969 and 1971. The different nature of the three regimes under attack in each case must not mislead the observer: in spite of the presence of anarchistic elements in their midst, on the whole all these youth movements are geared towards some form of 'democratic socialism' and towards the effective establishment of a freer polity.

II *The utopian political revolt*   In countries where a strong liberal constitution, a capitalist system, and a welfare state are well rooted, the revolutionary young are forced into new directions. 'Institutionalised' traditional left-wing parties—either Stalinist or social democratic—do not fulfil their needs any longer: they are seen as ossified bureaucracies which have 'sold out' to the 'imperialist establishment' and which control a working class indifferent to the students revolts against the 'system'. One of the results is the constant and fruitless political effervescence of countless splinter groups and local parties, often reviving once genuine revolutionary movements— Trotskyism, anarchism—or even embracing Maoism. Some semblance of unity occurs when an 'issue' manages to unite the student body of one or several institutions. If the issue is really a very important one—such as continued Gaullist ineptitude in French higher education, or the Vietnam war in the United States—the student movement may succeed in coalescing into an important social movement, whose long-run effects can be very beneficial for the country, bringing about positive changes in policy, ideological renewal and a better educational system. However, the students' alienation from the lower classes, the capacity of what they call the 'system' to reform itself and to give in to some of their demands without really transforming itself, the brief period in which a student is a student, all increase the utopian character of the most characteristic ideologies whose 'non-negotiable' demands belong to the realm of utopian communism. The plight of these groups seems more evident in democratic countries such as Great Britain where, in spite of the publicity of the mass media, student revolts have never reached the proportions of those of Germany, France, Italy or Japan.[3] For, as Colin Crouch concludes in his study of student revolts in the London School of Economics (1965–1970), 'the main import of the student revolutionaries' distinctive proposals for the improvement of our world are this: that we should organise our society in all its aspects according to principles that are by nature transitory and incapable of institutionalisation'.[3]

III *Authoritarian and fascist activism*   A section of the young may be ripe for authoritarian assimilation into violent organisations, where the crisis of confrontation with the shifting world is solved by over-identification with (rather than opposition to) what is considered traditional and sacred. The paramilitary *Hitlerjugend* organisation was, of course, an example of the extreme type of such organisations, but post-War Italian neo-fascists, and French right-wing violent groups such as *Occident*, are examples of the permanence of this pattern of reaction to the crisis. Their important role as *agents provocateurs* or in helping with the repression of other students often conceals the fact that these groups are small. Sociologically, though, authoritarian subservience to an established system, or even pressure towards the intensification of its right-wing is equally interesting in the study of possible responses to the modern crises.

IV *Withdrawal*   The most original aspect of generational cleavage in the modern world has been the apparent withdrawal of the young from a society that some of them regard as beyond repair or salvation. In spite of the outward spiritualist trappings of vague orientalist mysticism, the search for effortless bliss epitomised by drug-addiction shows the limits of such ventures. Trying to avoid its inherent quietism and moral indifference, certain groups within this diffuse movement have tried to find constructive alternatives to the 'immoral' and imperfect world in which they find themselves. For example, experimental communes have sprung up in several countries, but so far no evidence is forthcoming to show that they are feasible solutions except as small and not very lasting institutions in the midst of a vastly different world, whose democratic and tolerant traditions alone make their existence possible.

The sociological investigation of generational conflict is in its infancy[4] but the developments just mentioned show that the matter is far from superficial or unimportant. It is necessary to add, however, that much of the conflict just alluded to is only partially 'generational'. On the other hand simplistic, psychological formulas which seek to explain student activism by the child rearing practices and politics of the parents of active students ignore 'questions of variations in student goals, form and intensity of action'.[5] On the other many of the crises in which collectivities of young people actively engage in protest or revolt are just aspects of greater social conflicts and trends of change. In this sense they are more involved in these crises as a particularly embattled occupational, cultural and political category than as an 'age group' in supposed revolt against their elders.

## NOTES on Chapter IX, Section 6

1. 5. Schildkrout *Ethnicity. Kinship and Politics among Mossi Immigrants in Kumasi* (Unpublished Ph.D. dissertation, Cambridge University, 1969).
2. S. Giner 'Spain' in M. S. Archer ed. *Students, University and Society* (London: Heinemann, 1972) pp. 103–126.
3. C. Crouch *The Student Revolt* (London: Bodley Head, 1970) p. 241; cf. also A. Touraine *La revolution ... op. cit.*; E. Pinilla de las Heras *Reacción y revolución en una sociedad industrial* (Buenos Aires: Signos, 1970).
4. Apart from the works quoted in the three last notes cf. *Jnl. Contemp. Hist.* London, Vol. 5 no. 1, 1970; L. S. Feuer *The Conflict of Generations* (London: Heinemann, 1969); D. Bell and I. Kristoll eds. *Confrontation— the Student Rebellion in the Universities* (New York: Basic Books, 1969); P. Bourdieu and S. C. Passeron *Les Héritiers* (Paris: minuit, 1964); S. N. Eisenstadt *From Generation to Generation* (New York: Free Press, 1956); A. Cockburn and R. Blackburn eds. *Student Power* (Harmondsworth; Penguin 1969).
5. M. S. Archer, *Students, University ... op. cit.*

# X Social Change

## 1  THE DIMENSIONS OF SOCIAL CHANGE

The universality of social change has been apparent throughout the preceding pages. Time and again it has been shown that fluctuation, transformation, variation and mutation are an inherent aspect of every area of social life, even though these phenomena are themselves subject to certain regularities and definite causal relationships, which it is the task of sociology to unveil. This elementary fact of social life is so salient that it is convenient to give it some separate attention—keeping in mind, however, that its very generality creates serious difficulties. As a field—if indeed it is a substantive field of enquiry—social change 'occupies a kind of no-man's land between sociology and history', as Smelser points out. When we consider it as the 'systematic study of variations in social life' it is not very different from sociology as defined above; if it is viewed as the study of the 'unfolding of man's social arrangements through time, it appears to be indistinguishable from social history'.[1] And yet, as a distinct point of view, the study of social change remains a very attractive approach, never able to justify a sufficient degree of independence from the other fields of the discipline but stubbornly emerging in syllabuses, research projects and theoretical efforts as a special subject.

Social change may be defined as the observed difference between the earlier and the later states of a given area of social reality, or rather what happens between these two moments in time. Thus, change is not the final observed modification but the processes leading towards it. Also, for social change to be sufficiently interesting sociologically, it must refer either to significant transformations in social behaviour or to modifications in the patterns of social systems. Minor changes in the life of groups or even societies that are not real trends or die out without further effects are, strictly speaking, change, but may be excluded from its systematic study.[2] In general, social change can be considered as the consequence of three categories of phenomena:

I  Changes which occur in connection with the ecological and biological levels of society. Thus a change in climate may create a prolonged drought forcing steppe nomads into raids, banditry or even the conquest of other peoples. Great historical migrations have had this origin, with long-range consequences for many peoples and cultures. The growth or decrease of natural resources—game, grazing land, fisheries—affects the demographic trends of societies, with entirely unintended political, economic and military consequences. Plagues and epidemics are also part of this category. The social consequences of some are fairly well known. Thus, the Great Plague (or Black Death) of 1348–50 drastically checked the growth of towns and partially explains religious revivals and millennial movements in late medieval Europe as well as many of the new trends in the plastic arts of the period.

II  Changes which are explicitly willed and imposed by one or several social groups. The passing of a law, the carrying out of a military coup, the decision to build a motorway, the exclusion of an ethnic collectivity from political participation—all belong to this category, which, unlike its precursor, falls entirely within the discipline of sociology.

III  Changes which are the unconscious effect of sociocultural life itself. The attitudes, values and style of behaving that each group and collectivity possesses inevitably result in a given line of development. The same phenomena, belonging to either of the two categories just mentioned, elicit different responses in different peoples; the rhythm of economic activities, the pace of life, the educational values, all have a very real, if subtle, effect on the directions and the intensity of change. These factors can sometimes be observed sociologically, as various studies in the field of attitudes, beliefs and cultural patterns show. This unconscious level of social reality constantly impinges upon the world of conscious purposes, and colours and orients all its activities. But the latter cannot be solely explained as a simple, mechanical reflection of the former. As Morris Ginsberg has indicated:

> Neither . . . discloses a single pattern, both point rather to a series of groping efforts of men slowly becoming aware of their common needs and the possibilities of harmonious cooperation. The

results of their efforts are embodied in social structures which, in turn, react upon the individual concerned, creating new situations and generating new wants and strains which in their turn stimulate new efforts. Social forces thus consist of the energies of men in conscious or unconscious interaction. The individual will may be often powerless largely because it is thwarted or unaided by other wills, though on occasions, when opposing forces are equally balanced, the contribution of one or more determined men may be decisive ... Social processes are thus neither fatally predetermined nor free from limiting conditions. But the greater the knowledge of the limiting conditions, the larger is the scope offered to conscious direction and control.[3]

The purposeful transformation of the social order is a feature unique to man. It is largely for this reason that societies are social systems in the sense postulated earlier (III, 7), for social systems must cope with new situations created by themselves—or by active elements within themselves. And in this process they reach a new stage or level of order that differs from the earlier one substantially. This is true of every human society, including the most stagnant, with the sole difference that the latter possess a slower rhythm of change. Only animal societies do not change in the sociological sense of the word; their social changes, when they occur, are the effects of biological mutations. Now these specifically human changes (which occur without a corresponding change in the features of man as a species and are, therefore, cultural) do not necessarily possess one overall direction. Hence social change is not synonymous with development, much less with progress. The latter is merely a subclass of the former. *Development* is a growth in complexity; *progress* is development plus an improvement in the moral *and* aesthetic *and* cognitive dimensions of society—in a word, an improvement in the quality of life. Thus we may have development without progress. A country may develop economically with the help of great camps of forced labour. Another may make 'progress' in the field of knowledge (for instance, nuclear physics) without improving the trends towards peace or gaining greater freedom of artistic and political expression. These familiar distinctions, which seem so elementary, are systematically forgotten by many people, including social scientists. If a sociologist wants to measure progress in a particular country he must remember that the growth of the gross national product is only one datum among several, although it certainly is a very important datum if all he wants to assess is the broader category of change. The concept of *regression*, finally, points to the converse phenomenon of development; it is not ex-

actly a return to past, historically unrepeatable, societies, but it is a
loss in complexity. The decomposition of the Roman Empire and
the disintegration of city life, with the parallel transformation of
European peoples again into agrarian societies with hardly any
urban life, is a classical case. The disappearance of the Maya
civilisation and its substitution by a tribal, much more primitive,
world, is another. 'Retribalisation' is not the only process of regression. Amerindian tribes have often been impoverished by their
contact with Western societies: their myths and arts have disinte-
grated, their social structures have lost complexity, the pride of
their people has vanished, their economy has been destroyed. But
not all regressions are so dramatic and drastic. The collapse of
democracy in Greece in 1967 was politically regressive but perhaps
future history will show that it was only a temporary, though
serious, setback in the political modernisation and overall progress
of that country. The final defeat of the Spanish Republic in 1939
inaugurated a period of conscious political, religious, economic and
cultural regression: the country actually became less complex and
immensely poorer intellectually, artistically, and economically—
not to speak of the process of 'simplification' forced upon the polity
by the militaristic, fascist and reactionary elites which came to
power. And yet in the long run these very elites and the political
system they imposed have not been able to stop one of the most
rapid and intense societal transformations witnessed in Europe after
the Second World War.[4]

All this shows that social change in its several dimensions—progress, stagnation, regression, development, and the like—is a very
complicated affair indeed. Only very rarely does the whole society
move in one single direction. Depressed areas, 'pockets of back-
wardness', underdeveloped regions, slums, often develop in the
most industrialised and advanced countries as a consequence of—
rather than in spite of—certain types of overall progress. For all
these reasons, the construction of a cogent general theory of social
change is plainly a very difficult task whose completion perhaps
ought to await the more correct formulation of several partial
theories dealing with more particular (if still broad) aspects of
change, such as political revolution, the industrialisation in the
countryside, the effects of socialism, and the like.[5]

*NOTES on Chapter X, Section 1*

1. N. J. Smelser 'Social Change' in N. J. Smelser ed. *Sociology* (New York: Wiley, 1967) p. 674.
2. Cf. G. and A. Theodorson *op. cit.* p. 384.
3 M. Ginsberg 'Social Change' in *Essays in Sociology and Social Philosophy* (Harmondsworth: Penguin, 1968) pp. 129–161; quotation from p. 161.
4. S. Giner 'Spain' in M. S. Archer and S. Giner *Contemporary Europe: Class Status and Power* (London: Weidenfeld, 1971) pp. 125–61.
5. For a general treatment of social change cf. W. E. Moore *Social Change* Englewood Cliffs: Prentice Hall, 1963); G. K. Zollschan and W. Hirsch eds. *Explorations in Social Change* (London: Routledge, 1964).

## 2   SOCIAL EVOLUTION

The consideration of the broad sweep of human history as a whole may lead the observer to the conclusion that it possesses a definite pattern. That such a pattern exists has been taken for granted by most men. Mythologies, theogonies and cosmologies everywhere include some explanation of mankind's origin, predicament, and future direction. The growth of rationalist thought in ancient Greece did not put an end to such assumptions—on the contrary, philosophers of history thought it their task to give scientific explanations of such trends. Theories such as that of Hesiod, of mankind's continuous decay from an original golden age arose, to be followed by cyclical explanations of general social change, such as one finds in Polybius, in whose concept of history genesis (or regeneration) plays as important a part as decay (or degeneration).[1] But it was only the emergence of a generalised belief in progress among the educated in the Europe of the Enlightenment that made the concept of evolution finally possible. That the idea of evolution includes that of progress is quite plain; social evolution is more than change—it is change with a direction towards ever increasing complexity, richness and civilisation. To think of the history of mankind in terms of evolution is to assume that it has been developing, in spite of numerous setbacks and regressions, in the overall direction of higher and ever higher forms of civilisation. This has led some to assume that history as a whole is teleological—that it responds to some grand final design. Although many eminent social scientists such as Marx, Comte and Spencer, did embrace some definite form of teleological evolutionism, contemporary sociology has become much more cautious about this notion—which is not to say that it denies the possibility of evolution. On the one hand the teleological character of much social life is perfectly clear, as we saw earlier (III, 3); on the other, directions of development, long-range social trends, are also easily detectable over very long periods of history, and can only be ignored by extreme positivists lost in their fruitless pragmatical puzzles. But unfortunately modern sociology is not in a position to provide a final proof that a metaphysical social teleology exists. Together with the science of history it can only establish the presence of some very broad trends at given times: the formation of a feudal world, the passing of caste society, the rise of industrialism, and the like. All this does not mean that society is meaningless; it only means that, if we are eager to know its destiny, we must introduce extra-sociological and extra-historical elements, based on philosophical anthropology and social philosophy, amongst other sources of speculation and knowledge.

To renounce, *qua* sociologists, unwarranted conjectures about the possible teleology of the history of mankind does not hinder the search for general patterns in the past. It is clear that men have risen from an animal state to a barbarian state through many steps, and that from the latter they have developed important and highly complex civilisations; these, in turn, have shown an increasing degree of technological, industrial and scientific sophistication, although cumulative progress in art, poetry and philosophy is much more questionable. In these matters sociologists encounter serious difficulties, since linear or simple sequences of development from barbarism to civilisation are nowhere to be found. The very birth of civilisation in different parts of the world shows notable points of divergence, although common traits in the conditions that made it possible abound. The technological criteria followed by archaeologists in their efforts to define the lines of mankind's early sociocultural evolution are still far from furnishing us a satisfactory picture of it. And the all-too fragmentary evidence we possess of vast periods of even fairly recent history do not make the overall task too easy. Neither is the task simplified by drawing facile analogies between sociocultural and biological evolution. Culture and nature possess different internal dynamics. As Gordon Childe has stressed, only in some special cases are analogies acceptable. Thus the sequence 'variation-heredity-adaptation-selection' is a chain of phenomena in the realm of natural evolution which also occurs in cultural life. An invention is a variation—corresponding to a mutation in natural evolution—which unleashes this sequence in social life with even greater accuracy than a mutation does in the life of a species of the animal kingdom.[2]

The elaboration of an acceptable theory of the past evolution of mankind will have to be founded on the basis of isolated, if sometimes fairly broad, studies of its several aspects and epochs. This does not mean that the ambitious constructs of Ferguson, Morgan, Engels, Comte, and many other early theorists of evolution must entirely be ignored. On the contrary some of their contributions have withstood the passing of time remarkably well and are still a great help in our efforts to understand important general processes of social change, as frequent references to their work abundantly show. But classical evolutionary theory—even when weaned from its teleological assumptions—has had to undergo a drastic revision in the light of further evidence. William Ogburn started to move in this direction when he pointed to the important discontinuities one could notice between the 'material' and the 'symbolic' and moral aspects of culture. It was clear, he said, that the series of stages in the evolution of mankind seen as inevitable by the evolutionary theorists of every school was more than problematic, and that serious 'cultural lags' between these two spheres of social life could develop.[3] This was also Ogburn's way of expressing the disenchantment of intellectuals during the aftermath of the First World War by the (until then) widely accepted belief in the simultaneous technical and moral progress of man. But this proved a healthy disappointment, for it showed social scientists that a general evolution of mankind—if indeed it exists—is a very complicated phenomenon. It is in this context that the outstanding work of social anthropologists on primitive societies, followed by that of sociologists devoted to the study of the modernisation of traditional societies, has come to increase our knowledge of the serious gaps left by the work of the classical evolutionists (IV, 2).

It is not possible to give an account of these recent contributions to evolutionary theory, for that would mean giving a comprehensive and lengthy account of all the present studies on social change. Instead, it has seemed adequate to concentrate on one subject which is of undisputed interest for anyone involved in the problems of contemporary sociology—the directions of social change in our own world.[4]

*NOTES on Chapter X, Section 2*

1. R. A. Nisbet *Social Change and History* (London: Oxford University Press, 1969).
2. G. Childe *Social Evolution* (London: Collins, 1963) pp. 158–185.
3. W. F. Ogburn *Social Change* (New York: Huebsch, 1922); L. Sklair *The Sociology of Progress* (London: Routledge & Kegan Paul, 1970) chap. IV; R. Fletcher *The Making of Sociology* (London: Michael Joseph, 1971) Vol. 2, pp. 794–98.
4. For a good collection of studies linking the theme of evolution to that of modernization cf. S. N. Eisenstadt ed. *Readings in Social Evolution and Development* (Oxford: Pergamon Press 1970).

# 3 MODERN SOCIETY

*The process of modernisation*

What makes a society modern? Let us suppose we are faced with a society where social mobility is low, where families are patriarchal, where the number of children per family is high, where political authority is based on traditional justifications, where men earn their living by tilling the land by hoe and plough. No one will hesitate to define it as non-modern or, more likely, given the common prejudices of our times, as backward. If, on the contrary, we encounter the opposite traits—intense vertical mobility, birth control, legalistic political authority, sophisticated technology—we will call it a modern society.

And yet what is 'modernity'? For while, in a sense all these phenomena could be understood as the tangible consequences of a deeper dynamics that brings them all about simultaneously, their simple presence and coexistence is insufficient explanation for the demanding mind. In the foregoing pages several trends that could partially account for such phenomena have been mentioned or even been summarily described, such as tendencies towards rationalisation, the increase of the competitive ethos among individuals, bureaucratisation, the relative passage from the *Gemeinschaft* to the *Gesellschaft*. The truth is that all these diverse tendencies are in themselves an essential part of what for convenience is termed modernity. In these terms the explanation of modernity becomes a somewhat circular argument. To avoid this pitfall it is perhaps better to leave aside the question of the causes of modernity and simply define it as a state reached by certain technologically very advanced societies, which entails an interdependent series of historically unprecedented developments. Forced to find a single trait to define these we could perhaps state that they are all linked to a type of social change based on what Karl Deutsch has called 'social mobilisation'. *Social mobilisation* is the process whereby the traditional bonds of individuals with their pre-existing cultural, political, economic and primary institutions, are broken or weakened, so that they become available for new forms of behaviour and socialisation.[1] (The word 'mobilisation' in this context is somewhat misleading, for in ancient societies men and resources have often been mobilised on a great scale.) In the modern context mobilisation may be interpreted as meaning that the recruitment of individuals and resources into most institutions shows a tendency, but only a tendency, to occur on universalistic principles, and not according to criteria of locality, region, class, race, clan or even political affinity. As a matter of fact one of the constant sources of conflict in modern societies is the stubborn presence of attitudes that run counter to these tendencies—something which proves rather than disproves, the relatively high degree of overt acceptance of the universalistic principles by great numbers of people. This potential mobilisation of the population for the general social division of labour implies that one of the chief modern notions is that of the intrinsic value of any individual—so long as he is qualified—to perform certain tasks. Accordingly, in an ideally modern society, status would entirely depend on the individual's capacity for his role. Hypothetically, in the same society social positions are all open to universal competition. That this is still far from being a reality in actual societies is another matter. But the ideological, political and educational trends that have worked in that direction with a considerable degree of consistency over a long period of time and under several political and economic systems are undeniable. At any rate modern societies are those in which social change has become institutionalised, and for this institutionalisation an unprecedented degree of social mobilisation—in the specific sense given to this word here—had to occur.

'Modernity' is of course, an abstraction. Like 'industrial society', 'the nuclear age' and other general labels (each stressing a different aspect of the contemporary world) modernity cannot yet be identified with one single political or economic regime, even though it was once possible to identify its dawn with that of capitalism. However, although capitalism has been historically one of the main forces shaping the modern world, the expansion and consolidation of what can be strictly termed a fully modern society has come about with the very active help of welfare-state economics, new educational policies, and varying degrees of socialism or state control of the economy. In addition to this even the most modern societies in the world have not advanced in the direction of modernity along the same paths. Certain features of a country such as the Soviet Union—especially those relating to its artistic, intellectual and philosophical life—are strikingly old-fashioned, and lagging behind those of Holland, France or Sweden. In the United States, Alabama, Arkansas and Mississippi are areas several of whose cultural patterns remind us of the pre-modern bigotry that was typical of slave societies. Yet traits such as these are universally considered as vestiges of the past—attitudes, institutions or structures to be eroded by the profound social transformations we are all undergoing.

Such transformation is so intense now that full modernity seems to be really taking root in a great number of societies, that some sociologists have already begun to speak of a post-modern, or a post-industrial era, thus sharing in the impatience and anticipatory eagerness which is so typical of our contemporaries.[2] In this respect they may have been too rash, for in any case one can only surmise, *pace* our best and most fashionable futurologists, what society will be like in the future. For one thing, a great part of the world is striving towards modernity, but it does so in many different ways. China's path towards it and its moral and ideological image of modernity are very different from those prevalent in other countries, even those engaged in socialist transformation of their societies, such as Chile or Yugoslavia. For a great number of people in Europe, Australasia, and North America, pluralistic democracy ought to be a distinctive trait of modernity. Not so for the members of Communist Parties everywhere. With all these important reservations in mind, however, it is still possible to make some generalisations of what the world's most modern societies are like, and in so doing to indicate some of the most interesting sociological problems produced by their trends of change.

## The traits of modernity

A society can be said to be modern when its structure and culture include the following set of interdependent characteristics:

I *The presence of the centre in the periphery* In modern societies social space has a very low degree of correlation with geographical space. In a traditional society, the diverse centres—political, religious, cultural and economic—influence the several social areas unevenly. A region physically distant from one of these centres is also a region socially distant from it. In these societies technological innovation occurs in one place—often an urban setting—and spreads parsimoniously over the rest of the country. The administration of justice, religious reform, political decision, do not reach every area, or reach them refracted by several layers of power, influence and authority interposed between the source and the recipient of its action. Conversely, a social movement of distant origin may remain confined to its region, or spread very slowly to the centres in question. By contrast, as Edward Shils has stressed, modern society is a society where the presence of the centre in the periphery is an immediate structural fact.[3] And the presence of the peripheral zones in the centre is equally immediate. This not only indicates the emergence of a new type of social control, but also a new fact about communication, which results in the high degree of awareness of modern men about their membership of a wider and 'total' social system.

Seen from another angle the regular 'access' of individuals to the centres of society (through voting, getting information through the news media, receiving economic aid, paying taxes, standing for office, publicly expressing their opinion) is expressed in the very modern notion of citizenship. A modern society is a society of citizens, something easily revealed by those varied social movements which strive at greater equality and participation, fighting against the treatment of their members as 'second class citizens'. Originally citizenship might have been a legal conception leading to a political conception—political rights—but in the last stages of the development of this value citizenship has also come to mean economic, educational and welfare rights.[4] The fact that the actual degree of access to the centres of society is unevenly distributed amongst the citizenry does not rule out the phenomenon of citizenship itself. The lower classes participate less in the knowledge, power, and life chances generally enjoyed by the upper, but the very tension created by this contradiction of modern democratic societies and the constant pressure from many quarters for active policies to upset trends against egalitarianism in participation testifies to the relative involvement of the entire population in the essential central activities of the society.

II   *Rationalism, material development, economic and political interdependence* One of the meanings of rationalisation is the application of rational principles of logic and science to human action (III, 3 and VII, 7). It differs from science in that rationalisation does not attempt to investigate the nature of phenomena, but just to solve efficiently practical problems without taking account of moral considerations; it is the systematic application of technology to situations involving people. In modern society not all social and human problems are technically treated, nor are men always organised in rationalised patterns whenever they have to carry out a common task, but the scale on which this phenomenon occurs is unprecedented. Personnel management, psychological entrance tests for possible employees, productivity studies, organisation theory and research, systems analysis, are just so many names of techniques put into practice by private industry, governments, armies, health services, educational institutions in their efforts to maximise their efficiency in the attainment of their goals. The dangerous moral neutrality of these trends has been indicated at an earlier stage. Both the murderous gas chamber and the great modern hospital have been made possible by this tendency; countless less dramatic examples between these two extremes can be given, increasing either the misery or the happiness of modern man. The direction of these results of the technical treatment of human affairs is determined by forces which are not to be found in the inner logic of rationalisation but in the moral collective conscience of individuals and groups.

Rationalisation in the realm of the division of labour and in that of the production of commodities and goods of all sorts (for consumption, warfare, transport, enjoyment) has had the rapid effect of raising the *per capita* production of such goods to an enormous degree. Large scale rationalisation of production has meant that, in the decades following the Second World War, the social division of labour has undergone a further transformation, being partially absorbed by and entering into interdependence with automation and cybernetics (VI, 2). The success of these latter techniques has led to their application to immediate problems: the progressive cybernetisation of entire economic systems is an important trend,[5] even though modern economies are far from having fully reached that state. Nevertheless this has made possible a sufficiently sophisticated planning, market research, price control, and other devices to save enormous amounts of physical effort, just as machinery and fuel do.[6] The more these systems take deeper and deeper root, the more the entire economy resembles a network of interdependencies (rather than a radial system) where coordination, feedback and mutual consultation are essential, in contrast with the overtly competitive economies of the past. The common concern for the soundness of the market and the avoidance of crises seriously modifies the traditional patterns of economic competition. In the socialist countries, interestingly enough, a revision of old-fashioned centralisation along not altogether dissimilar lines is noticeable.

Political interdependence is not solely the consequence of increasing economic interdependence, as simplistic analysis of European efforts at unification have led some to believe. Ideological trends, communication, military and balance of power links are just as strong. They all take part in the vast process of increasing interdependence between states and their societies. The extension of these networks of interdependence is now such that even the countries which cannot be included among the modern ones have at least entered economically, militarily and politically into a world network of power relations.

III *Knowledge as a social force* Modern societies are those where a conscious effort is made towards the accumulation and systematic use of the knowledge emanating from science. This does not occur as a simple process of creation and application. Political elites often decide which kind of knowledge is wanted, and then agree to allocate greater funds to such endeavours as the development of better weapons, moon rockets and artificial satellites than to medical research, pollution control, or economic aid plans for the poor countries. Yet the growth in the importance of this kind of knowledge has set in motion new social processes affecting the social role of the men of science, their influence upon the decision-making bodies as well as that of experts generally in the shaping of all sorts of policies. Their alleged access to knowledge now acts as a legitimising source for their activity and as a basis for ever higher claims in status, influence and privilege. Although there are no signs that a technocratic and scientific elite controls society (one of the pet ideas of contemporary social science fiction) it is true that men in occupational groups based on scientific knowledge have special opportunities for sharing authority and power. The phenomenon is new, and the trends in this area are far from settled, as contemporary social crises in higher education and research show. This is a field still largely unexplored by the sociology of knowledge.[7]

IV *The preeminence of associations* It almost goes without saying that such developments cannot take place without the general consolidation of institutions based on *Gesellschaft* bonds, goals and structures. The expansion of such associations throughout modern societies has meant a considerable weakening or dissolution of many former communities, eroded and undermined by many decades of industrialisation and increasing social mobilisation. In many cases a state of anomy has existed for large sections of the population, increasing the rates of crime or pushing individuals towards extreme ideological allegiances where they hoped to find the lost world of community; in others, without falling into these extremes, vast numbers of people have sunk into the grey, meaningless, and fairly boring life of the affluent middle classes of the modern world.[8] But these negative trends, serious as they are, have not destroyed all community bonds: rather they have weakened or eliminated some types of traditional primary group bonds, especially the most tribal and parochial.

Instead of an 'eclipse of community' as one pessimistic intellectual would have us believe, there has been a reconversion of community ties in modern society.[9] This transformation has been made possible by virtue of the emergence of the values of individualism and citizenship. As was remarked earlier, 'elective affinities' can now play a much greater part in the formation of spontaneous primary groups, which are also based on freedom and sympathy. The transformation of the family in modern society is also a very good illustration of this point. Its disintegration is nowhere in sight, in spite of constant opinions to the contrary; instead we are faced with a change of traditional family patterns and the emergence of the conjugal family, while (as was indicated earlier) some extended family connections—aid, visiting, and general conviviality —remain (V, 3). In this connection, it is convenient to stress that the also widely accepted idea that the nuclear family is just a mere consequence of industrialisation may be wrong. As William Goode says:

> The argument as to whether political and economic variables ... generally determine family patterns is theoretically empty. ... Even the relation between the conjugal family and industrialisation is not entirely clear. The common hypothesis that the conjugal form of the family emerges when a culture is invaded by industrialisation and urbanisation—is an undeveloped observation which neglects three issues: (1) the theoretical harmony or 'fit' between this ideal typical form of the family and industrialisation; (2) the empirical harmony or fit between industrialisation and any actual system; and (3) the effects upon the family of the

modern (or recently past) organisational and industrial system, i.e., how the factors of the system influence the family.[10]

The nostalgic idealisation of past communities (patriarchal families, clans, idyllic villages) is a useless exercise in sociology— still indulged in, however, by a number of its practitioners who ought to know better. Moreover it is the undoubted preeminence of associational structures and the relegation of primary groups to a very secondary set of functions in the realm of politics, the production of goods or even the transmission of culture, that has made individualism a universalistic attitude, and social reform movements possible. These reform movements are a struggle for the re-establishment of stronger community bonds amongst modern men, to shelter them from the anonymity and helplessness people often feel in front of the modern Leviathans. That this struggle, if not easy, is perfectly possible in a number of advanced pluralistic democracies is evidence that the terms 'community' and 'association' are not incompatible. On the contrary, they seem to be mutually necessary in a fully modern civilisation.

V  *Technical and anonymous cultural transmission*  The mass media of communication characterise, for some, the modern world. It is true that it could not be conceived without its press, radio, television, communications satellites, and without much of its information stored in tapes, films, microfilms, libraries and computers. With the exception of some public proclamations carved on stone, and of art produced with a view to illustrate the people about myths or events, traditional cultural communication always necessitated the continuous effort of man—the storyteller, the preacher, the soothsayer, the teacher. These professions are all still about (often with other names) and show no sign of disappearing, especially since instead of being deterred by the mass media their practitioners have risen to the challenge and are now using them freely. It is through the mass media that the ultimate regular connection between centre and periphery, and the increasing interdependence of several subcultures have materialised. Political decisions, public responses to them, the effects of distant wars, fashion, advertising and marketing, ideological propaganda—they are all now communicated to the media and instantly arrive to that vast audience which is in a sense modern society.

These features present a series of very serious problems for the sociologist. In his essay *On Liberty* (1859) John Stuart Mill, wrote that people now read the same things, listen to the same things, see the same things, go to the same places, have their hopes and fears directed to the same objects, have the same rights and liberties, and the same means of asserting them. Great as are the differences of position which remain, they are nothing to those which have ceased. And the assimilation is still proceeding. All the political changes of the age promote it, since they all tend to raise the low and lower the high. Every extension of education promotes it, because education brings people under common influences, and gives them access to the common stock of facts and sentiments. Improvement in the means of communication promotes it, by bringing the inhabitants of distant places into personal contact, and keeping up a rapid flow of changes of residence between one place and another ...

The combination of these causes forms so great a mass of influence hostile to individuality that it is not easy to see how it can stand its ground ... The demands that all other people shall resemble ourselves grows by what it feeds on ... Mankind speedily become unable to conceive diversity, when they have been for some time unaccustomed to see it.[11]

Sociology has ever since shown a growing concern for the problems, social and moral, of mass communication—the dangers of the monopoly of the media by a totalitarian party, the possible relations between 'mass culture' and crime, the specific problems of leisure and entertainment, the manipulation of taste by commercial advertising, the dangers to democracy arising from party or private control of certain media, the vulgarisation and debasement of modern culture, and so on.[12] All these issues must be seen by sociologists above all as problems, and not as matters already decided. This might seem an unnecessarily elementary statement, but the fact is that passionate reactions about the mass media of communication and their alleged pernicious effects upon the public have been, and still are, very common. Pessimists forget that easy access to higher forms of culture, publications, music and science has also been made possible by the mass media. On the whole Mill's statement remains true, however, and no complacency in this matter seems justified.

VI *Worldliness, hedonism, humanism* The modern mentality appeared as a movement towards the consideration of nature within its own limits and on its own terms. When the development of this trend began to include man himself he began to be understood as a merely terrestrial creature. This in turn led to the elaboration of a lay humanism and to a new vision of the world, which now became his destiny rather than a stage in the life of his soul, and an uncomfortable and transitory vale of tears. The development of these notions, together with the acquisitiveness and industriousness originally fostered by the bourgeois ethos, became powerful cultural currents which gave rise ultimately to contemporary hedonism. Modern societies are openly hedonistic, in the common meaning of this word, not in the refined and philosophical sense. And modern hedonism is *sui generis* for it not only demands that public institutions be responsible for collective welfare but also that they provide the necessary fun and excitement that is the inherent, and perhaps the most vulgar part, of this complex of attitudes. Thus there are many aspects to the modern idea of the welfare state from which something more than progressive taxation, free education and health services is now demanded. Perhaps all this means the demise of the individualism of the early modern period, as David Riesman's study of contemporary American values seems to suggest, and its substitution by a far less competitive and adventurous society.[13] Once again, clichés and trite formulae are all too easy in this domain. The person who for the first time approaches these problems has to start with a healthy agnosticism, and without previous condemnation of the contemporary situation.

Enough has been said of the process of secularisation that has gone hand in hand with all these developments (VIII, 5). It remains to point out that secularisation has excluded the magic and supernatural interpretation of the world in some vital areas of modern life, while in others it has become compatible with it. And the rise of allegedly secular ideologies with metaphysical and historical claims of universal validity, inspiring millennarian and cataclysmic mass movements, indicates that these conceptions are totally incompatible with the necessary critical and lay spirit of humanism. Such ideologies often appear as *ersatz* religions which nevertheless the sociologist will do well not to treat strictly as religions. The truth is that in modern man the rational and the irrational still intermingle and coexist as they always have. This ought to be a warning against facile generalisations about the 'uniqueness' and 'unprecedented nature' of our times. Unique and unprecedented they may seem to be, but men's passions are still very much the same. As a matter of fact, man's great change of heart so eagerly expected by the believers in progress has not yet taken place. This much, sociology can testify. By the same token it is in no position to affirm that this noble hope will never materialise.

Modern humanism has not succumbed to the 'sensate' hedonism

of our era; both rather coexist in constant tension. The modern world is also a place which shelters a great critical and philosophical activity. And culturally a fully fledged modern society is pluralist; it is the society of dialogue. Thus one ought to speak rather of a number of humanisms, which is more congruent with the inner nature of Western culture and its best living traditions. Sociology itself has entered this intellectual arena and is now an essential part of the ongoing dialogue. It is not only a child of our times but also a very characteristic one at that. Sociology is a humanism.[14]

VII *The growth of destructiveness* One of the chief tasks of contemporary humanism consists precisely of making the effort to solve the grave contradiction that exists between the unprecedented civilised capacities of our society—citizenship, welfare, freedom— and the forms of repression, imperialism and war that emanate from them. Once upon a time a sociologist like Spencer could conclude that imperialist wars and militarism were mere—if harmful —relics of past ages, and find an intelligent audience for his claims. This is far from evident now, when the United States is constantly entangled in murderous wars in faraway countries, when the Soviet Union invades the socialist countries under its area of domination, and when lesser powers also show similar aggressive behaviour. Even traditional countries, striving for modernity, use their modern panoplies to engage in war, thus assimilating the ways, strategy and weaponry of modern armies sooner than other traits of modernity, such as industry, the equality of women, or freedom of speech. We are again faced with a situation of cultural lag (**X**, 2) which particularly affects statesmen and men of responsibility. Social change is too fast for the average man—and many rulers are indeed average men—imbued with nationalism, paranoic fears of (capitalist or communist) conspiracies, and old-fashioned notions of international domination, which just do not work in the modern world. The result, in terms of human suffering, is incalculable. The continued expansion of monopoly capitalism, with little or no brakes against its excesses, is a factor aggravating the dilatation of 'civilised' destructiveness: polluted rivers and oceans, the manufacture and international sale of arms, the creation of a useless abundance for a 'consumer' society at the price—to echo the words of John Kenneth Galbraith—of much public squalor and some private affluence, the hunt after 'defence' contracts with governments, these are only a few of such excesses. The record of most socialist countries is, at least in one sense, even worse, for theirs was the greatest ideal produced by modern man: the abolition of social inequality *and* the creation of the realm of freedom. The challenges to sociologists are very great here. It is time that, once they have learned the lessons of their classics, they turn to the specifically sociological problems posed by these new questions, instead of evading them, lest they become cynical in attitude and sterile in their science, for fear of getting into controversial issues. Moreover there are no serious grounds for complete scepticism in the matters of peace and war in modern times, for it is in the contemporary world that considerable efforts towards peace, greater freedom and a more humane civilisation in general assert themselves with unprecedented intensity.

VIII *The transformation of social structures* Under the influence of all these forces—and several others which have been hardly mentioned, such as population pressure—modern society has undergone deep structural transformations. The trends in social stratification are perhaps the best example of their range and significance.

In Western societies the transformations which took place during the first stages of the industrial revolution have taken a new turn: the trends in the nature and the volume of their social classes are now different. Under the continued impact of industrialisation, urbanisation and improved communications, the rural exodus has persisted, and the rural classes have diminished everywhere. A great part of this population has acquired a new status system, often mirroring the status system of urbanised society.[15] The poor rural proletariat—labourers and peons—has been drastically reduced without exception from the North Cape to Gibraltar. (In other Western societies such as New Zealand or Canada, rural society has evolved from other historical foundations since they never had a pre-industrial rural hinterland based on peonage (as in Sicily, Andalusia) or on slavery (as in Cuba, Puerto Rico and the Southern United States) and were from the start societies of farmers.) The industrial working classes have not continued expanding in volume, for the considerable growth in the services sector has absorbed a great part of the active population, now surpassing, in many countries, that of the working classes themselves. Besides which—and this is a decisive trait of modern stratification—the working classes have increased their internal differentiation into occupational strata. Accordingly, the differences in attitudes and the mentality between the unskilled and the skilled workers tend to increase.[16] The upward social mobility of skilled workers has created a 'work-

ing class aristocracy' with problems of political and economic behaviour which are a far cry from those of the traditional proletariat, although it is necessary to stress that these upper layers of
the industrial working classes have not by any means undergone
an *embourgeoisement*—they have not become middle class. Internal
differentiation is still more acute in the expanded middle classes,
where the petty bourgeois ethos of yore has shrunk to certain areas
within them (shopkeepers, small businessmen); a new professional-
ism—based on educational proficiency—is pervading these classes,
which have become the great recruiting ground of technological and
scientific manpower. Professional and occupational loyalties seem
to be stronger than class loyalties. Altruistic moral indignation is
also still more intense amongst the middle class (especially among
certain groups in them, such as schoolteachers, students) so that
disarmament and peace movements, left-wing activity, efforts towards racial harmony, hunger relief organisations, and so on are
largely dependent on them. Power elites are now often recruited
from the middle classes especially through technology, science and
the access to power of socialist parties. The very educational, technological and economic traits of modernity have opened high
status, power and authority to scientific and expert elites of all
sorts—economists, lawyers, nuclear scientists, educationalists, even
some sociologists. They have placed themselves side by side with the
traditional political, financial and bourgeois elites, who have largely
retained their power. The traditional upper classes have withstood
the onslaught of the welfare state remarkably well, helped by the
gradualism of contemporary socialism and the acute conservatism
of the Western communist parties. And they have certainly not
been taxed out of existence.

With the intense achievement-oriented ethos (III, 4) which per-
vades modern society, occupational stratification has become decisive. The occupational statuses of social classes have lost much of
their past congruence with other forms of status. In many cases
power itself does not depend on the social class to which one belongs.
Thus trade union leaders and their institutions certainly rank
very high in the economic and political power structures of many
countries—something which was not the case in the past—but they
are not members of the upper classes.

In the socialist countries the initial transformations have been
of a very different sign, but remarkable parallels can be traced with
the capitalist nations, especially as one looks at the criteria used
both in the recruitment and promotion of professional people in

industry, education, government, and the services. However, social structures in the socialist countries are not converging in a simple linear way with those of the West.[17] On the one hand their criteria of power and privilege are strongly connected with previous ideological commitment to the Party, and, on the other, recruitment from the lower classes into the professional classes is still higher: in this they are far more egalitarian.

The new social classes[18] are emerging in a world economically very rich and prosperous, but also threatened by the dangers and the destructiveness pointed out above. New class conflicts, new forms of anomy and alienation—often developing out of the subtle means of exploitation and manipulation which have developed in our midst—have created psychological tensions and have become the characteristic stuff of modern discontent. Increasing crime, police brutality, suicide, and defeatist escapism show that the task ahead is indeed immense.[19]

IX  *The institutionalisation of social change*  It would be a crude statement to say that in traditional societies technological and social change was not willed or planned, that it just happened, whereas in modern societies the opposite is the case. In fact both phenomena occurred in them as they occur now; but there is some fundamental truth in such a statement. As has been pointed out above, modern societies have institutionalised change and they are more than ready for it they call it forth. Also, as Samuel Eisenstadt points out, in those countries where the peaceful institutionalisation of the social transformation has not been relatively successful, the major challenge of modernisation is now how to deal with continuous social change and the sustained economic growth which is seen as essential to the process.[20] People in all these societies (often even the most conservative) tend to acknowledge the inevitability of change and the need to plan it ahead.

All societies are systems (III, 7), but modern societies are those that—more than earlier forms of human interaction—possess the systematic characteristics of wholeness, feedback, and change. If systems are distinct from structures not only in that they are more general (for they include them) but also that they have in themselves the capacity for change, it is modern society that best fits this description. Systems, it must be remembered, produce the conditions for their own change. This they do by raising themselves to another level of development, through a series of conflicts, re-adjustments, tensions and releases of energy. A fresh process starts again from this newly reached stage.

It would not be prudent to predict the future of modernity. The factors so briefly mentioned already make a considerable list, although they are only a limited part of contemporary social reality. The multitude of dynamic factors entering the picture show that social life may always develop along unsuspected paths, which often escape the most detailed descriptions of current ideologies. Even sociology, with its notable effort towards rigour and objectivity can make no large scale prognosis of the future situation. And yet it has an important place in the common task of making this society more humane and worthy of the human beings who are its members. It has no ready made formulas and no recipes for the resolution of our evils, for its nature is that of research, inquiry and endless questioning. But the generality of the scientific approach is precisely what is needed to combat the ossification of the modern spirit in the throes of ideology, the often numbing world of the mass media and the banality of so much public and private violence. Thus, apart from its practical applications, on the cultural level the sociological critique and imagination has an educational mission which it is already accomplishing. Its design is to understand and explain the social condition of man, thus putting some order and purpose into the consciousness of himself and his world that modern man possesses. This order and purpose must be undogmatic, agile and creative. Not only sociology, but some other humanistic endeavours have also set out to accomplish this task. Like them, sociology's effort and ultimate justification consists in an affirmation of our freedom. For the practice of sociology is the practice of liberty.

## NOTES on Chapter X, Section 3

1. K. W. Deutsch 'Social Mobilization and Political Development' in *Am. Pol. Sci. Rev.* (1961) no. 55, pp. 494–95; for a much more complex notion of mobilisation, cf. A. Etzioni *The Active Society* (New York: Free Press, 1968) pp. 387–427.

2. A. Etzioni *op. cit.* p. vii; A. Touraine *La société post-industrielle* (Paris: Denoël, 1969); Eng. trans. *The Post-Industrial Society* (New York: Random House, 1971).

3. E. A. Shils (Political Development in New States' in *Comp. Studies in Hist and Society* (Spring–Summer 1960). Also 'Center and Periphery' in *Selected Essays* (University of Chicago, Sociology Department, 1970) pp. 1–14.

4. T. H. Marshall *Citizenship and Social Class* (Cambridge University, 1950); D. Brogan *Citizenship Today* (University of North Carolina, 1960).

5. P. Naville *Vers l'automatisme social?* (Paris: Gallimard, 1963).

6. For an identification of modernisation with economic development cf. D. Lerner 'Comparative Analysis of Processes of Modernisation' in S. Rokkan *Comparative Research ... op. cit.* pp. 82–92.

7. However see *Minerva*, a journal largely devoted to exploring the relationship between policy and learning in the contemporary world. Cf. A. Etzioni *op. cit.* pp. 131–309.

8. C. W. Mills *White Collar* (New York: Oxford University Press, 1951).

9. S. Giner *Sociedad masa ... op. cit.*

10. W. J. Goode *World Revolution and Family Patterns* (New York: Free Press, 1963) pp 10–11.

11. J. S. Mill *op. cit.* pp. 550–51.

12. G. Trade *L'opinion et la foule* (Paris: Alcan, 1901) pp. 2, 3, 11, 17; J. Ortega y Gasset *La rebelión de las masas* (Madrid, 1929); Eng. trans. *The Revolt of the Masses* (London: Allen & Unwin, 1961); B. Rosenberg *et alii Mass Culture* (Glencoe: Free Press, 1957); N. Jacobs *Culture for the Millions?* (Princeton N. J.: Van Nostrand, 1961); D. McQuail *Towards a Sociology of Mass Communications* (London: Collier-Macmillan, 1970).

13. D. Riesman *et alii The Lonely Crowd* (New Haven: Yale University Press, 1963) also J. Dumazedier *Vers une civilisation du loisir?* (Paris: Seuil, 1962).

14. E. Gómez Arboleya 'Sociología, escuela de humanismo' in *Revista de Estudios Políticos* (1955) no. 79, pp. 3–24; R. Dahrendorf *Gesellschaft und Freiheit* (Munich: Pieper, 1965) p. 13.

15. S. Mallet *Les paysans contre le passé* (Paris: Seuil, 1962).

16. H. Popitz *Das Gesellschaftsbild des Arbeiters* (Tübingen: Mohr, 1961); J. H. Goldthorpe *et alii The Affluent Worker* (Cambridge University, 1968–1970); J. M. Maravall, *El desarrollo económico y la clase obrera* (Barcelona: Ariel, 1970); D. Caplovitz *The Poor Pay More* (New York: Free Press, 1967).

17. F. Parkin 'Class Stratification in Socialist Societies' in *Brit. Jnl. Soc.* (1969) Vol. XX, no. 4, pp. 355–74.

18. A. Touraine 'Anciennes et nouvelles classes sociales' in G. Balandier *et allii Perspectives de la sociologie contemporaine* (Paris: PUF, 1968) pp. 117–56.

19. For a comprehensive treatment of social stratification in contemporary Europe, both West and East, cf. M. S. Archer and S. Giner eds. *Contemporary Europe ... op. cit.* For the USA, P. Blau and O. D. Duncan *The American Occupational Structure* (New York: Wiley, 1967).

20. S. N. Eisenstadt *Modernization: Protest and Change* (New York: Prentice Hall, 1966).

# Author Index

*(The following list includes only those authors who are mentioned or directly quoted in the text, but not those referred to in the Notes.)*

# Subject Index